MW00803756

New Revised Cambridge GED Comprehensive Teacher's Guide

CAMBRIDGE Adult Education
Prentice Hall
Englewood Cliffs, New Jersey 07632

©1994 by Prentice-Hall, Inc.
A Simon & Schuster Company
Englewood Cliffs, NJ 07632

All rights reserved. No part of this book may be reproduced,
in any form or by any means,
without permission of the publisher

Printed in the United States of America

10   9   8   7   6   5   4   3   2   1

ISBN 0-13-388919-X

Prentice-Hall International (UK) Limited, *London*
Prentice-Hall of Australia Pty. Limited, *Sydney*
Prentice-Hall Canada, Inc., *Toronto*
Prentice-Hall Hispanoamericana, S.A., *Mexico*
Prentice-Hall of India Private Limited, *New Delhi*
Prentice-Hall of Japan, Inc., *Tokyo*
Simon & Schuster Asia Ptd. Ltd., *Singapore*
Editor Prentice-Hall do Brasil, Ltda., *Rio de Janeiro*

Contents

Preface

The Teacher's Guides for the New Revised Cambridge GED Program are intended to help teachers take advantage of the unique features of this series. There is a lesson-by-lesson guide for each of the five content-area texts, plus one for the Comprehensive book.

The thrust of the entire program is to integrate reading skills instruction with content area material in every lesson and to make the books as accessible and motivational as possible. The purpose of these guides is to provide a variety of suggestions for making use of every feature of this design.

These suggestions offer tips for using every part of every lesson. Since the magazine-like design contains a Prereading Prompt and Key Words list at the beginning of each lesson, a Lesson Warm-Up exploits these features with brainstorming and vocabulary tips. Many ideas for discussion of text, graphics and illustrations, headings and captions, as well as ideas for writing and read-aloud activities, will stimulate students to participate as a class, in small groups, or as individuals. Series of questions tied into the lesson as it unfolds give teachers a handy tool for moving students actively through the content. Proposed topics for debates, role-playing, narratives from student experience, applications of concepts to real-life problems—all these give the books an added dimension of relevance. They make the books not only student-friendly but decidedly teacher-friendly.

One feature that should prove particularly helpful to teachers are the detailed vocabulary activities throughout each lesson. Aware that the GED population has many students whose native language is not English, we have provided comprehensive brainstorming guides for vocabulary that might give these students difficulty.

Suggestions on how to use the reading practice exercises and the tests are also included. As part of our consistent test-taking emphasis, each lesson exercise is preceded by a practice GED item applying the reading skill just taught; the texts contain more full-length GED exams than any other series—three in each content-area book and two in the Comprehensive book. The Teacher's Guides offer tips on how to use the practice as a warm-up for the lesson exercise, and how to use the tests both as authentic GED exams and as homework.

Cambridge is proud to offer this new series, together with these guides to help teachers make full use of its many unique features.

Usage

Skill 1:   Subject–Verb Agreement

Learning subject–verb agreement is a process. The student has to come to terms with a number of concepts. Skill 1 presents these concepts in a logical order. In Lesson 1, the student learns to recognize subjects and verbs, write their plural forms, and apply this knowledge in subject–verb agreement.

Lessons 2 to 4 deal with those situations that students often consider "trick questions." Interrupting phrases, inverted sentence structure, and the use of expletives result in sentences that don't seem to follow the rules. These lessons show the student how to apply the rules even in these unusual situations. Finally, Lesson 5 introduces compound subjects. The material in this lesson will make the student's work with pronoun–antecedent agreement easier.

You may want to refer students who are having difficulty to Chapters 1, 7, and 10 of *On Your Own: Grammar*, and the *Threshold* writing skills text, Unit 1, Chapter 1. For more GED-level work, see *The New Revised Cambridge GED Program: Writing Skills*, Part 1, Unit 1, Chapter 1. These texts offer additional instruction and exercises at a Pre-GED level.

Lesson 1: The Basic Rules of Subject–Verb Agreement

Lesson Warm-Up

Vocabulary: An understanding of the following terms is necessary to do the work in Lesson 1.

- **Subject:** The subject tells who or what the sentence is about. Have the students write sentences about themselves using themselves as the subjects.
- **Action verb:** A word that tells what the subject does. Action verbs are verbs that can be acted out, as in a game of charades.
- **Linking verb:** A verb that shows a state of being. A linking verb is like an equals sign (=); it links another name or descriptive word to the subject. For example,

  Cathy is a good typist.   Cathy = good typist

Linking verbs are usually forms of *to be*, but the following sensory words can also be linking verbs: *look, sound, feel, smell, taste*. Other linking verbs are *seem, appear, become, stay*, and *remain*. For example,

  Donald looks tired.   Donald = tired

- **Singular:** One of something.
- **Plural:** More than one.
- **Consonant:** Any letter that does not produce the vowel sounds of *a, e, i, o, u.*
- **Irregular:** An exception to a rule.
- **Agreement:** The subject and the verb in a sentence are in agreement when both are either singular or plural in construction. Nouns, pronouns, and verbs have both singular and plural forms.

Activity: Write the following sentences on the board.

  John painted the cupboard with a small brush.
  His job provides excellent health benefits.
  The Greenbriar Hotel is the location for the wedding.

Ask the students to find all the nouns and verbs in the three sentences. Have the students identify the subjects of the sentences. Distinguish *painted* and *provides* as action verbs and *is* as a linking verb.

Answers:
Nouns: John, cupboard, brush, job, benefits, Greenbriar Hotel, location, wedding.
Verbs: painted, provides, is.
Subjects: John, job, Greenbriar Hotel

Activity: Read the following paragraph to the class. Ask the class if the paragraph "sounds" correct. Direct the class to make a list of any words that "sound" wrong.

  On the job, an effective worker are aware of what the boss expect of the employees. An effective employee uses good listening skills and ask questions often. Often workers is frustrated when the boss criticize their work, but good workers knows that listening to criticism are an opportunity to improve their work.

1

Give the class a copy of the paragraph or write it on the board. Did they find all the errors?

Correct Version: On the job, an effective worker *is* aware of what the boss *expects* of the employees. An effective employee uses good listening skills and *asks* questions often. Often workers *are* frustrated when the boss *criticizes* their work, but good workers *know* that listening to criticism *is* an opportunity to improve their work.

Discussion: Could you understand the meaning of the passage even though there were errors? (Yes, the meaning is still clear.) Do the errors detract from the passage? (Yes, errors always make the reader's or listener's job more difficult.)

Lesson Activity

Give the following list to the students. Ask them to fill in the blanks with verbs (or verb phrases). Have them write sentences that would happen or be true now.

My clothes _____.
The child _____.
Susan _____.
Most of the players _____.
Everyone _____.

List the responses on the board. Correct any incorrect statements by pointing out that singular subjects must use a singular verb.

Now give them the following list. Ask them to fill in the blanks with verbs (or verb phrases). Have them write sentences that would happen or be true now.

The teachers _____.
Her jeans _____.
We _____.
The news _____.
Their computers _____.

List the responses on the board. Correct any incorrect statements by pointing out that plural subjects must use plural verb forms.

Lesson Wrap-Up

Exercise and Answer Key Discussion: Ask for volunteers to write their corrected versions of the sentences in the exercise on page 69 on the board. Review the five-step method stated on page 68 for each sentence.

Discussion: When do people first learn about subject–verb agreement? Bring out the idea that as children, we listened to our parents in conversation, and this early experience formed our understanding of subject–verb agreement. If sentences that are wrong sound "right" to us, our only chance for improvement lies in learning the rules and applying them.

Error Analysis: Students who are having trouble may still be confusing other nouns in the sentence with the subject. Review the definition of a subject with these students. Another common error would be to consider the indefinite pronouns listed in Rule 1 to be plural pronouns. Remind students to refer to the list of indefinite pronouns if they are unsure.

Lesson 2: Interrupting Phrases

Lesson Warm-Up

Vocabulary: An understanding of the following terms is necessary to do the work in Lesson 2.

- **Phrase:** A group of words that have a relationship to each other
- **Interrupting phrase:** A group of words that comes between the subject and verb

Teach the students to find the interrupting words first and then determine whether the subject and the verb agree with each other. Remind the students to use the five-step test for subject–verb agreement on page 68.

Activity: Write the following sentences on the board.

1. The changes in weather in Seattle during the spring make it difficult to decide what to wear.
2. That dictionary, a 1965 edition, looks well-worn.

Ask the students to underline the interrupting phrases and identify the subjects and verbs.

Answers:

1. Changes (subject), *in weather in Seattle during the spring*, make (verb);
2. Dictionary (subject), *a 1965 edition*, looks (verb)

Lesson Activity

Write the following three sentences on the board.

1. Our workload for the next two weeks (looks, look) light.
2. The office manager, as well as the clerks, (goes, go) out for lunch every Tuesday.
3. Mr. Williams and Ms. Evans with great interest (examines, examine) the phone bill at the first of every month.

Ask the students to choose the correct verb form for each sentence. If they have difficulty, direct them to cross out the interrupting phrase first.

Answers: 1. looks; 2. goes; 3. examine

Lesson Wrap-Up

Exercise and Answer Key Discussion: Write the sentences on page 70 on the board. Ask for volunteers to cross out the interrupting phrases and edit the sentences for subject–verb agreement.

Discussion: Why don't we just write sentences without interrupting phrases? Wouldn't it be easier? In the discussion, point out that in conversation we often use interrupting phrases. Interrupting phrases add important information and variety to our writing.

Error Analysis: Remind students to follow a step-by-step process to edit the sentences.

1. Find the subject.
2. Find the verb.
3. Find the interrupting phrase and cross it out.
4. Determine if the subject and verb agree.
5. If the subject and verb do not agree, change the verb to agree with the subject.

Lesson 3:   Inverted Sentence Structure

Lesson Warm-Up

Vocabulary: A sentence has inverted sentence structure when the subject comes after the verb.

Activity: Write this sentence on the board.

> Does your children have a week off for spring break?

Ask the students to rewrite the sentence as a statement. Have the class identify the subject and verb. Ask the class if the subject and verb agree. Rewrite the sentence using correct subject–verb agreement. Then turn the statement back into a question.

> *Answer*
>
> *Original sentence:* Does your children have a week off for spring break?
> *Statement:* Your children does have a week off for spring break.
> *Correct subject–verb agreement:* Your children do have a week off for spring break. (Children is a plural noun that requires the plural verb *do* to agree in number.)
> *Corrected question:* Do your children have a week off for spring break?

Lesson Activities

Activity 1: Write the following phrases on the board.

> in my office
> on the wall
> at work
> behind my desk

Have the students make a sentence with each phrase. Then ask them whether or not it has inverted sentence structure. If the sentence has inverted structure, have them change it into normal structure; if their sentence has normal structure, have them change it into inverted structure. For example:

> She types letters at work. *Change to:* At work she types letters.
> At work she types letters. *Change to:* She types letters at work.

Point out that changing a sentence with inverted structure to its usual order is often the best way to check subject–verb agreement.

Activity 2: Have students put these sentences in usual order and say whether the subject–verb agreement is correct. Have them write questions using the verb *to be* and words listed in Rules 1 to 8 on pages 65–68 and do this activity.

> Are some of the meat bad?
> Is both of you good-looking?
> Is jeans worn by everybody?

Lesson Wrap-Up

Exercise and Answer Key Discussion: Ask for volunteers to edit the four incorrect sentences from the exercise on page 71 on the board. Identify the subject and verb in sentence 2. Also point out that sentence 2 is correct.

Discussion: If the subject comes after the verb, will the verb always be a linking verb? During the discussion point out the action verbs in sentences 2 and 4.

Error Analysis: A common error will be for students to identify nouns in introductory phrases as the subject. Remind students to cross out phrases to help them see the subject and verb.

Lesson 4:   "Here" and "There"

Lesson Warm-Up

Vocabulary: When either *here* or *there* begin a sentence, it is called an expletive. An expletive is an extra word placed at the beginning of a sentence. Sometimes expletives are called **filler words** because they have no real function except to get the sentence started.

Activity: Write this sentence on the board.

Here are the library books filled with pictures.

The word *here* begins the sentence, but it isn't the subject. The second part of the sentence has inverted sentence structure. It contains the subject and verb of the sentence.

Write this sentence on the board.

The library books filled with pictures are here.

Point out that the order of the words is changed but the meaning is the same. Now the subject *books* is obvious. Disregard the interrupting phrase, *filled with pictures*. The verb is *are*. This sentence shows correct subject–verb agreement.

Lesson Activity

Assign the students to write five sentences that begin with an expletive. Two sentences should contain errors in subject–verb agreement. Then trade papers with a partner. The partner should rewrite the sentence so that the subject and verb are in the usual word order. Then they are ready to check for correct subject–verb agreement.

Example

With expletive: Here are Mr. Allison's box of diskettes.
Usual word order: Mr. Allison's box of diskettes are here.
Correct subject–verb agreement: Mr. Allison's box of diskettes is here.

(The subject of the sentence is *box*. Disregard the interrupting phrase *of diskettes*.)

Lesson Wrap-Up

Exercise and Answer Key Discussion: Read aloud the exercise sentences on page 72. Correct each sentence with class input. Rewrite each sentence by moving *here* or *there* from the front of the sentence. Point out that sentence 4 is correct.

Ask: If you see *here* or *there* at the beginning of a sentence, will it ever be the subject? (No. When these words are used to show location, they are adverbs. They are not subjects.)

Error Analysis: Students who are having problems should be reminded to cross out interrupting phrases. Instruct students to rewrite the sentence by placing the subject before the verb. Point out that to do this they will sometimes have to change other words.

Lesson 5: Compound Subjects

Lesson Warm-Up

Vocabulary: An understanding of the following terms is necessary to do the work in Lesson 5:

- **Compound:** Two or more of something that join together to make one: For example, the word *salesperson* is actually made up of two words: *sales* and *person*. The two are joined together to make one word.
- **Compound subject:** Two or more subjects joined by a connecting word (*and, or,* and so on): Some compound subjects are singular and some are plural. The rules of subject–verb agreement also apply to compound subjects.

Activity: Tell the students to imagine that they are planning a party. They need to know how many guests to expect. Two of the invited families are the Olsens (8 people) and the Kramers (8 people). From the following statements, how many people from these two families should the students expect at the party?

1. Both the Olsens and the Kramers will attend the party.
2. Either the Olsens or the Kramers will attend the party.

If sentence 1 is true, the students should add 16 people to their guest list. *Both...and* signals the reader to combine the two subjects. If sentence 2 is true, the students should expect 8 people only. *Either...or* tells the reader that only one of the outcomes will happen.

Both these sentences have compound subjects. Even though a compound subject always contains at least two parts, the connecting words can affect the meaning of the sentence, resulting in a singular subject. Always analyze the subject before you choose the verb.

Tell students that a number of very common phrases—especially food combinations—are compound subjects that often take singular verbs: beans and rice, bacon and eggs, peanut butter and jelly. beer and pretzels, and fish and chips usually take singular verbs.

Lesson Activities

Activity 1: Ask the students to choose the correct verb form for the following sentences.

1. Neither Paula nor her roommates (plans, plan) to apply for the position.
2. Both Paula and her roommates (plans, plan) to apply for the position.
3. Not only the supervisors but also the shop steward (was, were) surprised by the announcement.

4. Both the supervisors and the shop steward (was, were) surprised by the announcement.

Ask for volunteers to write the correct verb forms on the board. Have the volunteers read the correct sentences aloud.

Answers

1. Plan   The word *roommates* is closer to the verb, so a plural verb form is needed.
2. Plan   *Both...and* creates a plural subject.
3. Was   The word *steward* is closer to the verb, so a singular verb form is needed.
4. Were   Again, *both...and* creates a plural subject.

Activity 2:   Give the students copies of the following skeletal sentences. Instruct them to fill in the blanks with words of their own choosing that correspond to the labels. They can add extra words as needed.

1. Neither (singular subject) nor (plural subject) (plural verb form) home early.
2. Neither (plural subject) nor (singular subject) (singular verb form) the games for the party.
3. Both (singular subject) and (plural subject) (plural verb form) about the baseball game.
4. Both (plural subject) and (singular subject) (plural verb form) to sign up for the workshop.

Ask for volunteers to share their sentences. Correct any wrong answers.

Sample Answers

1. Neither the receptionist nor the clerks go home early.
2. Neither her parents nor Ruth is planning the games for the party.
3. Both Clark and his friends are excited about the baseball game.
4. Both the managers and Ms. Foulks are planning to sign up for the workshop.

Lesson Wrap-Up

Exercise and Answer Key Discussion: Write on the board the five sentences from the exercise on page 74. With the students' input, underline the subjects and verbs. Ask the students to explain which rule applies to each sentence as they edit the sentences.

Error Analysis: If students are having difficulty, have them underline the subjects first and then the verbs. Remind the students to look at the rules and match the patterns of the exercise sentences to the patterns in the rules.

Skill 2:   Verb Tense

The students' experience with verb tense depends a great deal on the English they have heard during their lives. If you look over the list of irregular verbs on pages 78–79, you will notice that most of the irregular verbs are very common ones. Students who have heard these forms used incorrectly for the better part of their lives will have a difficult time with this chapter.

Some students have the advantage of knowing what "sounds right." To others, the right verb sounds wrong. The first step in helping students use correct verb tense is to help them evaluate their present skill level. Those who need help should rely on the rules, learning to apply them carefully. Others may need only a review; they should concentrate on those rules that help them compensate for a specific weakness.

One way to evaluate your students' skill with verbs is to assign them to write an essay on a topic from their past. Requiring them to use past tense and past perfect forms will reveal many trouble spots. Possible topics include writing about a favorite birthday celebration, family member, or vacation spot.

You may want to refer students who are having difficulty to Chapters 4 through 6 in *On Your Own: Grammar* and Unit 1, Chapter 2, of the *Threshold* writing skills text. These texts offer additional instruction and exercises at a Pre-GED level. For more GED-level work, see *The New Revised Cambridge GED Program: Writing Skills*, Part 1, Unit 1, Chapter 3.

Lesson 1:   Verb Forms

Lesson Warm-Up

Vocabulary: An understanding of the following terms is necessary to do the work in Lesson 1.

- **Tense:** Denotes time or duration of an action: The tense of a sentence tells the time frame of the action. Some actions happen at a certain point in time. Other happen over time. Verbs change their forms to show different tenses.
- **Present form:** A verb form used to write sentences that describe action taking place in the present
- **Past form:** A verb form used to write sentences that describe action that took place in the past
- **Past participle:** A verb form that is combined with a helping verb to make a verb phrase: Verb phrases are used in sentences that take place over a period of time
- **Regular verb:** A verb that follows a normal pattern in forming its past and past participle forms
- **Irregular verb:** A verb that forms its past and past participle forms in any way other than the regular one
- **Present tense:** Used to write about something that *happens* now or something that *occurs* regularly

- **Past tense:** Used to write about something that *happened* at a certain point in the past
- **Future tense:** Used to write about something that *will happen* in the future: The simple future tense always has the helping verb *will* or *shall.*

Activity: For subject matter, suggest the following:

1. *Simple present*—a routine activity or a strong like or dislike: "I eat at noon"; "I hate Stallone movies."
2. *Simple past*—a completed activity or part of life: "I bought food yesterday"; "She lived there during high school."
3. *Simple future*—an expression of a plan or prediction: "I will go to college"; "They will not change jobs."
4. *Continuing*—an action that goes on over a definite period of time in the present or the past: "He is waiting for the bus"; "She was working all night."
5. *Passive*—the subject does not do the action of the sentence: "The glass is broken"; "The letter was marked PRIVATE."

Lesson Activity

Ask the students to write three sentences for each of the following tenses: present, past, and future. Then ask the students to write three sentences that use the helping verbs: *have, has,* and *had*; and three that use the helping verbs *am, is,* and *was.* Collect their papers and randomly select sentences to read to the class. Have the class identify the verb in each sentence and the tense. Put the more difficult sentences on the board for discussion.

Lesson Wrap-Up

Exercise and Answer Key Discussion: Point out that all the verbs used in this exercise on page 79 are irregular. Challenge the students to complete the sentences using different verbs. Have them identify whether their new verbs are regular or irregular.

Error Analysis: If students are having difficulty, help them organize their thinking by first finding the verb. Then look for clue words that indicate the time the action is taking place, such as *yesterday, next week, ago.*

Lesson 2:   Using Verb Tenses Correctly

Lesson Warm-up

Vocabulary: No new vocabulary terms are presented in this lesson.

Activity: Give the following three sentences to the class. Have the class members figure out why each sentence does not make sense as written.

1. Maury decided to do the shopping first; then he walks to the bank.
2. Joan's guests come to the party on time and will eat the stuffed mushrooms quickly.
3. The Church will sponsor the fundraiser; then it builds a new homeless shelter.

Call on volunteers to read the sentences and explain what is wrong. Point out that using the wrong verb tense can cause confusion.

Lesson Activity

Direct the students to write five sentences, each containing two verbs. Two of the sentences should logically use the same verb tense for both verbs. Three should not.

Discussion: When does it make sense to use the same verb tense? When is it right to use different tenses within the same sentence?

Sentences that would use only one tense might describe two actions both completed in either the present("He runs and exercises regularly.") or the past ("Last night I ate dinner out and then went to the movies.") or the future ("My sister will finish high school and then will go to college.") Sentences with two tenses describe actions that are completed at different times. The two parts of the sentence can be connected by a semicolon and one of these (or other) time-words or time-phrases:

present	past	future
now	yesterday	tomorrow
today	recently	later
at present	in the past	next (week,
	last night (or	month, year)
	week, month,	
	year)	

For example:
"I am sick but later I'll go swimming." (present and future)
"Last night I stayed up late and this morning I am tired." (past and present)
"She lived in Mexico last year; now she lives in Los Angeles." (past and present)
"I came to the United States from Chile last year and next year I will go back."(past and future)

During the discussion, emphasize that whether you use the same tense or not depends on the relationship between the two verbs in the sentence. Compound verbs (usually joined by *and* or *or*) should be written in the same tense. When two separate ideas are joined in a single sentence, the ideas might not be written using the same tense. Often, one event takes place before or after the other.

Lesson Wrap-Up

Exercise and Answer Key Discussion: Write each sentence from the exercise on page 81 on the board and have the class correct (or complete) the sentences together. Discuss what verb tenses are needed for each sentence.

Discussion: Do you think it is more difficult to use verb tenses consistently in written or spoken communication? In the discussion point out that though there may be problems with verbal communications we usually can "hear" the correct form and say it correctly. Even when we do not, the listener grasps our meaning from other word clues.

Error Analysis: If a student is having difficulty completing this exercise, have the student first underline both verbs in the sentence. Then have the student identify the tense of both verbs. Next, the student should decide whether the sentence calls for consistent tenses and what that tense should be. The student is finally ready to make any necessary corrections. The most important key to success in working with verb tenses is to follow a set procedure instead of trying to "hear" the answer.

SKILL 3: Pronoun Reference

Pronoun problems are normal for most Americans. Many people remember being taught in grade school to say *John and I*, never *John and me*, yet there are at least five correct uses for objective case (*me*) and only two for nominative case (*I*).

Your students need to recognize where they have learned certain ways of speaking and writing that are often clear and useful but are not correct. The challenge for adult learners in learning to write correct English is often not the amount of new material they have to learn, but the amount they have to unlearn and relearn.

Another point to remember is that pronoun rules keep changing. Does this sentence sound right to you? *Everyone should remember to bring their textbooks.* It isn't right, but it reflects the way we speak. Your first battle in teaching the rules of this chapter is to convince students that they have a need to learn them. We don't always speak correctly, but we can learn to write correctly.

The rules in this chapter are not difficult to learn. Actually, the students have already learned a great many of the rules in Skill 1 during their work on subjects and verbs. Now they have only to apply their

understanding to pronouns. Encourage them to focus on their own particular need for improvement.

You may want to refer students who are having difficulty to Chapters 8 and 11 of *On Your Own: Grammar* and Unit 1, Chapter 3, Lesson 13, 16 and 17 of the *Threshold* writing text. These texts offer additional instruction and exercises at a Pre-GED level.

Lesson 1:   Pronoun Agreement: Number and Gender

Lesson Warm-Up

Vocabulary: An understanding of the following terms is necessary to do the work in Lesson 1.

* **Pronoun:** A word that can be used in place of a noun.
* **Antecedent:** The word a pronoun replaces or refers to in a sentence.
* **Gender:** A grammar characteristic that tells whether a word is feminine (she), masculine (he), or neuter (it).

Rules 1 through 5 give guidelines for correct pronoun–antecedent agreement. Point out that the rules for antecedent agreement are similar to the rules for subject–verb agreement.

Activity: Give the following sentences to the class as a handout or write the sentences on the board. Instruct the class to circle the correct pronoun from the choices in parentheses.

1. Both Robin and Denise do (her, their) work on this terminal.
2. Before a person pays a bill, (he or she/they) ought to read it carefully.
3. Most products must be paid for in full before (it, they) can be delivered.
4. Roslyn and the other employees chose to spend (her/their) Saturday at the workshop on word processing.
5. Either Joel or Marcus received $300 for (his/their) reward.

Ask five students to write the sentences on the board with the correct pronoun. Ask the students to explain their answers.

Answers

1. their   Rule 4
2. he or she   Rule 1
3. they   Rule 2
4. their   Rule 4
5. his   Rule 5

Refer to the rules on pages 82–83 to correct the exercises.

Lesson Activity

Write the following sentences on the board as examples or prepare a handout. Ask the students to explain why the sentence is correct. They may refer to the rules on pages 82–83.

1. Deirdre and Jamie worked on their project together.
2. Carlos forgot to bring his report to the meeting.
3. A receptionist should keep his or her desk tidy.
4. Dan and Justine performed their duet beautifully.
5. The players spent their afternoon at the restaurant.
6. Neither Mr. Cummings nor the employees turned in their complaints to me.
7. Either Ed or Paul left his receipts with the bookkeeper.
8. Neither the assistants or Ms. Bryant left her copy of the report on the desk.
9. Mrs. Merrill and her sons need to bring in their bank statements.
10. He needs to be more patient with his customers.

Answers: 1. Rule 4; 2. Rule 1; 3. Rule 1; 4. Rule 4; 5. Rule 2; 6. Rule 5; 7. Rule 5; 8. Rule 5; 9. Rule 4; 10. Rule 1

Lesson Wrap-Up

Exercise and Answer Key Discussion: Ask for volunteers to read the corrected sentences and identify which rule applies to that sentence. Point out that item 2 is correct because of Rule 1.

Error Analysis: Students who are having difficulty may benefit from the following procedure.

1. Underline each pronoun and draw an arrow to its antecedent.
2. Determine the number of the antecedent.
3 Make sure that the pronoun agrees in number.

Lesson 2:   Pronoun Agreement: Person

Lesson Warm-Up

Vocabulary: An understanding of the following term is necessary to do the work in Lesson 2.

• **Person:** The nouns in a sentence can be labels for the person speaking (first person), the person spoken to (second person), or a person or thing spoken about (third person). When pronouns are substituted for these nouns, they take different forms depending on the person they represent.

Activity: Ask the class to listen carefully as you read the following statement to them.

Guess what? I just heard about a great job opportunity. I could hardly wait to tell you about it.

Ask: In that statement, who was the person speaking? (The answer is *I*) Who was I speaking to? (The class, represented by the pronoun *you*. Remind the students that *you* can be either singular or plural.) What was I speaking about? (The job opportunity, represented by the pronoun *it*)

This statement uses person correctly. Identify the first-, second-, and third-person pronouns used.

Put this sentence on the board and ask what is wrong with it:

When we leave early, you have a better chance of getting a parking space.

Answer: The sentence begins in first person and then switches to second person. From the construction of the sentence, you can tell that *we* and *you* are supposed to refer to the same antecedent, which is incorrect.

Lesson Activity

Practice identifying person in sentences. Write the following sentences on slips of paper and hand them out to class members. As a student reads a sentence, ask the class to identify the persons used.

1. Our plan is to buy a car in the next two months.
2. Their price was the lowest offer of all the bidders.
3. I think these cassettes belong to you.
4. She wants me to work late for the next three days.
5. The 5-year-old on the left is ours.
6. It is the only song I know.
7. Your decision is going to affect him for many years.
8. I realized that my house needed painting badly.
9. The jury made its decision by noon on Friday.
10. You should compare all three brands before your purchase.

Answers: 1. Our (first); 2. their (third); 3. I (first), you (second); 4. she (third); 5. ours (first); 6. it (third); 7. your (second), him (third); 8. I (first), my (first); 9. its (third); 10. you (second), your (second)

Lesson Wrap-Up

Exercise and Answer Key Discussion: Ask for volunteers to explain the thought process they used to correct the sentences. Point out that pronouns must agree in person only when they refer to the same antecedent.

Person errors occur often in conversation. We don't bother to correct ourselves because our listeners can usually understand our messages anyway. Bringing more attention to the problem is often enough to correct it. If some students are having trouble seeing these errors, assign them to create five sentences of their own that have person agreement errors.

Error Analysis: Students who are having difficulty need to identify which pronouns share the same antecedent. Have them underline the pronouns first and connect pronouns that share an antecedent with arrows. Then they are ready to examine the connected pronouns for agreement errors.

Lesson 3: Relative Pronouns

Lesson Warm-Up

Vocabulary: An understanding of the following term is necessary to do the work in Lesson 3.

- **Relative pronoun:** A pronoun that introduces a group of words that describes a noun or pronoun. The word *relative* is similar to the word *relationship*. A relative pronoun tells you how the group of words relates to the noun or pronoun it describes.

Activity: Put the following examples on the board and ask the class to fill in the blank with the word that sounds best.

1. Jerry, _____ is very talented, is a standup comic.
2. Scott wrote the poem _____ was read by the mayor in her speech.
3. I made my father promise to take his old newspapers, _____ were piled to the ceiling, and recycle them.
4. Donna, _____ Mr. Gordon recommended for this project, cannot work overtime.

  Answers: 1. who; 2. that; 3. which; 4. whom

Lesson Activity

Discussion: There is often confusion about when to use *which* and *that*. Both can be used to refer to animals, places, or things. Generally, the pronoun *that* is used when the information is essential for identifying the noun. Use *which* to introduce information that is not essential to the identity of the noun.

  Examples

1. The book that you got from the library is due tomorrow. ("That you got from the library" tells you which book, so it gives essential information about it.)

2. The book, which was written in 1950, won the Pulitzer Prize. ("Which was written in 1950" is not essential for identifying the book, since we already know it is the book that won the Pulitzer Prize.)

Activity: Instruct the class to connect the following pairs of ideas by using the correct form of a relative pronoun.

1. Sheila is a pitcher for the Santa Monica Rockets. Sheila plays coed softball.
2. The vitamins should be taken daily. The doctor prescribed the vitamins.
3. The murals were commissioned by the city. The murals were painted by Harry Marshak.
4. The suit was made from gray wool. The suit cost less than $80.
5. Marsha is 40 years old. Hector made her the office manager.

  Answers: (Student answers may vary.)

1. Sheila, who plays coed softball, is a pitcher for the Santa Monica Rockets.
2. The vitamins that the doctor prescribed should be taken daily.
3. The murals, which were commissioned by the city, were painted by Harry Marshak.
4. The suit, which was made from gray wool, cost less than $80.
5. Marsha, whom Hector made office manager, is 40 years old.

Ask for volunteers to read their sentences, identify the relative pronouns, and explain their pronoun choices.

Lesson Wrap-Up

Exercise and Answer Key Discussion: Ask the class why item 3 is correct. Write the remaining sentences on the board and invite volunteers to edit them and explain their changes.

If students are having difficulty using who and whom correctly, have them try this procedure.

1. Take the word group out of the context of the sentence.
2. Replace the relative pronoun with either *he* or *him*.
3. If necessary, rearrange the words in the group to make a complete sentence.
4. If the word *he* sounds right, use *who*. If the word *him* is correct, use *whom*.

Error Analysis: If your students have had trouble with the exercise, first have them underline the group of words beginning with the relative pronoun. Then ask them to find the word that the relative pronoun describes. Use the following review questions to go over the correct use of relative pronouns.

1. Which relative pronoun should never be used to refer to people? (*which*)
2. Which relative pronouns should never be used to refer to things? (*who* and *whom*)
3. Which relative pronoun can be used to refer to people, animals, places, and things? (*that*)

Lesson 4: Avoiding Unclear Pronoun References

Lesson Warm-Up

Vocabulary: An understanding of the following terms is necessary to do the work in Lesson 4.

- **Vague:** In the context of this lesson, *vague* is used to refer to pronouns that have unclear meanings. Both relative and personal pronouns can be vague.
- **Ambiguous:** In the context of this lesson, *ambiguous* is used to describe a pronoun that is unclear because it could have more than one meaning. Remember, a pronoun is ambiguous if it could possibly be interpreted a second way.

Activity: The following sentences contain vague or ambiguous pronoun references. Read them aloud to the class one at a time. Ask the students to explain why the use of pronouns is unclear. Have them suggest possible antecedents for the pronouns. Point out that a pronoun with more than one possible antecedent is confusing to the reader. (The underlined pronouns are unclear.)

1. During the postgame interviews, <u>they</u> described the full extent of the quarterback's injuries.
2. Henry thought <u>it</u> said to use 3 cups of salt.
3. I always take vitamins when I am under stress because <u>they</u> say <u>they</u> help reduce anxiety.
4. The teachers voted against the directors, and <u>they</u> arrived back in the city the next day.
5. The postal worker and the customer discussed the postage and then <u>he</u> taped up the package.

Lesson Activity

One of the best ways to correct an unclear pronoun reference is to replace the pronoun with a noun. Write

sentences 1 to 3 from the lesson warm-up on the board and ask for volunteers to edit them.

Answers

1. During the postgame interviews, the trainers described the full extent of the quarterback's injuries.
2. Henry thought the recipe said to use 3 cups of salt.
3. I always take vitamins when I am under stress because doctors say vitamins help reduce anxiety.

The pronoun references in items 4 and 5 from the Lesson Warm-Up are ambiguous. Discuss the possible meanings of the underlined pronouns. Ask for volunteers to suggest corrections.

Possible Answers

4. The teachers who voted against the directors arrived back in the city the next day.
5. The postal worker and the customer discussed the postage and then the postal worker taped up the package.

Lesson Wrap-Up

Exercise and Answer Key Discussion: Write the sentences on the board. Circle the unclear pronoun references. Use an arrow to show that the pronoun does not clearly refer to an antecedent. Reword the sentences or substitute nouns for pronouns.

Activity: Divide the class into small groups (three or four students per group). Most unclear pronoun references are harmless because the reader is able to figure out the meaning from other clues in the sentence. Sometimes, however, bad writing can cost a company money or an employee a job. Assign the groups to write a sentence or short passage that contains a possible vague pronoun reference. Let the students select the most striking example of bad writing. Sometimes creating a bad example brings the right concepts into focus.

Error Analysis: Students who are having difficulty should be encouraged to circle every pronoun and make sure that each has a clear antecedent. If there is any doubt, the sentence should be edited.

Chapter 2 Sentence Structure

Skill 1:   Complete Sentences

Why do students have difficulty recognizing complete sentences? The answer is simple. Do you think in complete sentences? Do you speak in complete sentences? Most of us think and speak in fragments and run-ons. Our ideas continue to flow and we link them with whatever words and phrases seem convenient at the time. We don't notice the fragments and run-ons because our intent is to communicate. In other words, our focus is on content, not on structure.

Our students' ability to recognize and write complete sentences improves as soon as we shift their attention to the structure. The basic rules are simple. Seeing the patterns in the sentences is the thing that complicates the task. Students who have difficulty recognizing subjects and verbs at this point are likely to have difficulty working with complete sentences. You may need to review the appropriate lessons in Chapter 1. Otherwise, begin with the definition and structure of the complete sentence.

The lessons in this chapter center on common sentence errors. Lesson 1 shows how to correct fragments. Lesson 2 explains how to correct run-ons by separating them. Lesson 3 shows other ways to correct run-on sentences.

You may want to refer students who are having difficulty to Chapters 1, 2, and 3 of *On Your Own: Grammar*, and Unit 1, Chapter 3, Lesson 17 and Unit 1, Chapter 4, of the *Threshold* writing skills text. These texts offer additional instruction and exercises at a Pre-GED level. For more GED-level work, see *The New Revised Cambridge GED Program Writing Skills*, Part 1, Unit 2, Chapters 1 and 2.

Lesson 1:   Eliminating Sentence Fragments

Lesson Warm-Up

Vocabulary: An understanding of the following terms is necessary to do the work in Lesson 1.

- **Complete sentence:** A complete sentence has a subject and a verb, and it expresses a complete thought. It also starts with a capital letter and ends with a period (.), a question mark (?), or an exclamation mark (!).
- **Sentence fragment:** A fragment is a group of words that looks like a complete sentence, but it lacks one of the elements of a complete sentence. Usually, a sentence fragment lacks either a subject or a verb.

Activity: Read the following to the class. Have them vote on whether the ideas sound complete or not.

1. The supplies delivered by Office Standard.
2. Montana carried the ball across the line for a touchdown.
3. Is the major difference between you and me.
4. Two of the clerks in the post office.
5. Consuelo remained in the car.

Write the fragments (1, 3, and 4) on the board. Ask the students to explain why the ideas are not complete.

Lesson Activities

Activity 1:   Write the following fragments on the board. Have the students use the fragments to write complete sentences.

1. The company's plans.
2. Are the skills I need most on my job.
3. The empty lot on the corner of Broadway and Third Street.
4. Knowledge of grammar rules.
5. May arrive before we start.
6. All full-time employees the meeting on Saturday.

Ask volunteers to read their sentences. Have them explain what was missing from the original fragment.

Activity 2:   Have the students write a paragraph (on any topic) containing at least five sentences. Direct them to change two of the sentences to fragments.

11

The students should copy their paragraphs so that the fragments are not apparent. Each person should exchange paragraphs with a partner and edit the partner's paragraph.

Lesson Wrap-Up

Exercise and Answer Key Discussion: Identify sentence 3 as a complete sentence. Discuss why it is complete. For the remaining sentences, ask the class what is missing. Ask for volunteers to read their edited versions of each sentence.

Ask the students to describe the process they are using to detect fragments. Although fragments usually "sound" incomplete, how a sentence sounds is not the only test. Encourage the students to identify the subject and verb as well.

Error Analysis: If students are having a difficult time identifying fragments, have the students read the item aloud. Then ask the students if the item sounds complete. Have the students say their corrected versions aloud before writing anything down.

Lesson 2:   Separating Run-on Sentences

Lesson Warm-Up

Vocabulary: An understanding of the following terms is necessary to do the work in Lesson 2.

- **Run-on sentence:** This common sentence error occurs when two or more complete sentences are joined without punctuation or with incorrect punctuation. Point out that "on" spelled backward is "no." In other words, a run-*on* has *no* punctuation.
- **Comma splice:** This common sentence error occurs when two or more complete sentences are joined by only a comma.
- **Compound verbs:** Within a sentence, a subject can have two or more verbs. The verbs are joined using a connecting word. Remember, *compound* means two or more of something act as one. In a compound verb, two or more verb words act as one verb.

Activity: Prepare the following sentences as a handout. Point out that run-ons and comma splices must be seen to be detected. Tell the students to identify these items as either complete sentences, run-ons, or comma splices.

1. It was not an easy job I cleaned the garage myself.
2. Irma cooks dinner the first and third weeks, Samuel cooks the second and fourth weeks.
3. Ricardo carried his briefcase, the sack of groceries, his toddler, and his keys into the house.
4. Omri picked up his dry cleaning and returned his library books.

5. The bank closes early on Friday it will be open until noon on Saturday.
6. Julissa works on Mondays from noon to 8 P.M., she works on Tuesdays through Fridays from 9 a.m. to 5 P.M.

Answers: 1. run-on; 2. comma splice; 3. correct; 4. correct; 5. run-on; 6. comma splice

Lesson Activity

Write the following run-ons and comma splices on the board. Have the students underline each complete thought and circle the subject and verb pairs. Then correct the errors by separating the ideas into two complete sentences.

1. Ron was born in South Carolina, he went to college in Florida.
2. The contest ended Thursday, we will know the results on Friday.
3. That customer seems to be very angry she tore up the receipt and yelled at the manager.
4. Sophie ordered 1000 business cards, the printer spelled her name wrong on the cards.

Have the students check their work for run-ons and comma splices. Ask: What thought process do you use to check for run-ons and comma splices? The following steps are good suggestions:

1. Identify the two complete ideas in the sentence.
2. Find the subjects and verbs of each.
3. Identify the method used to join the two ideas.
4. Make a correction if necessary.

Lesson Wrap-Up

Exercise and Answer Key Discussion: Discuss why sentence 1 is correct. Ask for volunteers to write the remaining sentences on the board as two separate sentences. Point out the subjects and verbs in each sentence.

Error Analysis: Once the definitions of comma splice and run-on are known, students usually can identify them with little difficulty. The most common error is labeling a sentence with a compound verb as a run-on. Teach the students to find the subject and verb in each complete idea. Then direct them to find the point at which the first complete idea ends.

Lesson 3:   Correcting Run-on Sentences

Lesson Warm-Up

Vocabulary: An understanding of the following terms is necessary to do the work in Lesson 3.

- **Connecting words:** Also called conjunctions or coordinating conjunctions. These are words—*and, but, or, nor, so, for,* and *yet*—that with a comma are used to join two complete ideas in one sentence. The comma is used to mark the ending of the first complete idea.
- **Semicolon:** A mark of punctuation (;) that can be used to join complete ideas. When a semicolon is used, a connecting word is not needed.

Activity: Give the following items to the class with the instruction to edit all run-on sentences using punctuation and connecting words.

1. Jayne has finally decided to move to New York she will leave this summer.
2. The sales managers will meet in room 301, the floor personnel will meet in Mr. Rhode's office.
3. It is supposed to rain on Thursday and I hope it does.
4. Karla takes orders and types invoices Mike does the bookkeeping and handles customer relations.
5. Luke found the instructions in the box, however, the directions were too confusing.

Ask for volunteers to write each sentence on the board in its corrected form.

Possible Answers: (There are several right answers for each item.)

1. Jayne has finally decided to move to New York, and she will leave this summer.
2. The sales managers will meet in room 301; the floor personnel will meet in Mr. Rhode's office.
3. It is supposed to rain on Thursday, and I hope it does.
4. Karla takes orders and types invoices; Mike does the bookkeeping and handles customer relations.
5. Luke found the instructions in the box; however, the directions were too confusing.

Lesson Activity

Activity: Divide the class into small groups. Give the groups the following sentence pairs. Ask them to join the ideas in one sentence using the methods in the lesson.

1. I am going to the mall. I am not going to spend any money.
2. The diskette looked badly damaged. The right corner was bent.
3. Our team didn't win the game. It was fun competing.
4. Kirk set five goals at the beginning of the year. He has already accomplished three of them.

Ask for volunteers to write their answers on the board. Discuss with the class the process they used to write the sentences. What was the most difficult part of the task?

Lesson Wrap-Up

Exercise and Answer Key Discussion: Ask for volunteers to explain what is wrong with each sentence and to give one possible way of correcting it.

Discussion: Wouldn't it be easier to write only one complete idea in each sentence? Why should we combine ideas in a sentence? (Some ideas are related. Joining them in a single sentence helps the reader group ideas mentally. Also point out that too many short sentences make writing sound choppy.)

Error Analysis: If students are having difficulty, have them first underline the subjects and verbs in each item. This will help the student recognize both complete ideas. Then instruct the student to choose one of the methods from the lesson to connect both clauses. Remind the students that these are the only correct methods. They must learn how to use correct punctuation and connectors to form complete sentences. It is impossible to do the work based on what "sounds right."

After the students have edited the sentences, have the students read aloud the words on both sides of the punctuation. Point out that each side should sound like a complete idea.

Skill 2: Sentence Construction: Coordination and Subordination

Lesson 1: Equal Ideas: Coordination

Lesson Warm-Up

Vocabulary: An understanding of the following terms is necessary to do the work in Lesson 1.

- **Complete thought:** In the context of this lesson, a complete thought is an idea that could stand alone as a complete sentence.
- **Coordinators:** Words that are used as connectors in sentences. This lesson focuses on the coordinating conjunctions (*and, but, or, nor, so, for,* and *yet*) and the transitional words and phrases that can be used with a semicolon.

Activity: What is wrong with these sentences?

1. Computers make doing paperwork easier, and my brother likes to play computer games. (two unrelated ideas)
2. Manuel interviewed well, and he didn't get the job. (poor choice of coordinator)
3. In the past, fast-food restaurants have encouraged Americans to eat poorly, however, many fast-food restaurants are now becoming health-conscious. (punctuated incorrectly)

Lesson Activity

Assign the students to write ten sentences describing the events of their day yesterday. These should be short simple sentences. Then have them search their lists for items that could be combined into longer sentences. Assign them to choose appropriate connectors from the list on page 94. When they are finished, their lists will have become paragraphs. Point out that a paragraph made up of choppy, short sentences seems poorly written although the grammar is correct. Using connectors adds variety.

Lesson Wrap-Up

Exercise and Answer Key Discussion: Ask for volunteers to read their versions of each sentence. Point out that most sentences can be corrected in more than one way. Discuss how this applies to the GED test. During the test, they will have to choose an appropriate correction from the list of choices.

Discussion: What would be the best way to approach a sentence on the GED test that has a problem with coordination? (Once you have identified the error as a coordination error, read the answer choices to see which is a possible correction. Do not read only for the correction you would like to make.)

Lesson 2: Unequal Ideas: Subordination

Lesson Warm-Up

Vocabulary: An understanding of the following terms is necessary to do the work in Lesson 2.

- **Subordinators:** Words used to join ideas of unequal importance in a sentence. A subordinator can be used to begin a sentence.
- **Main idea:** A complete thought. The most important idea in a complex sentence.

Activity: Write the following sentences on the board. Ask for volunteers to underline the main idea and circle the subordinator.

1. Since I am going on vacation next week, I think I'll work some extra hours this week.
2. If you have any questions about the seminar, please ask me.
3. Charles must make a decision soon because he needs to send a reply by August 3.
4. Before I call the doctor, I'd better check with the insurance company.
5. Ms. Jordan called the Sacramento office as soon as she received the bill.

Answers:

1. (Since) I am going on vacation next week, <u>I think I'll work some extra hours this week.</u>
2. (If) you have any questions about the seminar, <u>please ask me.</u>
3. <u>Charles must make a decision soon</u> (because) he needs to send a reply by August 3.
4. (Before) I call the doctor, <u>I'd better check with the insurance company.</u>
5. <u>Ms. Jordan called the Sacramento office</u> (as soon as) she received the bill.

Lesson Activities

Activity 1: Divide the class into small groups. Have each group choose four subordinators from the lists on pages 95–96. Direct them to write sentences using the subordinators correctly. Then have them change the subordinators to make the sentences obviously incorrect. Create a master list of sentences that require revision for the class to edit.

Activity 2: Give the following sentences to the class as a review activity. Instruct the class to identify the items using these labels:

- A Correct sentence with two equal ideas
- B Correct sentence with ideas of unequal importance
- C Run-on or comma splice
- D Fragment

Have the students correct any run-ons and comma splices.

1. Carlos bought the wood and paint he forgot to pick up nails and hinges.
2. Victoria Lopez, the vice president of sales, in Los Angeles.
3. Because his office is so small, Mr. Tran decided to repaint it a lighter color.
4. Ms. Campbell will give Frederick another chance even though he missed his appointment.
5. We will meet our financial goals, and we will have extra money for the vacation.

6. Give Miguel a chance to prove his ability he is very talented.
7. As soon as we started to run.
8. Jeff set the table without forks, he forgot the glasses and napkins too.
9. If you need Mr. Lyons's help, you have only to ask him.
10. The music is written for a saxophone, trumpet, and drums; it sounds difficult.

Read the class the answers and discuss them. Students who are having trouble should review Skill 1 in depth.

Answers: 1. C; 2. D; 3. B; 4. B; 5. A; 6. C; 7. D; 8. C; 9. B; 10. A.

Lesson Wrap-Up

Exercise and Answer Key Discussion: Write sentence 3 on the board. Discuss why it is punctuated correctly. Ask for volunteers to describe what is wrong in each of the remaining incorrect sentences. Help the students analyze sentence 5. Although it is punctuated correctly, the sentence is incorrect because the two ideas are not related and should not be placed in the same sentence. Ask volunteers to write the corrected sentences on the board.

Activity: Divide the class into six groups. Assign each group a term to define. Each group of students should define a term in their own words and create three examples. Have the groups report to the class.

> *Terms*
> complete sentence
> coordinator
> subordinator
> fragment
> run-on
> comma splice

Error Analysis: If students are having difficulty, instruct them to underline the main idea first. Then have the students identify the subordinator. Have the class match the pattern of the sentence to the types of sentences on pages 94 and 95. This will help them determine if the punctuation is correct.
     Students may have difficulty learning the meaning of subordinators. The words on pages 95–96 are those subordinators that are commonly used on the GED test. Writing sentences using these words correctly is the best way to drill their meaning.

Skill 3:   Clear Sentences

There are two basic problems that can make a complete sentence difficult to understand. One, often-amusing problem occurs when a modifier (either a word or a phrase) is placed incorrectly within the sentence. These misplaced modifiers (and danglers) can be difficult to spot because the sentence retains some meaning even though it may be an unintended meaning. Lesson 1 shows how to recognize and correct misplaced modifiers.
     Sentences with parallel structure are easier to read and understand. Sentences that lack parallel structure can still be understood, but the reader has to stop and think. Lesson 2 shows how to use parallel structure and correct sentences that lack it.
     These qualities of a well-written sentence may seem subtle to students at first. As you use the learning activities in this guide, have the students focus on the mental images that a sentence gives them. Ask them how the image changes when the error is corrected. The three concepts presented in this chapter lead to clearly written messages.
     You may want to refer students who are having difficulty to Chapters 15 and 18 of *On Your Own: Writing Process* and Unit 1, Chapter 3, Lesson 17, and Unit 1, Chapter 4, Lessons 18 and 23, of the *Threshold* writing skills text. These texts offer additional instruction and exercises at a Pre-GED level.

Lesson 1:   Clarity of Thought

Lesson Warm-Up

Vocabulary: An understanding of the following terms is necessary to do the work in Lesson 1.

- **Clarity:** A sentence that has clarity is clear in meaning. Several common problems can make a sentence unclear. Using long words and unnecessary words are two common mistakes.
- **Modifier:** A word or phrase that explains or describes another word in a sentence.
- **Misplaced modifier:** An error that occurs when a modifier is placed too far from the word it is supposed to describe.
- **Dangling modifier:** An error that occurs when there is no word that can logically be modified or described.
- **Modification errors:** Errors made using modifiers; the two kinds are called misplaced modifiers and dangling modifiers.

Activity: Write the following sentences on the board. Tell the class to rewrite the sentences by correcting all modification errors.

1. Rushing to unload the groceries, the car parked on the front lawn.
2. Dodger Stadium is in Los Angeles, California, which seats about 50,000 people.
3. I found the recipe for homemade macaroni and cheese reading your mother's journal.

Have volunteers come to the board and rewrite each of the sentences. Have them explain their changes to the class.

Possible Answers

1. Rushing to unload the groceries, I parked the car on the front lawn.
2. Dodger Stadium, which seats about 50,000 people, is in Los Angeles, California.
3. I found the recipe for homemade macaroni and cheese while I was reading your mother's journal.

Lesson Activity

Put the following sentences on the board. Have the students explain what is wrong and offer a suggestion to correct the problem. All sentences have modification errors.

1. The robber was surprised to hear a gunshot trying to escape the attention of the police.
2. Skipping rope on our street, my father saw two little girls going for a walk.
3. Studying the driver's handbook, two rules were very confused.
4. The post office is located on Brand Avenue, which is red brick.

Possible Answers

1. Trying to escape the attention of the police, the robber was surprised to hear a gunshot.
2. While going for a walk, my father saw two little girls skipping rope on our street
3. As I was studying the driver's handbook, I became very confused over two rules.
4. The post office, which is red brick, is located on Brand Avenue.

Lesson Wrap-Up

Exercise and Answer Key Discussion: Write sentence 5 on the board. Discuss why it is correct. Underline the two prepositional phrases and draw arrows to the words they modify. Ask for volunteers to write correct versions of the remaining sentences on the board. Have the volunteers explain why they chose to correct the sentences as they did.

Discussion: Why are misplaced modifiers rarely a problem in conversation? Conversations include visual clues. In fact, some experts claim that less than 7% of a message comes through the words themselves. Words can be confusing. Because written language relies almost entirely on words, using correct grammar principles is very important.

Error Analysis: If a student is having difficulty completing these exercises, have the student read the sentence aloud. Ask the student whether the sentence

can be interpreted more than one way. If it can, the sentence probably needs correction. Your edits should help a sentence make sense. Determine what needs to change for the sentence to have only one meaning.

Lesson 2: Parallel Structure

Lesson Warm-Up

Vocabulary: An understanding of the following term is necessary to do the work in Lesson 2.

- **Parallel:** In the context of English grammar, the term *parallel* means similar or same. Sentences that express a series of ideas need parallel structure.

Activity: Write the following sentences on the board. For each sentence, ask the class to identify the series first. Then have them underline the words that lack parallel structure. Finally, make changes to correct the errors in parallel structure.

1. Babysitting, washing cars, and to do errands around the house are three ways my children earn money.
2. Dalida's new secretary is reliable, a friend to all, and efficient.
3. The house needs insulating, landscaping, and a new coat of paint.

Possible Answers

1. Babysitting, washing cars, and doing errands around the house are three ways my children earn money.
2. Dalida's new secretary is reliable, friendly, and efficient.
3. The house needs insulating, landscaping, and painting.

Lesson Activity

Give the class the following sentences as a handout. Instruct the class to correct all errors in parallel structure.

1. The campers will learn to swim, hiking, boating and to make crafts.
2. Selling, to handle customer problems, and word processing are three skills I am listing on my résumé.
3. My supervisor encourages creativity, productivity, and being on time.
4. Max baked a tuna casserole, mixed a fruit salad, and slicing pickles for the picnic.
5. My best friend is an author, a golfer and she paints things.

1. The campers will learn to swim, hike, boat, and make crafts.
2. Selling, handling customer problems, and word processing are three skills I am listing on my résumé.
3. My supervisor encourages creativity, productivity, and punctuality.
4. Max baked a tuna casserole, mixed a fruit salad, and sliced pickles for the picnic.
5. My best friend is an author, a golfer, and a painter.

Lesson Wrap-Up

Exercise Discussion: What types of sentence elements need parallel structure? Sentence 1 contains a list of adjectives. Sentence 3 has a list of clauses beginning with "how." Sentence 4 begins with a list of gerund phrases, and sentence 5 begins with a compound subject consisting of one gerund phrase and one infinitive phrase.

Point out that any sentence element can require parallel structure. Encourage the students to find the series and the elements involved before they begin to edit.

Divide the class into groups of three. Direct the members of the group to put into their own words each of the three methods of determining errors in parallel structure listed on page 101.

Error Analysis: If a student is having difficulty "seeing" the errors in parallel structure, have the student underline the words that are part of the series. Then ask the student if the elements separated by commas are in the same format. Have the student change any words that are not parallel.

Chapter 3 Mechanics

Skill 1:   Capitalization

This chapter follows a logical method of presenting the rules of capitalization. Lesson 1 gives an overview with ample examples to familiarize the student with the reasoning behind capitalization.

Lesson 2 applies these principles to the difficult area of names and titles. Capitalization gives importance to a word, so naturally we would all like our titles to be capitalized. However, the presence of too many capital letters is distracting. This lesson clears up the mystery of whether or not to capitalize titles—those other names we give ourselves.

In Lesson 3, the students learn the necessary details of capitalization. Specific rules that apply to time, dates, seasons, and special and historical events are given.

You may want to refer students who are having difficulty to Chapter 16 of *On Your Own: Grammar*, a volume in a Cambridge Pre-GED series. Additional exercises can be found in Chapter 23 of *On Your Own: Writing Process* from the same series. These chapters offer additional instruction and exercises at a Pre-GED level. For more work at a GED-level, see *The New Revised Cambridge GED Program: Writing Skills*, Part 1, Unit 3.

Lesson 1:   Proper Nouns and Proper Adjectives

Lesson Warm-Up

Vocabulary: An understanding of the following terms is necessary to do the work in Lesson 1.

- **Common noun:** A general name for a person, place, or thing. Do not capitalize a common noun (unless it is the first word in a sentence or part of a title).
- **Proper noun:** A specific name for a person, place, or thing. Proper nouns are always capitalized.
- **Proper adjective:** A word formed from a proper noun. For example, *English* (as in *English language*) is capitalized because it comes from the word *England*.

To help students understand the difference between common and proper nouns, suggest that proper nouns are official names. Official names appear on birth certificates, maps, billboards, and so on.

Example: When you cross the border as you enter a state, you usually see a billboard: "Welcome to the state of Colorado!" The noun *Colorado* is the official name of the state. It should be capitalized, but the word *state* is a general name. It should not be capitalized.

Activity: Write the following two sentences on the board. Ask for volunteers to underline all nouns. Then have them capitalize the proper nouns.

1. My husband, craig, played baseball for the houston astros last season.
2. The headquarters for egghead software is located in bothell, washington.

   Answers

1. My <u>husband</u>, <u>Craig</u>, played <u>baseball</u> for the <u>Houston Astros</u> last <u>season</u>.
2. The <u>headquarters</u> for <u>Egghead Software</u> is located in <u>Bothell, Washington</u>.

Lesson Activities

Activity 1:   Put the following list of proper nouns on the board.

Ask the class to think of an example of a common noun that could apply to the same person, place, or thing.

1. Mrs. Louise Young
2. Tilden Avenue
3. Monday
4. Kansas
5. Yellowstone National Park
6. Tulsa
7. *Jurassic Park*
8. French

Possible Answers: 1. woman; 2. street; 3. day; 4. state; 5. park; 6. city; 7. movie; 8. language

Activity 2: Put the following list of common nouns on the board.

Ask the class to think of an example of a proper noun that could apply to the same person, place, or thing.

1. man
2. highway
3. month
4. country
5. amusement park
6. award
7. book
8. team

Possible Answers: 1. Bill Clinton; 2. Pennyrile Parkway; 3. July; 4. Mexico; 5. Disneyworld; 6. Academy Award; 7. *The Grapes of Wrath*; 8. Chicago Bulls

Activity: Prepare a handout with the following sentences or put the sentences on the board. Have the students correct all capitalization errors.

1. wouldn't it be exciting to meet the queen of england?
2. on their honeymoon, ricardo and maria visited the golden gate bridge in san francisco.
3. jonathan mistakenly thought that the lincoln memorial in washington, d.c., was located in new york city.
4. ingrid was born in norway and speaks norwegian, french, and german fluently.
5. nora's granddaughter, letty, has memorized all the words to every song in the musical *the king and i.*

Answers

1. Wouldn't it be exciting to meet the Queen of England?
2. On their honeymoon, Ricardo and Maria visited the Golden Gate Bridge in San Francisco.
3. Jonathan mistakenly thought that the Lincoln Memorial in Washington, D.C., was located in New York City.
4. Ingrid was born in Norway and speaks Norwegian, French, and German fluently.
5. Nora's granddaughter, Letty, has memorized all the words to every song in the musical *The King and I.*

Lesson Wrap-Up

Exercise and Answer Key Discussion: Point out that sentence 3 is correctly capitalized. Ask the class to explain why the words *tourist attraction* in sentence 2

are not capitalized. Ask for volunteers to write the corrected versions of each of the remaining sentences on the board. Ask the volunteers to explain the rules that apply to each sentence.

Error Analysis: Have students underline the nouns in each sentence first. Then have the students determine if each noun is a specific name of a person, place, or thing. Remind the students that a proper noun is an official name. If they saw the noun on a billboard or a sign, would it be capitalized?

Lesson 2: Titles of People and Addresses

Lesson Warm-Up

Vocabulary: An understanding of the following term is necessary to do the work in Lesson 2.

- **Title:** People have both professional and personal titles. Most people are proud of their titles because they had to work hard to earn them. Using correct capitalization style with titles is important to make a good impression. In this lesson, the text makes a distinction between titles that come before a name (Aunt Mary, Captain Utley, General Adams) and titles that come after a name (Cynthia Adams, a professor at LMU).

Activity: Write the following two sentences on the board.

1. Julio used to work as a Gas Station Attendant at a business located East of Main street in Carson city.
2. Please send Your deposit to ms. elsye merced at 1600 south Alandele court, lincoln, Missouri 68543.

Ask for volunteers to come to the board and correct the capitalization errors.

Answers:
1. Julio used to work as a gas station attendant at a business located east of Main Street in Carson City.
2. Please send your deposit to Ms. Elsye Merced at 1600 South Alandele Court, Lincoln, Missouri 68543.

Lesson Activity

Prepare a handout with the following sentences or write them on the board. Direct the class to correct all capitalization errors.

1. the garcias announced the marriage of their daughter anna garcia to stephen r. brooks.

2. george c. scott portrayed general patton in the movie *patton*.
3. casey has worked as a dental hygienist for dr. kenneth grove for the past twelve years.
4. janice mendoza, president of kidcrafts inc., is sponsoring an art festival at 374 barton road in arlington park.
5. Mai can get extra credit in her history class if she visits the ronald reagan library in simi valley, california.
6. gregg wrote his report on sally ride, the first woman astronaut to travel in space.
7. My uncle says that he can easily see why florida is called the sunshine state.
8. doctor earl platter, aunt marie's doctor, strongly recommends that she move to the southwest to improve her health.

Answers

1. The Garcias announced the marriage of their daughter Anna Garcia to Stephen R. Brooks.
2. George C. Scott portrayed General Patton in the movie *Patton*.
3. Casey has worked as a dental hygienist for Dr. Kenneth Grove for the past twelve years.
4. Janice Mendoza, president of Kidcrafts Inc., is sponsoring an art festival at 374 Barton Road in Arlington Park.
5. Mai can get extra credit in her history class if she visits the Ronald Reagan Library in Simi Valley, California.
6. Gregg wrote his report on Sally Ride, the first woman astronaut to travel in space.
7. My uncle says that he can easily see why Florida is called the Sunshine State.
8. Doctor Earl Platter, Aunt Marie's doctor, strongly recommends that she move to the Southwest to improve her health.

Have the class exchange and correct each other's papers. When students find an error, instruct them to write the rule that applies (from Lesson 1 or 2) by the error.

Lesson Wrap-Up

Exercise and Answer Key Discussion: Point out that sentence 1 is correct. Have the class identify each error and state the rule that applies in the remaining sentences.

Error Analysis: Students who have difficulty with capitalization tend to use an intuitive method of making decisions. Remind the students that it is impossible to hear the need for capitalization. Capitalizing all "important" words won't work. Learning the rules is the only way to learn capitalization.

Lesson 3:   Times, Dates, Seasons, and Special Historical Events

Lesson Warm-Up

Vocabulary: No new vocabulary terms are presented in this lesson.

Activity: Instruct the class to correct all errors in capitalization in the following two sentences.

1. My Boss, tony Avakian, decided to add mother's day and Columbus day to our Holidays this year.
2. Katherine couric and bryant gumbel from the today show spent the week of may 10 highlighting the important events of the Sixties.

Answers

1. My boss, Tony Avakian, decided to add Mother's Day and Columbus Day to our holidays this year.
2. Katherine Couric and Bryant Gumbel from the Today Show spent the week of May 10 highlighting the important events of the sixties.

Lesson Activity

Dictate the following phrases to your class. Ask them to write them using correct capitalization style. (The phrases are shown correctly here.)

1. New Year's Day
2. Olympic Games
3. Monroe County Fair
4. Saturday, December 7, at 12:30 P.M.
5. the Vietnam War
6. the Freedom March of 1963
7. the fall and winter
8. St. Patrick's Day
9. the month of September
10. the Rose Bowl

Check the students' answers and discuss the rule that applies to each situation.

Lesson Wrap-Up

Exercise and Answer Key Discussion: Point out that sentence 4 is correct. Ask for volunteers to correct the remaining sentences on the board. Ask the class to identify which rules apply to each sentence.

Error Analysis: Have the students underline all the nouns first. Then have the students determine which nouns (and adjectives) are specific names.

Skill 2:   Punctuation

Part I of the GED test covers punctuation as it relates to revising or proofreading. The student is asked to read a sentence. The student is then asked to determine if anything is wrong, and if so, to choose the correct revision.

The lessons in Skill 2 teach the student about common punctuation errors. It isn't meant to be a reference manual. Instead, the reasons behind the rules are presented. Punctuation rules are easy to remember when they make sense. As you teach this chapter, avoid dwelling on exceptions. Punctuation rule exceptions are difficult for the best writers to remember. The GED tests only basic knowledge of punctuation.

There is another important reason to do well in this chapter. Learning the basics of punctuation will aid the student on the essay-writing portion of the test. You will notice that many of the activities call for students to write their own sentences. At times, the students are encouraged to write incorrect sentences to further see the purpose behind the rules. Incorporating writing activities now is good preparation for the students' work in Part II of this book.

You may want to refer students who are having difficulty to Chapter 16, Lessons 1 and 2, of *On Your Own: Grammar*, a volume in a Cambridge Pre-GED series. For more GED work, see *The New Revised Cambridge GED* Writing Skills text, Unit 3, Chapter 2.

Lesson 1:   Commas between Items in a Series

Lesson Warm-Up

Vocabulary: An understanding of the following term is necessary to do the work in Lesson 1.

- **Series:** A list of things arranged one after the other within the same sentence. A series may have as few as two items. When the items are separated by conjunctions, no punctuation is needed. When conjunctions are not used, the items in a series should be separated using commas.

Activity: Write the following sentences on the board. Instruct the class to correct all errors in punctuation.

1. Before I go home, I will go to the bank, the gas station, and, the grocery store.
2. The students can read *The Count of Monte Cristo*, or *The Grapes of Wrath*, or *The Phantom of the Opera* for extra credit.
3. This is the most difficult time-consuming project I've ever undertaken.

Answers

1. Before I go home, I will go to the bank, the gas station, and the grocery store. (Insert commas to divide the items in the series. Use the final comma before the conjunction, not after the conjunction. See Rule 1.)
2. The students can read *The Count of Monte Cristo* or *The Grapes of Wrath* or *The Phantom of the Opera* for extra credit. (Do not use commas in addition to a conjunction. See Rule 5.)
3. This is the most difficult, time-consuming project I've ever undertaken. (See Rule 2.)

Lesson Activity

Give the following sentences to the class as a handout or write the sentences on the board. Have the class add the correct punctuation to each sentence.

1. Joyce has lived in Chicago Detroit and New York.
2. Before you leave the house, turn off the television set the heater and the lights.
3. All the children in the preschool have had strep throat and ear infections this winter.
4. Enclose a self-addressed stamped envelope.
5. Geneen has decided to include aerobics bicycling dancing jogging and walking in her exercise program.

Answers

1. Joyce has lived in Chicago, Detroit, and New York. (Rule 1)
2. Before you leave the house, turn off the television set, the heater, and the lights. (Rule 1)
3. All the children in the preschool have had strep throat and ear infections this winter. (Correct. There are only two items listed; therefore, no comma is needed.)
4. Enclose a self-addressed, stamped envelope. (Rule 3)
5. Geneen has decided to include aerobics, bicycling, dancing, jogging, and walking in her exercise program. (Rule 1)

Ask volunteers to come to the board and write each corrected sentence. Have the student explain the rule that applies to each sentence.

Lesson Wrap-Up

Exercise and Answer Key Discussion: Ask the class which sentence is correctly punctuated and why. [Sentence 4: No punctuation is needed because there are conjunctions used between each item in the series (Rule 5).] Have volunteers explain the corrections used in each of the remaining sentences.

Error Analysis: If a student is having difficulty, have the student write the items in the series in a vertical list. This will help them "see" the series. Then have the student insert a comma after each item but the last.

Lesson 2: Commas after Introductory Elements

Lesson Warm-Up

Vocabulary: An understanding of the following terms is necessary to do the work in Lesson 2.

- **Introductory element:** A word or phrase that begins a sentence but is not part of the main idea of the sentence. An introductory element introduces the main idea.
- **Subordinate idea:** Subordinate clauses, sometimes called dependent clauses, are ideas that cannot stand alone.

Activity: Write the following sentences on the board. Instruct the class to copy the sentences on their papers. For each sentence, ask the class to underline the introductory element and add correct punctuation.

1. Finally the baby fell asleep around 2:30 A.M.
2. In addition will you call Mr. Potter before you leave?
3. Because of the smog Julia decided not to jog this morning.
4. If you use all the paper again this month I'll order two extra boxes.

Answers

1. *Finally*, the baby fell asleep around 2:30 a.m. (This sentence illustrates Rule 1. *Finally* is an introductory word beginning the sentence and followed by a comma.)
2. *In addition*, will you call Mr. Potter before you leave? (This sentence illustrates Rule 2. *In addition* is used as an introductory phrase.)
3. *Because of the smog*, Julia decided not to jog this morning. (This sentence illustrates Rule 2. *Because of the smog* is an introductory phrase. The remaining words form an independent clause.)
4. *If you use all the paper again this month*, I'll order two extra boxes. (This sentence illustrates Rule 3. *If you use all the paper this month* is a subordinate idea—a dependent clause—at the beginning of a sentence.)

Lesson Activity

Ask the class to write the following sentences.

1. A sentence that begins with the word *well* and demonstrates Rule 1.
2. A sentence that begins with the phrase *by the end of the day* and demonstrates Rule 2.
3. A sentence that begins with a subordinate idea (dependent clause) and demonstrates Rule 3.

Have volunteers read their sentences to the class. Point out that these words are introductory elements and must be set off by a comma in order to separate the elements from the main idea. Ask the students whether the introductory elements are read aloud differently than the main idea. (Most of us pause slightly at the end of an introductory element. Many people even lower their voices or speak at a lower pitch as the introductory element is read.)

Have the students turn their third sentences around so that the dependent clauses come at the end. Have them explore whether this change affects the meaning of the sentence. Remind them that it is not necessary to separate the dependent clause from the main idea with a comma when the dependent clause comes at the end.

Lesson Wrap-Up

Exercise and Answer Key Discussion: Point out that sentence 2 is correct because a comma is not needed to separate the main clause from the subordinate clause if the subordinate clause comes at the end. Have volunteers come to the board and underline the main idea for each remaining sentence. Then have the student point out which rule applies and add the correct punctuation.

Error Analysis: If a student is having difficulty, have the student read aloud each part of the sentence: the main idea and then the introductory element. Ask the student what part sounds complete. Identify this as the main idea. Next, have the student determine what rule applies to the sentence. Finally, have the student add the necessary punctuation.

Lesson 3: Commas with Sentence Interrupters

Lesson Warm-Up

Vocabulary: An understanding of the following terms is necessary to do the work in Lesson 3.

- **Essential:** In English grammar, this word means "necessary or important for understanding the meaning of the sentence."
- **Nonessential:** The opposite of essential. A nonessential element is not needed to understand the meaning of the sentence.

Activity: Write the following two sentences on the board. Ask the class to add punctuation to the sentences if punctuation is needed.

1. Dana and Kim in my opinion are very effective supervisors.
2. The only typewriter that needs a new ribbon is in Walter's office.

Have volunteers come to the board and add the needed punctuation.

Answers

1. Dana and Kim, in my opinion, are very effective supervisors. (Commas are needed because *in my opinion* is not essential to the meaning of the sentence. Have the student read the sentence without the interrupter. The main idea still makes sense.)
2. The only typewriter that needs a new ribbon is in Walter's office. (The clause *that needs a new ribbon* is essential to the meaning of the sentence and should not be set off by commas. Have the students read the sentence without the interrupting clause. Point out that the meaning of the sentence changes without the clause.)

Lesson Activities

Activity 1: Write the following sentence on the board.

Carol, who spoke to me yesterday, is going to cosmetology college.

Have the class read the sentence without the interrupter. Ask the class if the main idea of the sentence is still understood. Point out that *who spoke to me yesterday* provides extra information. The information may be interesting, the reader may want to know it, but it is not essential to the meaning of the sentence.

Activity 2: Write the following sentence on the board.

The man who is standing by the water cooler is the new sales representative.

Have the class write the sentence without *who spoke to me*. Ask the class if the identity of the man is clear. Point out that *who is standing by the water cooler* is essential information to the meaning of this sentence. The reader cannot identify the man without it.

Activity 3: Instruct the class to punctuate the following correctly and identify the clause by underlining it.

1. Mr. Flores is the only landlord that I've ever had who likes to do repairs.
2. Mrs. Kim who has been my neighbor for six years volunteers at Children's Hospital.

Answers

1. Mr. Flores is the only landlord that I've ever had who likes to do repairs.
2. Mrs. Kim, who has been my neighbor for six years, volunteers at Children's Hospital.

In the first sentence, the interrupting clause is needed. In the second, it is not. Remember, the decision to set off an interrupter must be based on whether the interrupter is needed to make the meaning of the sentence clear.

Lesson Wrap-Up

Exercise and Answer Key Discussion: Point out that Sentence 4 in the exercise is correct because *that overlooks the entire Seattle area* is essential. The main idea still makes sense without it.

Have volunteers write the remaining sentences on the board with corrections. For each sentence, discuss whether the interrupter is essential or nonessential to the meaning of the sentence.

Error Analysis: Have the students read the sentences aloud. This will help the student "hear" the interrupters in the sentences. After identifying the interrupter, have the student determine whether the information is essential or nonessential. Can the information be taken out of the sentence without changing the meaning of the sentence? If so, the interrupter needs to be set off by commas.

Lesson 4: Avoiding Overuse of Commas

Lesson Warm-Up

Activity: Write the following sentences on the board.

1. The rocking chair in the bedroom, sounds like a frog when I rock in it.
2. Marianne loaded the truck, and trailer and drove to Tennessee.
3. Glenn decided to hold the meeting in May, because everyone was taking a vacation in June and July.

Ask the students to identify the comma errors and correct the punctuation in each sentence.

Answers

1. The rocking chair in the bedroom sounds like a frog when I rock in it. (Do not use a comma between the subject and the verb of a sentence.)
2. Marianne loaded the truck and trailer and drove to Tennessee. (Do not use a comma between compound nouns.)

3. Glenn decided to hold the meeting in May because everyone was taking a vacation in June and July. (Do not use a comma before the word *because*. It always introduces important information that should not be separated from the rest of the sentence.)

Lesson Activities

Activity 1:   Write the following sentence on the board:

I read Jerry the instructions from the manual, he did not follow the correct procedures.

Ask the class what is wrong with the sentence. (Two complete sentences are joined by a comma only.) Ask a student to correct the sentence using a conjunction.

Activity 2:   Write the following sentence on the board:

My ten-year-old daughter is taking swimming lessons this summer and, she is still struggling with breathing correctly.

Ask the class what is wrong with the sentence. (Do not use a comma after a coordinator that joins two complete sentences.)
Have the class rewrite the sentence using correct punctuation style.

Activity 3:   Write the following sentence on the board:

The two linebackers ate lunch at, Taco Bell, Burger King, Pizza Hut, and Winchell's Donuts.

Ask the class what is wrong with the sentence. (Do not use a comma before the first item in a series.) Have the class rewrite the sentence using correct punctuation style.

Activity 4:   Write the following sentence on the board:

Deadliest of all reef creatures, the stonefish has a slimy, warty, back.

Ask the class what is wrong with the sentence. (Do not use a comma to separate an adjective from the noun it describes.) Have the class rewrite the sentence using correct punctuation style.

Lesson Wrap-Up

Exercise and Answer Key Discussion: Point out that sentence 4 is correct. Remind the students not to separate an adverb from the adjective it modifies. Have the class identify the corresponding rule from pages 110 and 111 for each sentence.

Have the students create sample incorrect and correct sentences of their own for each of the rules on pages 110–111. Writing incorrect and correct sentences will help solidify the rules for them.

Error Analysis: If students are having trouble, first have them circle each comma in the sentence. Then ask them to state the purpose of each comma. If they believe that a comma has been used without a reason, they should consult the rules in Skill 3 for an analysis of the error.

Skill 3:   Spelling

Learning spelling rules requires a combination of hard work and insight into word groups. Although there are many spelling exceptions in the English language, most words can be organized into groups that share similar letter patterns.

In the past, many students have been labeled as bad spellers. Much like those who suffer from math anxiety, the "bad spellers" among us don't expect to do any better. The first step in successful spelling is awareness. Although there are many difficult words, most of us know how to spell a great many words. The trick is becoming aware of the words that are difficult and seeing what they have in common.

Memory tricks, or mnemonic devices, are often a great help to students. The familiar "*i* before *e* except after *c*" works (although there are many exceptions) because it rhymes. You may have learned to remember the *e* in *stationery* because a stationery store is a place to buy *envelopes*. Once students know their weak spots, they can create their own tricks for remembering correct spelling.

This chapter also presents the use of the apostrophe in forming contractions and apostrophes (Lessons 2 and 3). Although the apostrophe is a mark of punctuation, learning its rules as part of the spelling process is the most efficient for GED test preparation.

You may want to refer students who are having difficulty to Chapters 16 and 17 of *On Your Own: Grammar*, a volume in a Cambridge Pre-GED series. For more GED work, see *The New Revised Cambridge GED Writing Skills* text, Unit 3, Chapter 3.

Lesson 1:   Basic Spelling Rules

Lesson Warm-Up

Vocabulary: An understanding of the following terms is necessary to do the work in Lesson 1.

- **Singular:**   A word form meaning one of something.
- **Plural:**   A word form meaning two or more of something.

- **Vowel:** A letter that makes an open sound. The vowels in the English language include *a, e, i, o, u,* and sometimes y.
- **Consonant:** A letter that represents a sound made with the lips, tongue, and/or teeth.

Activity: The class may use dictionaries for this lesson. Write the following sentences on the board.

1. They ordered hambergers, potatoe chippes, salades, and drinkes.
2. Colin sorted the quarteres, dimes, nickeles, and pennys into the cash drawer.
3. They say that cats have nine lifes, and my tabby is useing up her nineth life today.

Have the class copy the sentences and circle the spelling errors in each sentence. Then have the class rewrite the sentences with the words spelled correctly. If they are unsure of any spellings, the students should check the words in the dictionary.

Answers

1. They ordered hamburgers, potato chips, salads, and drinks.
2. Colin sorted the quarters, dimes, nickels, and pennies into the cash drawer.
3. They say that cats have nine lives, and my tabby is using up her ninth life today.

You may want to take time to show the class how to look up a plural form in the dictionary (particularly if you have a class set of dictionaries for the students' use). Irregular plurals are given in the dictionary in parentheses shortly after the main entry word. If a plural is not given, the noun follows Rule 1 presented in the lesson.

Lesson Activities

Activity 1:   Give the following list to the class. Have the students form the plural of each word and explain the rule number that applies from Lesson 1. (Plural forms and rule numbers are for teacher's reference only.)

		Plural form	Rule
1.	purse	purses	#1
2.	nobility	nobilities	#2
3.	earnings	earnings	#3
4.	inventory	inventories	#2
5.	stray	strays	#2
6.	holiday	holidays	#2
7.	cattle	cattle	#3
8.	fox	foxes	#1
9.	church	churches	#1
10.	leaf	leaves	#4
11.	thief	thieves	#4
12.	proof	proofs	#1
13.	clothes	clothes	#3
14.	statistics	statistics	#3
15.	courtesy	courtesies	#2

Have volunteers give the plural form of the noun and the rule number.

Activity 2:   This activity helps the students apply Rules 5, 6, and 7 from the lesson. Ask the students to form the *-ing* verb form of the following words. (*-ing* verb forms are for teacher's reference only.)

		-Ing verb form
1.	circle	circling
2.	educate	educating
3.	handle	handling
4.	delve	delving
5.	relieve	relieving

Activity: Have the class form the past tense (*-ed* ending) and *-ing* verb form for the following words. (Verb forms are for teacher's reference only.)

		Past tense	*-Ing verb form*
1.	ship	shipped	shipping
2.	bag	bagged	bagging
3.	jam	jammed	jamming
4.	scrub	scrubbed	scrubbing
5.	drip	dripped	dripping
6.	refer	referred	referring
7.	travel	traveled	traveled

Lesson Wrap-Up

Exercise and Answer Key Discussion: Point out that sentence 5 is correct. The word *offered* has been spelled correctly. The *r* is not doubled because the stress is not on the last syllable. Write the corrected words from the remaining items on the board. Identify which rules apply to each word.

Discussion: When you see a word misspelled in a letter, what do you think of the writer? When you see a word misspelled in an advertisement, what do you think of the business?

Error Analysis: If students have difficulty applying the spelling rules, make sure they know the difference between vowels and consonants. Often students find understanding the rules more difficult than simply memorizing the words. The rules will help if the student can see the reasoning behind them.

Lesson 2: Possessives

Lesson Warm-Up

Vocabulary: An understanding of the following term is necessary to do the work in Lesson 2.

- **Possessives:** A word that shows that something belongs to something or someone. Possessive nouns are formed using apostrophes. Possessive personal pronouns are not.

Activity: Give the following sentences to the class. Have the class correct all errors in the spelling of possessive nouns and pronouns.

1. I read Steinbecks book *The Red Pony* in Mrs. Eisenbergs' ninth grade English class.
2. The records jackets' are ripped and unreadable.
3. The childrens' voices were sweet but off-key.

Ask for volunteers to come to the board and rewrite the sentences with the corrections.

Answers

1. I read Steinbeck's book *The Red Pony* in Mrs. Eisenberg's ninth-grade English class. (Rule 1: Add an apostrophe and the letter *s* to make a singular noun possessive.)
2. The records' jackets are ripped and unreadable. (Rule 2: Add an apostrophe after the *s* to form the possessive of a plural noun.)
3. The children's voices were sweet but off-key. (Rule 3: Add an apostrophe and the letter *s* to a plural noun that does not end in *s*.)

Lesson Activities

Activity 1: Have the class rewrite the following phrases to show possession.

1. the program for today
2. the store owned by Mr. Montenegro
3. the book written by Ken Follett
4. the schedule of the class
5. the sleeping bag of Ross
6. the coats of the women
7. the decision of the jury
8. the animals belonging to the zoo
9. the offices of the nurses
10. the home of the Hernandezes

Have the class exchange and correct each other's papers.

Answers: 1. Today's program; 2. Mr. Montenegro's store; 3. Ken Follett's book; 4. the class's sched-

ule; 5. Ross's sleeping bag; 6. the women's coats; 7. the jury's decision; 8. the zoo's animals; 9. the nurses' offices; 10. the Hernandezes' home

Activity 2: Give the class the following sentences with the instruction to underline the possessive pronouns and correct the spelling if necessary.

1. Please bring you're dictionary to our class.
2. Her middle name is the same as mine.
3. They're car is losing its' bumper.

Answers

1. Please bring *your* dictionary to *our* class.
2. *Her* middle name is the same as *mine*.
3. *Their* car is losing *its* bumper.

Ask for volunteers to come to the board and rewrite the sentences.

Lesson Wrap-Up

Exercise and Answer Key Discussion: Point out that sentence 4 is correct. The rule that most people have trouble with is putting an apostrophe after the *s* to make a plural word possessive. Remind the students that this looks odd because we seldom write using possessives. Think about it. Our speaking is full of possessives, but most formal writing tends to avoid them. Ask for volunteers to rewrite the remaining sentences on the board. For a review of possessive forms, see Unit 1, Chapter 3, Lesson 1.

Error Analysis: If the students are having difficulty, they are probably skipping steps. Before they can spell a possessive correctly, they must decide whether the word should be singular or plural. Once the singular or plural has been handled correctly, making a noun possessive is fairly simple.

Lesson 3: Contractions

Lesson Warm-Up

Vocabulary: An understanding of the following term is necessary to do the work in Lesson 3.

- **Contraction:** The word *contraction* usually refers to something tightening or squeezing together. In English grammar, a contraction is a word formed when two words are combined to make one word by omitting one or more letters.

Activity: Give the following sentences to the class. Have the class correct the errors in each sentence.

1. If your waiting for the noon bus, its late.
2. Its all right, I do'nt want anymore.

3. Horatio and Will are'nt here; their at the game right now.

Have volunteers come to the board and write the corrected sentences. For each sentence, have them rewrite the contractions as two words to demonstrate how the contraction was formed.

Answers

1. If *you're* waiting for the noon bus, *it's* late. (you are, it is)
2. *It's* all right, I *don't* want anymore. (It is, do not)
3. Horatio and Will *aren't* here; *they're* at the game right now. (are not, they are)

Lesson Activity

Give the following sentences to the class. Have the class form common contractions when possible and correct any errors.

1. We would appreciate you're feedback about our presentation.
2. Kenneth must have rushed out in a hurry; he has left the doors open.
3. Three weeks ago, Cherisse decided she would send Christmas cards.
4. They have eaten all the shrimp rolls. I should have made three dozen.
5. That is a beautiful ring. It's color is so vibrant.

Answers

1. We'd appreciate your feedback about our presentation.
2. Kenneth must've rushed out in a hurry; he's left the doors open.
3. Three weeks ago, Cherisse decided she'd send Christmas cards.
4. They've eaten all the shrimp rolls. I should've made three dozen.
5. That's a beautiful ring. Its color is so vibrant.

Ask for volunteers to suggest possible contractions and correct the errors. Point out that some contractions are acceptable when we are speaking but are too informal for writing (for example, must've and should've).

Lesson Wrap-Up

Exercise and Answer Key Discussion: Point out that sentence 3 is correct. *It's* is the correct spelling for the contraction of *it is*. Have volunteers identify the errors and corrections for the remaining sentences. Write the corrections on the board so that the class can see how the contraction is formed.

Using a "spelling bee" format, quiz the class from the chart on page 117. For instance, ask a student to spell the contraction of *is not*. As time allows, use all of the items from the chart.

Error Analysis: Remind the students that the apostrophe takes the place of letters. If the student cannot decide where the apostrophe is placed, have the student write both words of the contraction. Then have the student cross out the letters that are left out from the example. For example: does not = doesn't.

Lesson 4: Frequently Confused Words

Lesson Warm-Up

Vocabulary: An understanding of the following term is necessary to do the work in Lesson 4.

- **Homonyms:** Words that are pronounced the same (or nearly the same) but are spelled differently. One of the first sets of homonyms children learn is *to*, *too*, and *two*. These words are indistinguishable by their sound alone.

Activity: Write the following sentences on the board. Have the class circle the correct word in parentheses.

1. Remember not (too, to, two) buy (too, to, two) many plants at the (too, to, two)-for-one sale.
2. If (your, you're) going to the (stationery, stationary) store, please pick up some (plane, plain) white paper for me.
3. Allow me to (compliment, complement) you on this (desert, dessert); (its, it's) (altogether, all together) the best I've ever tasted.

Answers:

1. Remember not to buy too many plants at the two-for-one-sale.
2. If you're going to the stationery store, please pick up some plain white paper for me.
3. Allow me to compliment you on the dessert; it's altogether the best I've ever tasted.

Lesson Activity

The students will each need a dictionary for this activity. Divide the class into two groups. Give the first ten homonyms to the one group and the last ten to the second group. Have the groups look up in their dictionary the definitions of the following words. Have them write sentences using each pair of words correctly.

1. affect/effect
2. aid/aide
3. allowed/aloud

4. almost/all most
5. always/all ways
6. bare/bear
7. bases/basis
8. cereal/serial
9. correspondence/correspondents
10. do/due/dew
11. flour/flower
12. guessed/guest
13. heal/heel
14. knew/new
15. patience/patients
16. personal/personnel
17. poor/pore/pour
18. read/reed
19. right/write
20. seen/scene

Have each group read their sentences to the other group and ask the students in the other group to state which word belongs in each sentence. For further practice, have students select words from the lesson which they feel they need to do work on, and have them write sentences with them.

Lesson Wrap-Up

Exercise and Answer Key Discussion: Ask the class to identify which sentence is correct (sentence 4). Ask for volunteers to come to the board and write the corrected versions of the remaining sentences. The students should be able to explain why changes in the sentences are necessary.

Ask the class if there are any words that they now know that they have been misspelling frequently without realizing it. Have the class share their examples.

Error Analysis: Instruct the class to use their dictionaries rather than "guess" at correct spelling. If there is any word that they are not sure of, now is the time to learn its spelling and meaning. These words come up frequently on the GED test both in passages and in distractors for test items. The students must be familiar with most common homonyms to do well on the test.

Personal Writing

The purpose of this chapter is to get students into the habit of writing regularly. Many of us freeze up when we face a blank piece of paper. Many of your students' fears about the essay portion of the GED are based on their concern that they won't have anything to say. Writing the first sentence of an essay can be the hardest part. The trick is to start writing.

This chapter teaches a technique called *freewriting*. The goal in freewriting is to write quickly with the knowledge that no one will judge your work. It is not necessary to worry about grammar rules, sentence structure, and punctuation. This is harder than it sounds. Most of us hate to make mistakes. The need to go back and correct our mistakes is strong. However, letting go of rules and restrictions opens our creativity. Students who consider themselves "bad" writers may be the most creative ones.

Doing the freewriting exercises in this chapter is a good way to get over the fear of freezing under pressure. Help your students take this step by giving them time in class to do the activities. Don't skip this important step; it will free their imaginations and build their confidence.

For instruction and practice at a Pre-GED level on personal or daily writing, see the *Threshold* writing skills text, Part II, Chapter 1. For more GED work, see *The New Revised Cambridge* Writing Skills text, Part 2, Chapter 1.

Lesson 1: Introduction to Personal Writing

Lesson Warm-Up

Vocabulary: An understanding of the following term is necessary to do the work in Lesson 1.

- **Freewriting:** Getting your ideas on paper quickly without worrying about grammar, sentence structure, or punctuation rules.

Activity: For the following activity, choose an excerpt from any appropriate work of fiction. Read this passage to the class for several minutes. Then have the students write down all the ideas that they can remember. Give them three minutes to write the ideas of the story in their own words. The goal is to write as quickly as possible while the story is fresh in their minds.

You may want to repeat this activity with different excerpts from time to time. The goal is to increase the students' tolerance for freewriting.

Lesson Activity

Each student will need a blank piece of paper and pen. Tell the class that the goal in this activity is to write as fast as they can without correcting mistakes or rewriting.

Tell the class that their assignment is to write for two minutes describing themselves. Their "essay" can include a physical description, experiences about themselves, their history, and their feelings.

Lesson Wrap-Up

Exercise Discussion: Ask the class how the experience of freewriting felt to them. Allow the class to express their positive and negative reactions to the activity.

Discussion: Remind the class that freewriting is just one of the techniques that can help them become better writers. Its purpose is to help them overcome some of the blocks that prevent writers from getting ideas down on paper. People experience many different kinds of obstacles to their writing.

Ask: What are some of the reasons that people might not enjoy writing? Ask the students what types of obstacles they have experienced.

Lesson 2: Keeping a Daily Journal

Lesson Warm-Up

Activity: Journal entries and first-person accounts have the unique ability to reveal an author to us in two ways. Not only do we learn what happened (the facts of the story), but we also see through the words to the author's personality and feelings.

Choose a selection from a journal or autobiography to read to the class. Your local bookstore or public library will have many accounts to choose from. Choose a selection that can be read in no more than five minutes. If possible, the selection should tell of an important event or emotional experience.

After you are finished reading, have the students write their impressions and feelings about the reading. They might include their feelings about the author and the event. They might write about whether they agree with the author's viewpoint. The objective of the exercise is to write as many of their ideas and feelings as they can in three minutes.

Lesson Activity

Ask the class to picture themselves as six-year-olds. Have the class picture the clothes they wore as six-year-olds, their school, their teacher, any pets, favorite activities or toys, and so on.

For 10 minutes have the class write an imaginary journal entry for a day in their lives as a six year-olds. Tell the class that a perfect memory of an actual day is not necessary. Using the freewriting technique, the students will "make up" a day and write as many words as they can.

Discussion: Following the activity, begin a discussion with the following questions.

1. Do you feel successful about this writing experience?
2. How did it feel to write as a six-year-old? How was it different from the freewriting experiences you have had so far?
3. Were there any surprising memories?
4. How has the freewriting technique helped you in your writing?

Lesson 3: Enjoying Your Writing

Lesson Warm-Up

Activity: Each student will need a blank piece of paper and pen. Remind the class of the freewriting "rules." The objective is to write down as many words as possible without worrying about mistakes in sentence structure.

Have the students write for two minutes on the following topic: If you won a million dollars today and you had to spend all of the money on yourself, what would you buy, and why?

Discussion: Was it hard to keep writing? Why or why not? How did this experience compare with that of the previous lessons?

Lesson Activity

Each student will need a blank piece of paper and pen. Write the following on the board:

> I will commit to writing for 10 minutes every day.
> When will you write?
> Where will you write?
> What could stop you?
> What will you do about it?
> How do you feel about this goal?

Give the class five minutes to set goals that will help them develop a daily writing habit. Have them write the answers to the questions on the board.

Lesson Wrap-Up

Activity: Help the class meet their goals by writing a journal entry now. After the students have written for 10 minutes, point out that they have met their goal for the first day.

Chapter 2
Planning the Essay

The students in our classes have a specialized goal: They need to pass the GED test. To do that, of course, they need to write successful essays. Because their goals have a particular focus, our students want to skip steps if they can. They don't necessarily want to learn to write; they want to learn to write an essay that will help them pass the test.

Our challenge as teachers is to convince our students that learning the writing process will help them write a good essay. Writing is a process. The students who do poorly on the GED essay are those who ignore parts of the process. This chapter gives the students opportunities to practice all parts of the writing process. Encourage your students to put the process first for the time being, and they will see positive results in their test-taking abilities soon enough.

For a full-scale and detailed treatment at a Pre-GED level of prewriting activities essential to planning a one-paragraph essay, see *On Your Own: Writing Process,* Unit 1. For another Pre-GED treatment on gathering and organizing ideas for a paragraph, see the *Threshold* writing skills text, Unit 2, Chapters 2 and 3. For further instruction and practice at a GED-level, see *The New Revised Cambridge GED Program: Writing Skills,* Part II, Chapter 2, Lessons 1-4.

Lesson 1:   The Writing Process

Lesson Warm-Up

Activity: Imagine that you have been asked to write an essay on the effect of beer commercials on drinking and driving. You are asked to decide whether you think beer companies should be allowed to advertise their products on television. The essay instructions tell you to support your opinion with reasons and examples.

Ask: What kinds of things would you do to get ready to write the essay? (The students will probably mention thinking of ideas and organizing the essay. Point out that these are part of the prewriting step.)

Ask: What should be your goals as you actually write the essay? (Following the outline and responding to the topic are two ideas. Point out that these are part of the writing step.)

Ask: What will you do after you have completed a draft of your essay? (The students should mention revising and editing. Point out that these are the final steps in the writing process.)

Lesson Activity

Have the students follow the three steps to write the essay referred to in the Lesson Warm-Up. Tell the students not to worry about the amount of time that any step takes at this point. The important thing at this early stage in learning to write essays is to make sure that each step is complete before going on to the next.

Lesson Wrap-Up

Have the students answer the questions in the Lesson 1 activity regarding the essay they have just written.

Discussion: Which steps did you skip? Which steps do you need to learn and practice?

Discuss the importance of making an organizational plan. Point out that without a plan, it is impossible to write a good essay. Very experienced writers may take less time to plan and organize, but their plan and organization still clearly show in their essay. Emphasize this point: If the person who grades your GED essay cannot see evidence of an organizational plan, you probably will not receive a passing score.

Lesson 2:   Understanding Essay Topics

Lesson Warm-Up

Activity: Write these three statements on the board in this order.

A. Decide on your own point of view and state it in one sentence.

B. Underline any other key words that help you decide what you are to write about.

C. Make sure that you understand your purpose in writing.

Tell the class that these are the three steps for understanding an essay topic. Have the class put the steps in logical order. To correct their answers, have the class refer to the steps listed on page 133.

Lesson Activity

Have the class work in small groups to analyze Topic 2 on page 133. Each group should do the three steps together and be able to state the topic in their own words. Invite students to share the sentences they have written expressing the key ideas and their points of view.

Lesson Wrap-Up

Activity: To help your students focus on the structure of GED essay topics, assign each student to write an essay topic statement. Remind them to make sure that the person writing the essay would know exactly what they should write based on the sentences in the topic. Then have the class members exchange topics and follow the three steps to analyze each other's topics.

Lesson 3: Generating Ideas

Lesson Warm-Up

Vocabulary: An understanding of the following terms is necessary to do the work in Lesson 3.

* **Brainstorming:** Thinking of many ideas and writing the ideas down without censoring or revising them.
* **Clustering:** A visual method of showing the relationship between ideas. Circles are drawn around words and phrases which are then connected with lines to larger circles, which represent main ideas.

Lesson Activity

Ask the class to brainstorm as many "controversial" essay topics as they can in 15 minutes. Assign a volunteer to list the ideas on the board. Remind the class to be careful about not passing judgment on the ideas at this point. Laughter, shrugs, and even sudden silence can convey disapproval and restrict the flow of ideas. After the brainstorming session, have the class work together to select ten topics that can be used for extra essay-writing practice.

Do the Lesson 3 activity on page 138. Remind the students to save their work for use in future lessons.

Supplementary Activities: If the students need additional help with the brainstorming technique, the following list can be used for either individual or group brainstorming sessions. Instruct the class not to revise their ideas as they write them down. The brainstorming sessions can be either given a time limit or students can set a goal to write a certain number of ideas. Encourage the students to take even silly ideas seriously. The purpose of brainstorming is to free your imagination, not restrict it.

1. What would happen if we also had two eyes in the back of our heads?
2. What if it were essential that we reduce the number of automobile accidents that occur? How might we do it?
3. If money were not a problem, what improvements would you make in the design and construction of your home?
4. What would happen if men and women were not allowed to marry until they were 30 years old?
5. What would the consequences be if our bodies could heal themselves?
6. What changes might occur if the 40-hour work-week were changed to a 60-hour workweek one time per month for every worker?
7. What would happen if all food and drink were the same color?
8. How could we solve the communication problems that result from the existence of so many different languages in the world?
9. How would it affect people's lives if they were assigned a career at birth?
10. How would our lives change if everyone were required to move to another state or city every five years?

Lesson Wrap-Up

Discussion: Ask the class if they see any similarities between freewriting and brainstorming or clustering. How have these techniques changed their approach to writing?

Lesson 4: Organizing Ideas

Lesson Warm-Up

Vocabulary: No new terms are presented in this lesson.

Activity: Have the students brainstorm answers to the following question: What actions could we take if it became imperative to stop drunk driving? Brainstorm a list of at least twenty ideas.

Discussion: Imagine that we are going to present our ideas to the President of the United States. How could we group them to catch his interest and make the ideas seem stronger? Proceed to arrange the ideas into four or five groups. Point out that the process the class has just used is similar to the work of organizing the ideas for an essay.

Lesson Activity

Have the class use the ideas they generated in Lesson 3 to do the Lesson 4 Activity (page 142).

Discussion: Why is grouping important? Why is it important to throw out ideas that don't seem to fit into any category? What might happen if a person generates many ideas but neglects to put them into categories? What effect might this have on an essay?

Lesson Wrap-Up

In reviewing the students' work, the following checklist will help determine whether the students are understanding the grouping techniques.

1. Do the groups of ideas seem related?
2. Have the categories been given a title?
3. Has the introduction been labeled?
4. Have the remaining paragraphs been marked as supporting ideas?
5. Have the supporting paragraphs been assigned an order?

Chapter 3

Writing, Revising, and Editing the Essay

Finally, your students will see how their work in Part I will pay off not only on the GED test but in their writing. In this chapter the students will apply the grammar rules they have learned to their own essays.

This isn't as complicated as it might sound. People do express themselves in patterns. Some students might use mostly simple sentences, while others write in complex sentences. Some are fond of transitional phrases, and others begin nearly every sentence with **I**. Your students don't need to become great writers to pass the GED. They do need to organize their thoughts well and write in complete sentences. Don't try to eliminate their natural patterns. Instead, show them how to use their patterns to write competent essays.

For a full-scale treatment of writing, revising, and editing a one-paragraph essay at a Pre-GED level, see *On Your Own: Writing Process*, Unit 1, Chapter 6, and Units 2, 3, and 4. For another Pre-GED treatment, see the *Threshold* writing skills text, Unit 2, Chapter 2, Lessons 33-35, and Chapter 3. For work at a GED level, see *The New Revised Cambridge GED Program: Writing Skills*, Part II, Chapter 2, Lessons 5-7, and Chapter 3.

Lesson 1:   Writing the Essay

Lesson Warm-Up

Activity: Have the students read the essay on page 145. You may want to read the essay aloud to the class.

Ask: What key elements should every good essay contain?
Now ask the class to find the following elements in the essay on page 145.

1. The introductory paragraph
2. The author's point of view
3. The referral to supporting ideas in the introductory paragraph
4. Supporting paragraphs
5. Examples and reasons in the supporting paragraphs

6. The concluding paragraph
7. The point of view restated in the concluding paragraph.

Lesson Activity

Have the class complete the Lesson 1 Activity on page 144. Point out that the preliminary work from Chapter 2 has prepared them for this step of writing the essay. Remind the class that the next step in the writing process is revising. The students should write their essay quickly, remembering they will have a chance to revise and rewrite later.

Lesson Wrap-Up

After the class members have completed their essays, have them check their work to make sure that they have included the following:

1. An introductory paragraph
2. A point of view
3. A referral to supporting ideas in the introductory paragraph
4. Supporting paragraphs
5. Examples
6. A concluding paragraph
7. A restatement of the point of view in the concluding paragraph

Lesson 2:   Revising the Essay

Lesson Warm-Up

Activity: Use the demonstration section on pages 144–147 to illustrate the revision process. Point out that the author is not concerned with grammar, sentence structure, and punctuation at this point, although these types of corrections certainly could be made if they are noticed. The emphasis is still on tightening the organization of ideas.

Discussion: Is organization really that important to a successful essay? It certainly is. A student who writes perfect sentences about the wrong topic might know grammar, but he or she will never pass the GED essay portion of the test.

Lesson Activity

The activity on page 148 takes the students through the revision process using their essays from Lesson 1. Point out that the students should refer to the questions on page 144 and their explanation on page 146 as a guide to revising their essays.

Discussion: What is the difference between revising and editing? (Editing focuses on the grammar, sentence structure, and spelling errors.) Why is it important to concentrate on revision first? (Correcting errors in sentences that should be eliminated from the essay is a waste of time. First decide what ideas belong in the essay; then correct them.) Point out that Lesson 3 covers the editing process in greater detail.

Lesson Wrap-Up

Have the students do the Lesson 2 Activity. For more revision practice, divide the students into small groups. Have each group choose a topic from the list generated on pages 134–136. The members of the group should work together to write an essay. When the groups are finished, have them trade essays and revise them using the questions on page 144.

Lesson 3:   Editing the Essay

Lesson Warm-Up

Vocabulary: An understanding of the following term is necessary to do the work in Lesson 3.

- **Editing:** Reading a piece of writing to correct errors in usage, sentence structure, capitalization, punctuation, and spelling.

Discussion: Why is it harder to find errors in your own sentences than in someone else's?

Lesson Activity

Have the students edit their essays from the previous lessons as the activity for Lesson 7. Encourage the students to use the questions on pages 148–149 to better edit their work.

Lesson Wrap-Up

The following is a list of the most common errors in essay writing. The students can use this as another aid in editing their essays. The page numbers in the text that cover these topics are included.

1. Comma usage: pp. 158–69
2. Run-on sentences and sentence fragments: pp. 98–101
3. Subject–verb agreement: pp. 65–74
4. Spelling: pp. 112–22
5. Verb tense: pp. 75–81
6. Word usage—homonyms, synonyms: pp. 119–22
7. Parallel structure: pp. 100–101
8. Misplaced and dangling modifiers: pp. 98–99
9. Plurals and possessives: pp. 65–66, 115–16
10. Capitalization: pp. 102–5
11. Contractions: pp. 117–18
12. Pronoun usage: pp. 82–87

Chapter 1

Social Studies

Brainstorming: Read aloud and discuss with the class the Prereading Prompt on page 154. Paraphrase the question in the last sentence: "Do you think human beings would have made as much progress as we have if we had always lived separately from each other instead of in groups?" Ask students to brainstorm a list of accomplishments that human beings have made as the result of cooperative effort. Accept all reasonable responses and write them on the board. Guide students to understand that all important accomplishments—from the discovery of lifesaving medicines to the exploration of space—are the result of individuals and groups sharing their knowledge and building on the work of others.

Lesson 1: The Social Sciences that Make Up Social Studies

Lesson Warm-Up

Vocabulary: Write on the board the five Key Word items from page 156 (*history*, *geography*, *economics*, *political science*, and *behavioral science*). Point to each of the five Key Words in turn as you ask the following related questions. Allow as many students as possible to give answers to each question.

- **History:** Where did your family come from originally? How long ago did they come here?
- **Geography:** Where were you born? What rivers and mountains are near your birthplace?
- **Economics:** Why do you think there are homeless people in many U.S. cities?
- **Political Science:** Name the President and Vice-President of the United States, and the governor of this state.
- **Behavioral Science:** What information from psychology or economics are you aware of from movies, television, and what you read?

Read aloud the Key Word definitions in the book and discuss them with the students, answering any questions they may have. After that, reinforce the meaning of each term by providing factual statements concerned with one of the five areas of social science and asking students which of the five Key Words each statement is most closely related to. For example, say "Columbus landed in America in 1492." This is a historical fact, so it is most connected with the word *history*. An example of a statement about *geography* might be: "The ocean in the cold areas near the North and South Poles is frozen solid all year long." A statement about *economics* might be: "In the United States, people pay an average of 30% of their income to the government in taxes." A statement about *political science* might be: "In some countries a single leader makes all the decisions, whereas in the United States many people have a voice in major decisions." A statement about *behavioral science* might be: "Behavioral scientists sometimes use mice to study how the learning process works." Ask students to make up other factual statements related to each term and write them on a piece of scrap paper. Collect the papers and read them to the class, asking students to say which Key Word each statement applies to.

Lesson Activities

Lesson Review: Divide the class into pairs and have students take turns reading paragraphs to each other. Suggest that they underline any words they don't know as they go along and stop after each paragraph to clarify the meaning of each. Suggest that they ask for your help if they are not able to figure out the meanings of any words. Then work with the entire class as you review the reading paragraph by paragraph.

Paragraph 1: Ask students to close their books. Then ask several students to name the five social sciences from memory.

Paragraph 2: Explain that later the class will choose a new example of an important event and look together at how each branch of social science relates to it.

Paragraph 3: Ask students what types of things history is concerned with. (names, dates, facts)

Paragraph 4: Ask students to name as many aspects of geography as they can. (landforms such as mountains and rivers, climate, weather, soil conditions, etc.)

Paragraph 5: Ask students to explain why the economy of the U.S. South depended on slaves. (The landowners could not have made any money on farming if they had to pay for their labor.)

Paragraph 6: Ask students what they think of when they hear the word *political.* (They will probably mention elections and political parties. Point out that political science is the study of how all aspects of a government operate, not just the election process.)

Paragraph 7: Ask students to name the three areas of behavioral science mentioned in this paragraph. (psychology, sociology, and anthropology)

Application: Paragraphs 3 through 7 of this lesson use the American Civil War to provide concrete examples of the types of information each of the five social sciences are concerned with. With the class, choose an important situation that is relevant to the students' lives, such as the civil rights movement or the economic recession of the 1990s. Divide the class into five groups and put each group in charge of one of the five social sciences. As you talk about the situation, members of each group raise their hands when you mention something that relates to their branch of social studies. One member of the group then repeats the fact and describes the connection to their branch. Help students put into words the connections between your description and their area of social science. For example, if you talk about the civil rights movement, you might say: "Many U.S. schools were segregated in the 1950's." (The history group should raise their hands. This is a historical fact.) "Dr. Martin Luther King, Jr. was an important civil rights leader." (history/person) "Dr. King was killed in June 1968." (history/date) "Many African Americans who were being discriminated against were still living in the South because their ancestors had been brought to that part of the United States to do agricultural work, and the climate and soil in the South are ideal for growing cotton and other crops." (geography/Climate affected where African Americans were living.) "African Americans often had to take menial jobs at low wages. Few African Americans were able to own businesses." (economics/Lack of educational opportunity and racial discrimination meant that African Americans were poorer than other Americans.) "President Kennedy began a series of antipoverty programs after he was elected." (political science/Social problems reflected in political programs) "Some people in the South, both African American and white, seemed to feel that the system of separation of the races should be continued." (behavioral sci-

ences/People had lived under the system for many years and feared change.)

Reading Strategies Instruction: Ask students to take turns reading aloud the section called "Using Context Clues." Ask students to refer back to the reading passage on pages 157–158 each time it is used to illustrate a point. Then have students read the practice item and choose the correct answer before looking at the explanation that follows. Ask students which answer they chose, and why. Discuss differences among the answers chosen and ask students to explain in detail how they came to their conclusions. Then read aloud the explanatory paragraph and elicit any final questions or comments. For students having difficulty, extensive instruction and practice at a Pre-GED level can be found in the *Threshold* social studies text, Unit 2, Chapter 1. For GED-level work, see *The New Revised Cambridge GED* social studies text, Chapter 1, Lesson 1, and *The New Revised Cambridge* science text, Chapter 1, Lesson 1.

Lesson Wrap-Up

How to Do the Exercise: Before students complete the Lesson 1 Exercise, remind them that they will have a limited amount of time to answer the questions on the GED exam, so they will need to work as efficiently as possible. Give them the following instructions:

1. Always look over the reading passage first. Glance through it, looking for repeated words.
2. Read the questions. They will help you focus on the specific information you need to look for.
3. Read the passage carefully.
4. Answer the questions using the process of elimination to discard obviously incorrect answers.

Complete the Exercises: Ask students to complete the exercise individually. Then go over together the answers and explanations on page A-14.

Lesson 2: How Social Scientists Report Information

Lesson Warm-Up

Discussion: Ask students to respond to the following questions with a yes/no answer. Then confirm the correct answer and elicit an explanation or some further information about the question from a student. If no student is able to give this additional information, supply some hints and, if necessary, provide the information yourself. Use simple blackboard drawings to illustrate answers as necessary.

1: Is a *graph* a picture? (Yes. It's a special kind of drawing in which the parts of the picture represent numbers.)

2: Is there more than one type of graph? (Yes. Some graphs use lines, some use bars, and some use circles divided into pieces.)

3: Are *statistics* always given as numbers? (Yes. Statistics are facts in the form of numbers.)

4: Is the statement "Less crude oil was produced in 1982 than in 1981" a statistic? (No. This statement contains dates but it doesn't contain numerical information about crude oil production.)

5: Is the statement "Twenty-seven million gallons of crude oil a day were produced in 1980" a statistic? (Yes. It gives an exact number to describe crude oil production.)

Brainstorming: Ask students to brainstorm a list of statistics that they already know. Some students may be able to describe how a favorite baseball player is doing in terms of his batting average, or how one football team is performing as compared to others in the league. You might try to elicit the exact price of this year's most popular athletic shoes or a statement of how much monthly rent a student is paying this year versus last year. Point out that students are already familiar with a lot of statistics and that this lesson will show them how to use graphs to be able to understand even more information.

Lesson Activities

Vocabulary: As you work through the reading passage with students, several vocabulary items may need special attention. List the following words on the board and stop to define them and use them in sample sentences as they appear in the reading. Suggest that students copy in their notebooks any words they have trouble with together with their definitions.

- **Scientifically controlled study:** Research in which the facts are gathered in a very careful way and the results of the study are checked thoroughly before they are released
- **Trend:** Movement in a certain direction, as in "a trend toward higher prices"
- **Vertical axis:** Line with numbers on it that runs up and down the left side of a graph
- **Horizontal axis:** Line with numbers on it that runs across the bottom of a graph
- **Ethnic group:** Group of people with a common racial or cultural background

Lesson Review: Ask students to take turns reading aloud the paragraphs on pages 161–163. Pause after each paragraph (or after a group of three or four sentences in the long paragraphs). Ask comprehension questions and clarify any new vocabulary words contained in the passage.

Paragraph 1: Ask students if they know what the U.S. Census Survey is. If not, explain that it is an official count of how many people are living in the country. The Census also gathers information about the size and furnishings of our homes, how much money we make, and so on. Ask a student who has completed a Census form to tell about some of the questions that were on it. Explain that the answers given by each person are combined with the answers given by millions of other people to come up with *statistics* about life in the United States.

Paragraph 2: Ask students what use social scientists make of statistics once they have gathered them. (They use them to diagnose the causes of problems and to decide on possible solutions.)

Paragraph 3: Ask students to repeat the definition of a *graph* given in this paragraph. (pictures that show numerical information)

Paragraph 4: Clarify what is meant by *average income* per year. (This is a statistic obtained by adding up the annual incomes of all the people living in Alphaville and dividing it by the number of households in Alphaville.)

Paragraph 5: Draw a large circle on the board and ask students to shade in pieces of the circle representing 25%, 50%, 75%, and so on.

Paragraph 6: To make it easier for students to read the graph, point out that slices of the circle on page 163 going down its left side (0.8%, 3.9%, etc.) are arranged in the same order as the color key boxes going down the right side (Native American, Eskimo, Aleut, followed by Other, etc.).

Paragraph 7: Ask students to read off the percentages of other ethnic groups in the United States in 1990 in the circle graph on page 163.

Paragraph 8: With regard to the graph on page 164, ask students to trace across from the dot above each year to the vertical axis and tell about how many million gallons of oil per day were being produced that year. (1980 = about 27,000,000, 1981 = about 23,000,000, etc.)

Application: Ask students to contribute information from their own lives as you create several original graphs on the board.

Bar Graph: Put a blank grid on the board and label it "School Attendance." List the last five years on the horizontal scale (labeling it "Years") and put the numbers 1–10 (or more if necessary) on the vertical scale (labeling it "Number of students." Then poll the class and find out how many students attended school, either part-time or full-time, during each of the years indicated. Go through the years asking students to raise their hands if they were in school at any time during that particular year. Make bars over each year as tall as the number of students attending school. Then review the graph asking such questions as: "In which year were the most people going to school? Is the number of people going to school growing or shrinking?"

Circle Graph. Draw a circle on the board and label it "Family Budget"—"Circle Graph." Elicit information from one student on what proportions he or she spends on food, transportation, day care, and so on, and divide up the circle to represent these approximate proportions. Label the segments and discuss the graph.

Line Graph: First make a blank grid and label it "Enrollment in GED Classes—Line Graph." Mark off the intervals 10, 20, and so on, on the vertical scale and label it "Students enrolled." On the horizontal scale mark off 12 divisions and label them "Past 12 months." Using information from your attendance book (or school records), make a dot over each month on the horizontal scale to show how many students were enrolled in GED programs in that month. Connect the dots and review the graph asking such questions as: "When were the most students enrolled? When were there fewest?" "Does it look like more people or fewer people are starting to study for the GED?"

Lesson Wrap-Up

Reading Strategies Instruction: Read aloud the first two paragraphs of "Finding Details in Text and Graphs." Ask students what questions they should ask themselves as they search for detailed information in written material. (Who? What? Where? When? How?) What should they do before they try to extract information from a graph? (Look at the title, the description on each axis, and the type of statistics shown.) Ask students to complete the two questions on page 165 individually. Then go over their answers referring back to the timeline to check the answers. For students having difficulty, see the Pre-GED *Threshold* social studies text, Unit 1, Chapter 3, Lessons 6, 9, and 10; and the *Threshold* science text, Unit 1, Chapter 3, Lesson 7, and Chapter 6. See also the Pre-GED *On Your Own: Reading*, Unit 2, Chapter 6, and Unit 4, Chapters 17 and 18. For more GED-level work, see *The New Revised Cambridge GED Program*: the social studies text, Chapter 1, Lesson 2 and Chapter 2, Lesson 3; the science text, Chapter 1, Lesson 2 and Chapter 2, Lesson 3.

How to Do the Exercise: Before students complete the Lesson 2 Exercises on page 166, ask several students to take turns reading details from each graph in the lesson. Answer any questions they may have about this procedure. Then point out that question 1 refers to the paragraph at the top of page 166, questions 2 and 3 refer back to pages 161–162 of the reading passage, and that question 4 refers to the graph on page 164.

Complete the Exercise: Ask students to complete the Lesson 2 Exercise individually. Set a five-minute time limit. Then discuss each question with the class and go over the answers and explanations on page A-14.

Lesson 3:   The Making of the United States

Lesson Warm-Up

Brainstorming: Read aloud the Prereading Prompt. Then ask students to think back to a time when they joined a new group. Perhaps some students were born in another country or in another city in this country, and recently moved to their present city. Or they may have worked in one place for several years and later taken a job with a new company. Ask them how they felt at first in the new setting. Were they excited? Scared? Did they feel part of the group right away? How long did it take them to feel comfortable? What were some of the arrangements they had to make with the people they met in order to fit in? Then compare their experiences with those of the British colonists arriving in the United States and starting to build a new life here. Some were scared. At first food was scarce and there were threats from the Native Americans who were already here; there was conflict with the monarchy back in Britain. Eventually, they had to break away from England's rule and figure out a new form of government for this new country. The newly organized states also had to figure out how to get along with each other. How much power should they give to the federal government? How much should be reserved for the individual states? Point out that this lesson will give a picture of what the early colonists did that allowed them to survive and prosper.

Vocabulary: Write on the board the three Key Words from page 167 and ask students to read the definitions aloud. After each one, ask questions about specific terms within the definitions. For example, What is an *incident*? (a happening, an important event) What is a *rebellion*? (an uprising against a ruler, a show of resistance against a current government) What are *amendments*? (additions to the Constitution) Then ask the students to restate each definition in their own words. Have one student write these paraphrases on the board.

Lesson Activities

K–W–L: Introduce Lesson 3 using the K-W-L technique described in Chapter 14 of the Cambridge Pre-GED book *On Your Own: Reading* by Donna Stelluto. Read aloud the two headings (*From the Colonies to the Revolutionary War* and *State's Rights and the Federal Government*) and ask students what they know about each element in these titles. Ask what they think some of the boldface words mean. Accept all reasonable answers. Then make three columns on the board with the headings "What I Know," "What I Want to Learn," and "What I Learned." Ask students to suggest things for you to write in the first column. Possible responses might be: (1) The first colonists came from England on the *Mayflower*. (2) The United States became independent of Britain on July 4, 1776. (3) The colonies had to pay taxes to England. Then help students come up with questions for the "What I Want to Learn" column. Possible responses might be: (1) What actually caused the Revolutionary War? (2) What was the Stamp Act? (3) Why did we need a Constitution if we already had the Articles of Confederation? Add other "What I Want to Learn" questions of your own, such as: (4) Why wasn't the Constitution approved quickly? Was something wrong with it?

Vocabulary: List the following terms on the board.

  Drafted
  Representatives
  Felt justified
  Printed matter
  Repealed
  Currencies
  Compromise

Add a second list featuring the definitions of these words in random order.

  People who are elected to speak for a group
  Any paper with words printed on it
  Forms of money
  An agreement in which each side gives up part of what it wants
  Did away with an unpopular law
  Thought they were correct
  Wrote the first version of something

Ask students to match up each word with its definition. Discuss each term and definition, giving students a chance to ask questions. Then supply a sample sentence or ask students to make up sentences using each word. Write one of the sample sentences for each word on the board. Ask students to copy these sample sentences in their notebooks and to watch for these words as they appear in the reading passage.

Lesson Review: Divide the class into pairs and have students take turns reading paragraphs to each other. Suggest that they underline any other new words as they go along and stop after each paragraph and ask you about anything they don't understand. Then work with the entire class as you review the reading paragraph by paragraph. You can use the following questions to guide the discussion.

Paragraph 1:   Who wrote the Mayflower Compact? (the colonists who sailed to America on the *Mayflower*) What kind of government did they plan to have? (majority rule)

Paragraph 2:   What were *town meetings*? (meetings in which the people living in a town voted on how the town was to be run) What higher-level meetings came later? (meetings among several colonies) Did England try to stop these meetings? (not at first) Why were the colonies costing England a lot of money? (England was fighting a war with the French and the Native Americans to keep control of the colonies.)

Paragraph 3:   What kinds of things did England tax after the Stamp Act was repealed? (tea, glass, paint, and paper) Why did this anger the colonists? (They couldn't make these things for themselves. They had to import them and now the prices would be higher.)

Paragraph 4:   What did England do that caused the Americans to form an army? (England closed down the port of Boston and tried to stop Massachusetts from governing itself.)

Paragraph 5:   What document ended the Revolutionary War? (the Treaty of Paris)

Paragraph 6:   What problems did the colonies have after the war? (The various states were taxing each other, the central government was weak, and the individual states disagreed with each other on many issues.)

Paragraph 7:   Where and when was the Constitution adopted? (in Philadelphia in 1790)

Paragraph 8:   What two problems caused problems after the Constitution was ratified? (Many people were afraid of a strong central government and small states didn't want representatives to the federal government to be chosen based on population.)

Paragraph 9:   What did the Connecticut Compromise provide for? (a two-house legislature) Why did this make both sides of the debate on representation happy? (Representatives to one house would be elected based on population; each state would send two representatives to the other house.)

Return to the K-W-L lists that you put on the board earlier. Answer questions from the second column and fill in key items in the third.

Reading Strategies Instruction: Explain that being able to repeat someone else's idea in your own words is a good test of whether or not you really have understood what they said. If you repeat the idea using the exact words the other person used, you may be just "parroting"—repeating words, without understanding the ideas behind them. If you are able to put the other person's thoughts into your own words, it proves that your mind has taken in the other person's ideas and processed what the person said until you were able to restate the idea in your own way. Many GED questions will ask students to pick out correct answers that are not stated in exactly the same words as they appear in the reading passage. Read aloud the section called "Restating Information: A Detail" on page 169 and complete the practice exercise and followup explanation with the whole class. For students having difficulty, suggest more instruction and practice at a Pre-GED level in the *Threshold* science text, Unit 1, Chapter 3, Lesson 8. For more GED-level work, see *The New Revised Cambridge GED* social studies text, Chapter 1, Lesson 2, and *The New Revised Cambridge GED* science text, Chapter 1, Lesson 2.

Lesson Wrap-Up

Complete the Exercise: Ask students to complete the Lesson 3 Exercise on page 171 individually. Set a 10-minute time limit. Then discuss each of the questions with the class, eliciting opinions about what the correct answers are and why. Also encourage students to explain why each incorrect response is incorrect, giving reasons for their opinions. After a consensus is reached, go over the answers and explanations on page A-15.

Lesson 4:   Regional Differences

Lesson Warm-Up

Brainstorming: Read aloud the Prereading Prompt on page 172. Ask what other parts of the United States class members originally came from or have visited. What sectional attitudes did people from that area have? (Californians think their climate is the best. Southerners think people from other parts of the country are impolite. Northerners think that Southerners are racially prejudiced.) Why do some Southerners want to continue to hang the Confederate flag over state buildings? (They are proud of their Southern heritage.) Why are others against it? (To some it represents a return to pre–Civil War days when slavery was an accepted way of life.)

Vocabulary: Write on the board the words *sectionalism* and *secede* from the Key Words section. Lead students through a discussion that will illustrate clearly what sectionalism and secession are. Look at the root word *section*, within the term *sectionalism*. Remind students of the definition of nationalism from Lesson 3. (Nationalism is an intense feeling of pride in your country.) Lead them to understand that sectionalism is a feeling of pride for one section of the country that is stronger than the person's feeling for the country as a whole. Point out that slavery has existed for thousands of years among people of the same race. (Some

Africans had slaves. Some rich women in Greece and Rome had slaves who were white.) Contrast the word *succeed* with the word *secede*. Ask students to define *succeed* and to use the words *succeed* and *success* in sentences. Point out that *secession* comes from the root word *secede*. Explain that when a state seceded from the union, it left the union. Now ask students to restate the meaning of the words *sectionalism* and *secede* in their own words.

Lesson Activities

Vocabulary: As you work through the reading passage with students, several vocabulary items may need special attention. List the following terms on the board and stop to define them and use them in sample sentences as they appear in the reading. Suggest that students copy in their notebooks any words they have trouble with, together with their definitions.

- **Deep-seated:** Beginning a long time in the past
- **Moral disgrace:** Situation that is embarrassing because it goes against our idea of how human beings should be treated
- **Abolitionists:** People who wanted to do away with slavery immediately
- **Identified with:** Felt the same as
- **Tariffs:** Taxes on items purchased from other countries
- **Flocked to:** Went to in great numbers
- **Sue:** Go to court to try to get your way
- **Emanicpation:** Freedom
- **Constitutional rights:** Freedoms guaranteed by the U.S. Constitution
- **Ruthless:** Tough, without any sympathy; cruel

Discussion: Ask each student to read a paragraph to the class. After each reading, ask other students to list one or two details that were in the paragraph in their own words. Be sure that everyone understands these details. Then ask a volunteer to say what he or she thinks to be the main idea of the paragraph. Here is an example of the types of responses you may expect.

Paragraph 1 Details: The Northeast made money on manufacturing and sales. The Southern economy depended on agriculture. The West made money selling food to the Northeast.

Paragraph 1 Main Idea: The various sections of the United States got along because each had something the other needed.

Paragraph 2 Details: Southerners felt that slavery was necessary for their economic survival. People from the North and West ran successful farms using mostly family labor. Northerners and Westerners thought slavery was wrong. Some people, called abolitionists, wanted to stop slavery immediately.

Paragraph 2 Main Idea: The various areas of the country disagreed strongly on the issue of slavery.

Continue the reading and discussion in this manner throughout the reading.

Lesson Review: Divide the class into small groups. Assign each group two or three paragraphs as their focus. Their task is to read it aloud together, discuss what they have read, and come up with three or four questions about the facts contained in their material. When they are ready, ask them to have one representative from the group write out their questions on the board. Then conduct a discussion with the entire class in which students try to answer each other's questions. Help students discover the answers in the reading passage and point out the location of any answers they can't find.

Students working on paragraphs 3 and 4 may come up with questions such as these: What is sectionalism? (putting the good of your particular part of the country ahead of the good of the country as a whole) Did Americans in the early 1800s put the welfare of the country as a whole first? (No, they pushed for laws that would help their particular part of the country, not the country as a whole.) What did the Northerners want to do? (They wanted to sell their goods for high prices even if it hurt other parts of the country.) What did Southerners want? (They wanted to continue slavery even though it was morally wrong.) What did Westerners want? (They wanted the government to spend a lot of money on roads and canals in their part of the country so that they could make more money.) Who was elected President in 1828? (Andrew Jackson) What did he do that angered Southerners and Westerners? (He enforced the tariffs on foreign goods.) Why were the people in the South and West angry? (These tariffs made goods more expensive for them.) Why were the Northerners happy with the tariffs? (It meant that things they manufactured could be sold for less than the imported goods.)

Reading Strategies Instruction: Read aloud the first two paragraphs of the section entitled "Finding the Main Idea of a Paragraph" on page 174. After finishing paragraph 2, divide the class into small groups and ask each group to apply the information about stating the topic of a paragraph to other sections of the reading passage. Assign each group one or two paragraphs to work on. Then have the groups report back to the class and ask the other students to comment on whether they agree or disagree with that group's choice of topic, main idea, and topic sentence for each paragraph. (The explanatory material discusses the topic sentences of the first three paragraphs of the reading passage, so assign group work beginning with paragraph 4.) Then read aloud the paragraph on locating the topic sentence. After discussing how to locate topic sentences with the class, ask them to go back to the same groups they were in before and

locate the topic sentences in the paragraphs they worked on. Go over their findings with the class. Then ask students to read the sample paragraph on page 175 and answer the questions individually. Go over the explanation of the correct answers together in class. For students having difficulty, refer them to three Cambridge Pre-GED volumes: *On Your Own: Reading*, Unit 2, Chapter 7, the *Threshold* social studies text, Unit 1, Chapter 2, and the *Threshold* science text, Unit 1, Chapter 4, Lessons 9 and 10. For more GED-level work, see *The New Revised Cambridge GED* social studies text, Chapter 2, Lesson 1, and the science text, Chapter 1, Lesson 3.

Lesson Wrap-Up

How to Do the Exercise: Before students complete the Lesson 4 Exercise on pages 176–177, remind them that they will have a limited amount of time to answer the questions on the GED exam, so they will need to work as efficiently as possible. Give them the following instructions:

1. Always read the question items before reading the passage. This will help you focus on the information you need to look for.
2. As you read the passage, focus on information relating to the questions.
3. Use the process of elimination to discard obviously incorrect answers.

Complete the Exercise: Ask students to complete the Lesson 4 Exercise individually. Set a 10-minute time limit. Then discuss each question with the class, eliciting opinions about which answer is correct and why. Also encourage students to explain why each incorrect response is incorrect, giving reasons for their opinions. After a consensus is reached, go over the answers and explanations on page A-15.

Lesson 5: Industrial Growth of the United States

Lesson Warm-Up

Brainstorming: Ask students to list as many facts as they can about the city in which they live. (If they live in a rural area, choose the nearest large city as the focus for this exercise.) Encourage them to include the population, the kinds of manufacturing and other businesses that are located there, educational opportunities, entertainment available, medical care facilities located in this city, and similar factors. Then ask students where the people living there came from and why they are now living in this particular city. Draw connections between the employment and other opportunities offered by cities and the movement of great numbers of people from the countryside to urban areas. Then read aloud the Prereading Prompt and discuss the question posed in the final sentence. Refer back to the brainstormed material on the board during the discussion.

Lesson Activities

Vocabulary and Major Concepts: Ask students to take turns reading aloud a few sentences each. Pause after each set of sentences and ask comprehension questions about the passage just completed. Also pick out vocabulary items that may not be clear to students and elicit or supply definitions for them.

Paragraph 1: What caused the rapid expansion of manufacturing and business from the time of the Civil War until the 1920s? (the need for weapons and ammunition for the war, the growth of the railroad system, the strong demand for food and manufactured goods all over the country) What does *crucial* mean? (very important) Was the Industrial Revolution happening only in the United States? (No, it was also taking place in Europe.)

Paragraph 2: What does *sprang up* mean? (grew quickly) What is *mass production*? (It's the manufacturing of goods in very large quantities; before this most goods were handmade.) What is an *assembly line*? (a system in which the item being manufactured passes from one worker to the next, with each worker doing a specific part of the process) What is a *conveyor belt*? (It is the moving platform that carries the item being manufactured from one worker to the next.) What is *division of labor*? (It is the system in which assembly line workers divide up the work, with each person doing a special job over and over.) *Paragraph 3:* What is a *lifestyle*? (It is the way a group of people spend their lives—the work they do and the way they spend their leisure time.)

Paragraph 4: Why were so many more people needed in cities after the Civil War? (Millions of factory jobs were created by the Industrial Revolution and most factories were located in or near big cities.)

Paragraph 5: Where did many immigrants come from in the late 1800s? (Asia and southern Europe) What is *oppression*? (the opposite of freedom) What does *fled to* mean? (moved rapidly to)

Paragraph 6: What does *brutal* mean? (tough and cruel) What were some of the problems experienced by different groups of workers? (Textile workers developed lung diseases. Some coal miners breathed gas and got sick; others were killed when mines collapsed. Steelworkers were killed when they were burned by fires or melted steel. What is a *labor union*? (a group organized to protect workers) When was the first union formed in the United States? (in 1886)

Paragraph 7: What was the *Progressive Movement*? (an attempt to improve the lives of factory workers in the

United States) How many hours a week did some children work in 1900? (twelve hours a day, six days a week) Didn't children have to go to school? (No, there were no laws saying that children had to attend school.)

Paragraph 8: What is a *monopoly*? (complete control of one type of business by a single company) What is a *bribe*? (money paid to someone in order to gain an advantage—here, paid to a lawmaker so that he or she would pass laws favorable to a certain industry)

Paragraph 9: What is *stock*? (certificates that show that you have paid for ownership of a small part of a big company) What does on *margin* mean? (using borrowed money to buy an object, often stock) What was the *stock market crash*? (It happened when prices of stock fell; many people lost a lot of money, and many companies went out of business.)

Paragraph 10: What was the *New Deal*? (a plan to end the Great Depression) What were some parts of the New Deal? (a system to control the stock market, a system to help out older people—Social Security—and several projects to create government-funded jobs for the unemployed.)

Lesson Review: Divide the class into four groups. Assign each group one of the four sections of the reading passage as their focus. Their task is to read it aloud together, discuss what they have read, and come up with a summary of the content of their section. Ask them to come to a group consensus and have one representative from the group write out on a piece of paper, in a sentence of two, their summary statement. Set a 10-minute time limit on this activity. When the summaries are complete, ask one person from each group to write their summary on the board. Then review them with the class. Ask other class members to review each section of the reading passage and compare what they find with the summary given. Encourage students to critique the summaries, stating what is accurate about each, adding key elements that were omitted, and suggesting deletions in cases in which a less important detail was given too much attention.

Application: Ask students to list as many work rules as they can. Those who are working can use their own experience. Others can cite the experiences of friends and family members. They may come up with rules such as these: (1) You must be paid at least the minimum wage for all work you do. (2) You must be 16 years old to work in a factory. (3) If you work more than 40 hours a week, you must be paid overtime pay. (4) You must be allowed to take a 15-minute coffee break each morning and each afternoon. Ask students how they think these rules came about. Lead them to understand that at one time factory owners and others treated workers very badly and that the workers and the government demanded that these unfair practices stop.

Reading Strategies Instruction: Ask students to read with a partner the section entitled "Find the Main Idea of a Passage." Suggest that they put a mark by anything they don't understand and that they ask you for an explanation when they have finished reading. Then go over the five main idea choices they are given after the sample paragraph on page 181. Review the reasons given for eliminating each incorrect choice. For students having difficulty, see the Pre-GED volume, *On Your Own: Reading*, Unit 2, Chapter 10, and the Pre-GED *Threshold* science text, Unit 1, Chapter 4, Lesson 11. For more GED-level work, see *The New Revised Cambridge GED* social studies text, Chapter 2, Lesson 2, and *The New Revised Cambridge GED* science text, Chapter 2, Lesson 1.

Lesson Wrap-Up

How to Do the Exercises: The passages on pages 182–183 illustrate clearly the importance of working quickly and efficiently. Explain that on the actual GED test students will have approximately a minute and a half to answer each question. Since each of the Lesson 5 exercises takes up a full page, students will have to make the best possible use of their time. Give them the following instructions:

1. Glance at the passage to get an idea of what it is about.
2. Read the question carefully. This will help you focus on the information you need to look for in the paragraph.
3. Read the passage looking only for the main idea. Don't be distracted by unimportant details.
4. Use the process of elimination to discard obviously incorrect answers.

Complete the Exercises: Give students six minutes to complete the Lesson 5 Exercise. Then read and discuss each question, writing on the board the number of people who choose each answer. Encourage students to refer back to the reading passages and to ask questions to help clarify exactly what each distractor is saying. Then go over the answers and explanations on page A-15. Remind students that the key to doing well on the test is to be able to eliminate the obviously wrong answers very early on, and to concentrate on choosing the best answer from the choices that remain.

Lesson 6: Government and Political Science

Lesson Warm-Up

Brainstorming: Read aloud the Prereading Prompt. Ask students if they had ever thought of our government as an experiment. Explain that the fact that the

U.S. Constitution provides for amendments and that there have been over 40 of them in 200 years shows that the United States knows that its government must be open to change. The founders of the country realized that there was no one perfect way to govern a land as large and diverse as ours. Then make two columns on the board. At the top of one write the heading "Positives" and at the top of the other "Negatives." Reread aloud the sentence "Some governments have people's best interests in mind, some don't." Ask students to brainstorm lists of ways in which they feel that our government has their best interests in mind, and another list of ways in which they feel the government is not looking out for them. (Students may appreciate the fact that the federal government operates an army to protect the country and allows 18-year-olds to vote. On the other hand, they may not think that the amount of tax they pay is fair or they may feel the federal government should offer more aid to education programs.) Elicit as many items as possible in a five-minute period. Then go back and briefly discuss each contribution.

Vocabulary: Write on the board the four Key Words from page 185. Refer back to the negatives on the list just brainstormed and explain that although our government can't always meet all the needs of all the citizens, there are much worse forms of government that don't even attempt to take individual rights into account. As you point to each term on the board, ask a student to read aloud the corresponding definition from the book. Ask students to try to come up with examples to illustrate each term. If they can't, supply one of your own. (The kings and queens of England were a *monarchy*. Hitler was the leader of a *dictatorship* in Nazi Germany. Spain was ruled by an *oligarchy* in which General Franco allowed the church and some rich people to have some of the power.) Point out the terms *direct democracy* and *representative democracy* under the term *democracy*. Ask students which form the U.S. government is. (It is a representative democracy.)

Lesson Activities

Discussion: This lesson contains five subtopics: Types of Modern Government, The American Constitutional System, Political Science Statistics, Public Opinion Polls, and Statistical Studies. Divide the class into groups and ask each group to become expert in the material about their particular topic. They will do this by reading the passage aloud together and making notes about any word or idea they don't fully understand. (One group can handle more than one of the short topics.) Then their task is to master the material on their assigned topic(s) through rereading, group discussion, and teacher input. The next step is for each group to come up with two or three questions per topic to ask the rest of the class members. They should write these questions on a piece of paper so that you can collect them and use them to quiz the rest of the class. You can use some of the questions listed below to get them started, if necessary.

Read and Question: After the groups have studied their assignments and produced the questions, read the lesson aloud, section by section, with the class. Answer any questions that students may have about vocabulary or concepts, using the list below as a guide. Then use the questions that were formulated by the various groups as a way of checking comprehension and reviewing the main points in each section. Be sure to cover the following points.

Types of Modern Government:

1. What is the difference between an absolute monarch and a constitutional monarch? (An absolute monarch rules without limits. A constitutional monarch does not really govern; he or she is more of a symbolic leader.)
2. What is *propaganda*? (It is the use of untruths or half-truths to make a group of people do what someone else wants them to.)
3. What is a *police state*? (a country in which the government uses military and police power to make people to obey its absolute authority in most parts of their lives)
4. What is the difference between a *dictator* and a *totalitarian dictator*? (Both have total power, but the totalitarian leader insists more on thought control and is seen by many citizens as a godlike figure.)
5. What is the difference between *direct democracy* and *representative democracy*? (In direct democracy every person can vote on every decision. This is possible in very small towns. In representative democracy an elected agent ideally carries out the wishes of the people who elected him or her. This type of democracy is needed when there are millions of people and millions of decisions to be made and direct democracy is impossible.)

The American Constitutional System

1. What is a *federal system*? (one in which the various states give up some powers and keep others for themselves)
2. What is the difference between the *separation of powers* and the *division of powers*? (*Separation of powers* refers to the fact that the various states have some laws and systems that are not under the control of the central government. These laws and systems are *separate from* the central government. *Division of powers* refers to the fact that the power of the national and state governments is *divided into* branches: the legislative branch, executive branch, and judicial branch.)
3. What is the main responsibility of each branch of government? (The legislative branch makes laws, but the judicial branch interprets what they

mean, and the executive branch chooses how to enforce them.)
4. Using the chart on page 187, give some examples of how one branch of government can limit the power of another. (The President can veto a bill passed by Congress, but Congress can override the President's veto. Congress can pass laws, but the Supreme Court can declare them unconstitutional.)

Political Science Statistics:

1. Why are statistics important to politicians? (Statistics help to show what people want.)
2. What does *gleaned* mean? (gathered, taken)
3. What does *media* mean? (newspapers, radio, television)

Public Opinion Polls:

1. What is a *poll*? (a survey)
2. What is a *breakdown*? (It shows how large each part of a whole thing is. A religious breakdown would show what percent of people in a given city follow each religion.)

Statistical Studies:

1. Restate the purpose of statistical studies in your own words. (They show whether or not the information gathered through polls and interviews is likely to be accurate or not.)
2. What does the word *valid* mean? (true, accurate)

Reading Strategies Instruction: Ask students what the word *graphic* means. (A graphic is a picture or a chart that helps make complicated information easier to read.) Then read the paragraph under "Finding a Detail in a Graphic" aloud, referring to the pie chart to illustrate each point. To make it easier for students to read the graph, point out that slices of the circle going down the left side (the 1%, 2%, 5%, 13% slices) are arranged in the same order as the color key boxes going down the right side (i.e., "Other City Salaries—1%" corresponds to the narrowest slice, "Repairs to Water System—2%"corresponds to the next slice to the left of the 1% slice, and so on). Ask students to complete the Practice item on page 190 before looking at the explanation that follows the answers. Ask students which answers they chose, and why. Then read aloud the explanatory paragraph on page 190 and elicit any final questions or comments. Students having difficulty can find further instruction and practice at a Pre-GED level in *On Your Own: Reading*, Unit 3, Chapters 17 and 18, the Pre-GED *Threshold* social studies text, Unit 1, Chapter 3, and the *Threshold* science text, Unit 1, Chapter 6. For more GED-level work, see *The New Revised Cambridge GED Program:* the social studies text, Chapter 2, Lesson 3 and the science text, Chapter 2, Lessons 2 and 3.

Lesson Wrap-Up

Complete the Exercises: Set a five-minute time limit on the Lesson 6 Exercise. Emphasize the importance reading the title above each graphic and looking over the figure to get a clear idea of what kind of information is being presented. The next step is to read the questions and answers and eliminate any impossible distractors. Read the question again and go back to the graphic to find the answer. When students have written their answers, review the explanations on page A-16.

Lesson 7:   Economics: Systems and Measures

Lesson Warm-Up

Brainstorming: At the extreme left of the board write the words "Very controlled," and at the extreme right write the words "Not controlled." Ask students how they handle their own money supply. At the extreme left would go such comments as "I write out a budget every month" or "When I get paid I put aside $50 a month for food and $20 for bus fare." At the extreme right would go comments such as "I don't know where my money goes" or "I always run out of money halfway through the week." Ask students whether they think the government is able to keep the country's money supply in control. (Accept all reasonable responses. At this point you can briefly describe the Federal Reserve system as the government's own bank, which it uses to control the country's money supply.)

Debate: Discuss the two Key Word phrases, *free-enterprise system* and *welfare state services*, with the class. Divide the class into two groups. Give them five minutes to prepare a list of the positive aspects of the system they have been assigned. Then stage a debate between the two sides in which they try to convince each other of the benefits of each system. At the end, summarize the positive and negative points about each type of system that have emerged during the discussion.

Lesson Activities

Brainstorming: Before reading the section entitled "Types of Economic Systems," make three columns on the board, headed Capitalism, Socialism, and Communism. Then make a list down the left side of the board with the following phrases: Who owns businesses? How are prices set? How high are individual taxes? Who controls the media? Ask students to tell you anything they can about each system. Make notes about what they say under the appropriate columns. Then read the passage aloud together, pausing after each paragraph to summarize what it said and to answer any student questions. After you finish read-

ing the section, go back to the chart on the board and try to fill in something in each section of the grid in response to the questions along the left side. For example, for the question "Who owns businesses?" the capitalist column would read "Mostly individuals," the socialist column would read "Mostly the government," and the communist column would read "Only the government." When you have filled in the entire grid, review the findings with the class.

Creating an Advertisement: Divide the class into three groups and ask each group to create a magazine-style advertisement for one type of economic system: capitalism, socialism, or communism. Assign to each group one of the systems and ask the students to reread the paragraphs that describe the three systems. Their task is then to come up with as many positive things as they can about their system, and as many negative things as possible about the other systems. Have them write down all the ideas people in the group can think of. Hand out blank white paper and ask the group to work together to create the ad, complete with headlines, catchy phrases, graphs, or cartoonlike drawings. When the groups are finished, have a representative from each group present the ad to the rest of the class. Ask others in the class to offer ideas for elements that could be added to each advertisement.

Application: Read aloud and discuss with the class the section titled "The Free-Enterprise System." Answer any questions that students may have. Then divide the class into two groups, one called the high-supply group, and another called the low-supply group. Ask each group to try to come up with the names of three items that fit their group's name. For example, the high-supply group might notice that a certain fruit is plentiful right now and that all the stores have a lot of country and western CDs to sell. The low-supply group might list a certain brand of athletic shoe or a certain fast-food item that is difficult to find. Have each group put its list on the board. Then compare the lists, looking at the prices of each item. Are any of the high supply items very high priced? (probably not) Are any of the low supply items high priced? (some may be) Review with students the concept that high demand–low supply keeps prices high, while low demand–high supply drives prices down. Ask students to make up their own examples using products they frequently buy for themselves.

Graphics: Read aloud and discuss with the class the section titled "Business Cycles and the Federal Reserve System." Review the vocabulary used to describe the economy by drawing a long horizontal line on the board. Label the area above the horizontal axis "Good times" and the area below it "Bad times." Ask individual students to choose one of the boldface words from the reading passage, state in their own words what it means, and then write it in the appropriate area on the board. The words *recession, depres-*

sion, and *unemployment* should appear below the line. *Recovery* should appear above the line and *inflation* should be on or just below the line.

Summary Discussion: Review the function of the Federal Reserve System by asking the following questions:

1. What is *tight money*? (It means that the Federal Reserve is not making much money available for loans.)
2. Why does the Fed sometimes have a tight money policy? (Inflation sometimes starts to grow very rapidly, and the Fed wants to slow it down.)
3. What is an *easy money* policy? (It means that the Fed makes a lot of money available for loans.)
4. Why would they do this? (The economy has slowed down. There may be unemployment. The Fed wants to make loans available so that businesses can start growing again.)
5. What is the *discount rate*? (It is the rate of interest the Fed charges its best customers.)
6. How does it affect the economy? (A high interest rate will mean that fewer people will borrow, so it has almost the same effect as limiting the amount of money that the Fed makes available for loans.)

Vocabulary: Read with the class the section entitled "Two Economic Measures." Write on the board the words *gross national product* and *consumer price index*. As a way of reviewing this section, break down each phrase into its individual words. What does *gross* mean? (When you are talking about people, it means fat or very large. Point out that when you are talking about money it means the total or entire amount of money involved in a transaction.) What is a *product*? (Explain that the *product* in *gross national product* includes all goods and services produced in a country during one year.) Ask students to rephrase the definition in their own words. Ask what a *consumer* is. (someone who buys something) Ask what an *index* is. (Students may say that it is a list of all the words in a certain book. Explain that when we talk about numbers, an index consists of numbers that show certain patterns in information about a topic. Point out that the Consumer Price Index shows how much the cost of things changes from time to time. It shows us whether we're paying more or less for the same items from year to year.

Reading Strategies Instruction: Ask students to work in pairs. Have them read together "Finding the Main Idea of a Graphic: Graphs." Then call on individual students to say in their own words what they think the steps in answering main idea questions about a graph should be. Steps should include:

1. Look at the title to see what information the graph is communicating.
2. Briefly look over the entire graph to see what time period it covers and what units of measure it uses.

3. Look over the questions and distractors and eliminate any distractors that don't make sense at all.
4. Look at the sensible distractors and compare them with the information presented in the graph. The same steps can be followed with a cartoon, except that cartoons usually don't have titles. For students having difficulty, try the Pre-GED volume *On Your Own: Reading*, Unit 4, Chapter 19. For more GED-level work, see *The New Revised Cambridge GED Program*: the social studies text, Chapter 2, Lesson 4 and the science text, Chapter 2, Lesson 4.

Lesson Wrap-Up

Complete the Exercises: Ask students to complete the exercise on pages 200–201. Set a five-minute time limit. Then discuss each question with the class. Go over the answers and explanations on page A-16.

Lesson 8:   Geography

Lesson Warm-Up

Vocabulary: Write on the board the five terms under Key Words and review each term with the class. When discussing *landforms*, ask students to give examples of the types of landforms listed in the definition (e.g., have them name some specific mountains, valleys— say, river valleys—or plains). Ask them to use simple line drawings on the board to illustrate what each one looks like.

Some people become confused regarding the difference between *longitude* and *latitude*. A trick that may help them remember the difference is to remember that longitude has an *o* and lines of longitude go from the top to the bottom of the map. To help illustrate the concept of degrees of longitude, draw and label a 30° angle on the board facing a simple outline of a globe of the world. Connect the ends of the angle to the globe itself. Then draw and label a 60° angle on the other side of the globe and connect the lines to the globe. Point out how much higher (farther from the equator) the 60° angle hits the globe. Point out the longitude and latitude measurements on the map on page 203.

Ask students what the difference is between *climate* and *weather*. (*Climate* is the general weather pattern for a certain geographical area. *Weather* refers to the specific temperature, wind, and precipitation at any given moment.) Ask students to give examples of five different *ethnic groups*, including all groups represented by class members.

Lesson Activities

Discussion: This lesson contains four subtopics: Physical Geography, Latitude and Longitude, The Zones of Climate, and Cultural Geography. Divide the class into groups and ask each group to become expert in the material about a particular topic. They will do this by reading the passages aloud together and making notes about any word or idea they don't fully understand. (One group can handle more than one of the short topics.) Then their task is to master the material on their assigned topic through rereading, group discussion, and teacher input. The next step is for each group to come up with two or three questions per topic to ask the rest of the class members. They should write these questions on a piece of paper so that you can collect them and present them to the rest of the class. You can use some of the questions listed below to get them started, if necessary.

Read and Question: After the groups have studied their assignments and produced the questions, read the lesson aloud, section by section, with the class. Answer any questions about vocabulary or concepts that students may have, using the list below as a guide. Then use the questions that were formulated by the various groups as a way of checking comprehension and reviewing the main points in each section. Be sure to cover the following points.

Physical Geography:

1. What is topography? (a detailed description of the landforms in a given area)
2. How is topography usually pictured? (with different colors on a map to show how high or low each area is)
3. Why is topography important? (It shows landforms that influence the way that people live their lives.)

Latitude and Longitude: On the board draw a simple map of the world similar to the one on page 203, showing the outlines of the continents, but leave off all latitude and longitude lines. Ask a student to come to the board and add arrows showing the four directions (north, south, east, and west). Reread the material with the class and point out that east longitude is east of the Prime Meridian, and west longitude is west. Similarly, south latitude is south of the equator and north latitude is north. Then ask individual students to come to the board to label the following items. (Some items will have to be drawn in or circled or indicated by brackets before they can be labeled.)

1. Equator
2. Prime meridian
3. Northern hemisphere
4. Southern hemisphere
5. 30° East longitude
6. 60° North latitude

Ask students to practice giving some very general coordinates. For example, ask them to name any coordinates that fall within the United States. (40° north latitude and 120° west longitude) or within Africa (the Equator and 30° east longitude). Divide the class into pairs. First, one person names a set of coordinates, and the other tells what continent or country the location is in. Then they switch roles.

The Zones of Climate:

1. Which locations on the Earth are generally warmest? (those nearest the Equator)
2. Which areas are coldest? (those farthest from the Equator)
3. Use the map that was used to discuss latitude and longitude (or a standard wall map) and point out the location of the Tropic of Cancer and the Tropic of Capricorn. (23.5° north latitude and 23.5° south latitude, respectively)
4. Name some countries that are "in the tropics." (Vietnam, Thailand, Jamaica, the Bahamas, etc.)
5. What is the difference between an *arid* climate and a *marine* climate? (An arid climate is very dry and a marine climate is very wet.)
6. Why are the arctic zones so cold? (They get very little direct sunlight.)

Cultural Geography:

1. Ask students to define cultural geography in their own words. (They might say that it is the study of the ways in which people live in a certain part of the world and how the physical environment affects their lives.)
2. Ask them to give examples other than those in the book of how cultural geography works. Encourage students to think about other areas of the United States. Students from other countries can look for examples from their homelands. (The Texas plains have rich oil reserves and a large area of grass-covered plains for grazing cattle, so the lives of many people there are affected by the fortunes of the oil industry and the beef market. The Sahara Desert didn't allow for the raising of crops or animals, so many people who lived there became traders and moved from place to place making a living by buying and selling.)
3. Draw a large circle on the board and ask students to make it into a pie chart showing the percentages of the world's population that belong to each race.
4. Put a chart on the board listing the major religions of the world and have students fill in the numbers showing how many people follow the four major religions of the world.

Reading Strategies Instruction: Ask students to take turns reading aloud the section "Making Inferences" on page 205. After reading the first two paragraphs, review the difference between facts and inferences. Make two columns on the board labeled "Facts" and "Inferences." Give the students some sets of facts and help them come up with possible inferences that might explain them. For example, a student who lives alone comes home to an empty apartment and finds the door unlocked and the lights on. (A thief has broken in.) If time permits, give students additional practice with creating inferences to go along with factual information. Then ask students what they should look for before trying to answer questions based on a map. (Look at the title so that you'll understand the reason for the map. Review the legend so that you will know how the map works.) Ask students to read the practice item and choose the correct answer from the choices on page 206 before looking at the explanation that follows the answers. Then ask them which answer they chose, and why. Discuss differences among the answers chosen and ask students to explain in detail how they came to their conclusions. Then read aloud the explanatory paragraph on page 206 and elicit final questions or comments. Students having difficulty might benefit from more work at the Pre-GED level in *On Your Own: Reading*, Unit 3, Chapter 11, and also Chapter 16 ("Making Predictions"), the *Threshold* social studies text, Unit 2, Chapter 2, Lesson 15 and the *Threshold* science text, Unit 2, Chapter 1. For more GED-level work, see *The New Revised Cambridge GED Program:* the social studies text, Chapter 2, Lesson 5, and the science text, Chapter 2, Lesson 5.

Lesson Wrap-Up

Complete the Exercises: Ask each student to complete the Lesson 8 Exercise on page 207. Set a five-minute time limit. Then discuss each question with the class, eliciting opinions about what the correct answers are, and why. Also encourage students to explain why each incorrect response is incorrect, giving reasons for their opinions. After a consensus is reached, go over the answers and explanations on page A-17.

Lesson 9:   Anthropology and Sociology

Lesson Warm-Up

Brainstorming: Read aloud and discuss the Prereading Prompt with students. Then ask students to brainstorm a list of all the groups that they or members of their family belong to. Emphasize that membership in some groups is a formal and organized affair. You must decide to join this kind of group and you may support it with regular attendance at meetings and with donations of money. When you join a church or a bowling team, or take a course, you become involved in this type of group. There are other, very different types of groups to which we all belong. We were born into these groups, or we belong to them because of the place we happen to live in or because of our personal likes and dislikes. You are a member of a group of people that live in a certain city and speak a certain language. You root for a particular

football team. You did not consciously join the groups that do these things, but you are a member just the same. Set a five-minute time limit and gather as long a list as possible during that time. Then ask students to look at each membership listed and put a *J* after the ones that the person purposely *joined*, and an *A* after the ones in which membership was *automatic* and the person became a member without realizing it. Discuss briefly the influences that these groups may have on our lives.

Vocabulary: Ask students what they think the word anthropology means. They may use the description given in the Prereading Prompt as a starting point. Help them differentiate between *sociology* and *anthropology* at this point. Explain that anthropology looks at the history, physical characteristics, and lifestyles of human beings as a whole, over many years, perhaps thousands of years. Sociology, in contrast, studies how the various human groups interact with each other in one specific society, usually in a more limited period. Review the definitions of *physical anthropology* and *cultural anthropology*. List the following areas of interest on the board and have students label them *P* for *physical anthropology* or *C* for *cultural anthropology*:

Buddhism (C)

Marriage customs (C)

The origin of Native Americans (P)

The effect of climate on physical behavior of an agricultural population (P)

Men's roles in family life (C)

Lesson Activities

Lesson Review: Divide the class into two groups. Assign group 1 the section "Anthropology" as their focus. Their task is to read the five paragraphs describing anthropology aloud together, discuss what they have read, and come up with a summary of what each paragraph says. Ask them to reach a group consensus and have one representative from the group write out on a piece of paper, in a single sentence, a summary statement for each paragraph. Ask them to spend about five minutes per paragraph on this activity. Group 2's job is to follow the same steps for the section on "Sociology". When the summaries are complete, ask one person from each group to write their summary on the board. Then review them with the class. Ask class members to review each paragraph in the book and compare what they find with the summary given. Encourage students to critique the summaries, stating what is accurate about each summary and adding key elements that were omitted. During the discussion allow students to add any relevant facts they may know and to ask any questions they may have. First refer the questions to the "expert" group, supplying any additional explanation or clarification yourself. As each group gives its report, review the following concepts:

Paragraph 1: Students should write out their own statement of the difference between physical anthropology and cultural anthropology.

Paragraph 2: What is evolution? (Guide students so that they avoid the creationism versus evolution conflict, but understand that the physical forms of plants and animals change over time in response to environmental factors. For example, Caucasians living near the sunny Mediterranean developed complexions that are darker compared to complexions of Caucasians living farther north.)

Paragraph 3: When students give their summary of this paragraph, ask them to list some examples of their own values, beliefs, and attitudes that would be of interest to cultural anthropologists. (These may include the value placed on a good education, the belief in a single god, and the attitude that women should receive equal pay for equal work.)

Paragraph 4: What is a creed? (a fundamental set of beliefs that form the basis for all the other beliefs of a given society) What is America's basic creed? (individual freedom and individual initiative and in theory, equality of opportunity)

Paragraph 5: How do physical and cultural anthropologists collect their information? (They both use the same methods—they observe everything they can, ask questions, and make up theories that describe how the society works.) What is an *artifact*? (an object made by human beings)

Paragraph 6: Review the definition of sociology given in the Lesson Warm-Up. (Sociology studies how the various human groups interact with each other in a specific society.) How are the neighborhood groups mentioned in this paragraph divided up? (by national background)

Paragraph 8: What is a *peer group*? (a group of people who are about the same age and think the same way about a lot of things) What peer group are you in? (Students may belong to a teenage, an urban group, a "twentysomething" suburban working-parent group, etc.) What do peers in a peer group do in the same manner? (They may dress similarly, have the same interests, and even have a special set of vocabulary words that people outside the group don't understand.)

Paragraph 9: What does the term *socioeconomic group* refer to? (It refers to groups of people who have about the same amount of education, the same level of jobs, and the same standard of living.) What are some socioeconomic levels? (working class, middle class, and upper class) What does *lifestyle* mean? (It represents the way a person or group lives. It includes what they eat, where they live, what they do for a living, and how they spend their leisure time.) What is *social mobility*? (It is the ability to move from working class to middle class, or from middle class to upper class.)

Paragraph 10: What is a *norm*? (an accepted standard of behavior in a given society) What is *deviant* behavior? (any action that doesn't fit in with the norm) What is *socialization*? (learning the values of the society in which a person lives) How is a person socialized? (through the home, school, and religious training)

Reading Strategies Instruction: Read and discuss "Inferring the Main Idea of a Paragraph" on page 210 together. Review with the class the techniques you used to locate the main idea of a paragraph when the main idea was contained in a single sentence within the paragraph. (First, determine the topic of the paragraph. What is the subject of the paragraph? Second, locate the sentence that gives the most important idea about the topic. You can do this by looking at each sentence and deciding which ones give less important supporting details that support the topic sentence. When you have found the topic sentence, you have located the main idea of the paragraph.) Explain that the procedure for inferring the main idea of a paragraph is almost the same. However, instead of being able to locate the topic sentence surrounded by sentences containing details, you have to make up your own topic sentence. Refer students having difficulty to the Pre-GED instruction and practice in *On Your Own: Reading*, Unit 3, Chapter 12, the *Threshold* social studies text, Unit 2, Chapter 2, Lesson 15, and the *Threshold* science text, Unit 2, Chapter 2, Lessons 24 and 25. For more GED-level work, see *The New Revised Cambridge GED Program:* the social studies text, Chapter 2, Lesson 6, and the science text, Chapter 2, Lesson 6.

Complete the Practice Exercise: Have students work on the Practice item on page 211 individually and select the correct answer from the choices before looking at the explanation that follows the answers. After they have finished, ask them to share their answer with a partner and then read through and discuss the explanation with a partner.

Lesson Wrap-Up

Complete the Exercises: Ask students to complete the exercises individually. Go over the answers with the entire class, asking individual students to explain why they answered each question as they did. Then go over the answers and explanations on page A-17.

Lesson 10:   Psychology

Lesson Warm-Up

Brainstorming: Read aloud the Prereading Prompt. Ask students to guess at the meaning of the terms *anxiety, neurotic, repressed,* and *conditioned,* and accept all reasonable ideas. Do not get into detailed explanations at this point, but mention that each term will be explained and illustrated later in the lesson. Read aloud the question "Have you ever observed someone's behavior and been unable to figure out the reasons behind it?" Then help students brainstorm a list of such behaviors and write them on the board. For example, a student may know someone who finished all but one course needed for high school graduation and then quit, or someone may have a friend who has enough money to live on but sometimes takes things from a store without paying for them. Ask students to come up with possible reasons for each action on the board. Do not try to provide complete psychological explanations, but point out that psychology can provide some possible reasons for each of these actions.

Lesson Activities

Vocabulary: Write the words *anthropology, sociology*, and *psychology* on the board. Ask students to explain the differences among the three terms. (Anthropology is the study of cultures and groups of people. This means that it studies many different societies spread out across the globe. Sociology is the study of how various groups operate within a single society. Psychology is the study of the mental and emotional life of individual human beings. Ask students why psychology is placed in the area of social studies. Isn't it really a medical area? (The answer is that it is a medical specialty because it deals with healing people. However, it is also a social studies topic because it helps explain how people live in a society. The behavior of millions of individuals ultimately establishes the behavior of our entire society.)

Lesson Review: Read aloud the material on pages 214–216. As you encounter new technical terms, stop to explain them and ask students what help they need with them.

Paragraph 2: Help students take apart the word *psychoanalysis*. The first part, *psycho*, has to do with the mind. The second part, *analysis*, has to do with figuring something out. So the term means figuring out how the mind works. Who was Freud? (a doctor in Austria) What was special about the people he worked with? (They were blind or paralyzed, but there was no physical reason for these illnesses.)

Paragraph 3: What is a *trauma*? (something very upsetting that happens to a person) Help students list some childhood traumas. (A child's parent dies when he or she is very young; a child is repeatedly abused by a parent or sibling; a child has a long, painful illness.) What does *repressed* mean? (When a thought is repressed it is put out of the person's mind because it is too painful to think about.) What did Freud think was the connection between traumas and physical illness? (He thought that

repressed traumas could sometimes cause physical illnesses such as blindness and paralysis.) How did Freud cure his patients' illnesses? (He had his patients talk about the trauma behind the physical illness. Gradually, by recalling and understanding the sources of the illness, the patient might be freed from the illness.)

Paragraph 4: Discuss the differences among the *id*, the *ego*, and the *superego*. Write the following actions on the board and ask students to state which of these three forces seems to be causing the action.

1. A man repeatedly womanizes and indulges in sexual harassment. (id)
2. You eat ice cream only once a week, although you would like to have it every day. (superego)
3. You act with appropriate friendliness and respect toward your boss and fellow employees. (ego)

Debate: Divide the class into three groups and assign one of the three aspects of the mind to each group. Allow them a few minutes to review the definitions of the id, ego, and superego. Then tell the class that you are going to list some activities on the board. The task of each group is to figure out how their particular aspect of the mind might respond to each suggestion, and then try to convince the other groups that they are wrong. Use the following suggestions or make up your own.

1. It's a beautiful day. I'm going to skip school and go swimming. (The id says, "Why not? It's important to enjoy life. You're not hurting anyone." The superego says, "That's wrong. It's against the rules. You should attend class." The ego says, "Why don't you go to class for two hours and then take a ride in the park?")
2. I hate to step inside hospitals, but my friend's mother is ill and I should visit her.
3. The man offering me a "bargain" is really not offering me any savings.

Lesson Review: Continue reading aloud the material on behaviorism on page 215.

Paragraph 6: Why do behaviorists think that human behavior can be changed? (They think that behavior is learned and therefore that people can learn to act differently.)

Paragraph 7: Ask a student to explain how Pavlov taught the dog to salivate at the sound of the bell. Point out that associations can be created without anyone realizing that it is happening. Ask students to think of some associations that have been created in their lives. (A student may have the urge to light a cigarette whenever he or she smells coffee. Someone else may feel happy every time they hear a certain song on the radio.)

Paragraphs 8 through 10: What did Skinner add to the study of behaviorism? (He showed that rewards could be used to encourage desired behaviors and punishments to discourage unwanted ones.) Did he experiment on human beings? (No, he worked with animals.) What rewards did he use? (food) What punishments did he use? (a mild electric shock) Ask students to think of ways they have used behaviorism to try to change the behavior of a friend or family member. (They may have told a child he couldn't have candy because he hit his sister, or they may have given a child five dollars for every A she got on her report card.) Then ask students to think of ways that you may have used behaviorism to try to change their behavior. (You may have frowned when a student walked in late, or you may have given a student a "no homework" day when he or she got 100% on a test.)

Role-Playing: Divide the class into groups of three or four students. Ask each group to think of a situation in which they can show how one person uses behaviorism to change the actions of another person. When they have decided on a situation, have them choose two students from the group to act out the scene. Next, they should decide on the words and actions they will use in their presentation. Allow them a few minutes to prepare and rehearse their demonstrations. Then have each group present its situation. Encourage other class members to ask questions and comment on the action.

Reading Strategies Instruction: For further work at a Pre-GED level, see the *Threshold* social studies text, Unit 2, Chapter 3, Lesson 18 and 19, and the *Threshold* science text, Unit 2, Lesson 26. For more GED-level work, see *The New Revised Cambridge GED Program:* the social studies text, Chapter 2, Lesson 7, and the science text, Chapter 2, Lesson 6.

Lesson Wrap-Up

How to Do the Exercises: Before students complete the Lesson 10 Exercise, remind them that they will have a limited amount of time to answer the questions on the GED exam, so they will need to work as efficiently as possible. Give them the following instructions:

1. Always look over the reading passage first. Glance through it, looking for repeated words. This passage contains two paragraphs, so keep in mind that the answer must include both paragraphs.
2. Read the question and look at the distractors. They will help you focus on the specific information you need to look for.
3. Read the passage carefully.
4. Answer the questions using the process of elimination to discard obviously incorrect answers.

Complete the Exercises: Ask each student to complete the Lesson 10 Exercise on pages 218–219. Set a 10-minute time limit. Then discuss each question with the class, eliciting opinions about what the correct answers are, and why. Also encourage students to explain why each incorrect response is incorrect, giving reasons for their opinions. After a consensus is reached, go over the answers and explanations on page A-17.

Chapter 2 Science

Brainstorming: Have students look at the photo on page 229 as you read the introductory paragraph and the Prereading Prompt. Then ask students to say in their own words what they think science is all about. Read aloud the material on page 221, explaining any difficult terms (such as *scientific method*, *hypothesis*, *experiment*). Then ask students to brainstorm any words or phrases that come to mind when they hear the term *science*. Provide a few phrases of your own, such as *figuring out what happened to the dinosaurs*, *looking for a cure for cancer*, *test tubes and microscopes*. Write all student responses on the board. Write the four main sciences and Key Words at the bottom of page 221 on the board and review the meaning of each (biology, earth science, chemistry, physics). As you point to each word, ask the following questions (and allow as many students as possible to suggest answers).

- **Biology:** What are some rules for good health? How do plants help you stay alive?
- **Earth science:** How do weather forecasters predict the weather? How far is the Earth from the sun?
- **Chemistry:** What is air made of? How does air change when it becomes polluted? (Some students may indicate that these questions are also related to earth science. Point out that there is actually a lot of overlap between the various areas of science and the questions they attempt to answer.)
- **Physics:** How does your stove work? Why are some types of energy better than others?
- **Hypothesis:** We are not sure why alcoholism tends to be more common among certain families than among others. What are two possible reasons?
- **Theory:** Many experiments have been done to figure out why children tend to resemble their parents. What do you know about how traits such as eye color are passed down from parent to child?

Read aloud the definitions of these six terms provided in the textbook and discuss them with the students, answering any questions they may have. After that, reinforce the meaning of each term by providing factual statements concerned with one of the four areas of science and asking to which area each statement relates. For example, say, "All living things are composed of cells." This is an important fact from biology. An example of a statement about earth science might be, "The climate in tropical regions tends to be hot and humid." A statement about chemistry might be, "The atom is the basic building block of matter." A statement about physics might be, "An object in motion will tend to continue in motion." Have students come up with their own factual statements related to each term, if they can.

Application: Present students with the following situation and have them explain how they could use the scientific method to learn more about the phenomenon. One day, several people who drank cider from a roadside stand end up in the hospital with stomach pains and vomiting.

1. *Raise a question:* What is making these people sick? Suggest a hypothesis: Could the cider have made the people sick?
2. *Perform an experiment:* Analyze samples of cider that the patients drank and compare them with samples of cider that do not make people sick.
3. *Examine information from the experiment:* Was there something unusual in the cider that the patients drank? Sure enough, germs that cause food poisoning are detected.
4. *Reach a conclusion about the hypothesis:* The hypothesis is correct; the cider made the people ill.

Lesson 1:   Cells: The Basic Units of Life

Lesson Warm-Up

Brainstorming: Suggest that students draw up a K-W-L chart with this format in their notebooks:

What I Know	What I Want to Learn	What I Learned

After reading aloud the Prereading Prompt, preview the lesson with students to help them get an idea of what the lesson will be about (by pointing out titles, key words, words in bold print, diagrams). Then have students jot down and share what they already know about cells. (To help students realize what they already know about cells, ask: How big are cells? What do they do? Have you ever seen a cell? What do you need to see one? Do all plants and animals have cells? How many cells do you have in your body? How many cells do tiny plants and animals have? Why are cancer researchers interested in cells? What happens to your cells when you have an infection?)

To elicit ideas about what students want to learn, suggest a few questions that were raised in your mind by the preview: Why is a cell called "the basic unit of life"? What is the cell membrane for? What happens when cells die? (Tell students that they will jot ideas in the "What I Learned" column after reading the lesson.)

Vocabulary: Write the Key Words (*cell, nucleus, photosynthesis*) on the board, read them aloud, and discuss them with the class. Point out the diagrams of animal and plant cells on page 223 and have students locate the nucleus in each. Ask what students know about photosynthesis, and point out that only plants can make food by this process—not animals.

Lesson Activities

Brainstorming: Have students predict whether the following statements are true (T) or false (F) and discuss all that comes to mind when they hear each statement. Then tell them to check their predictions as they read the lesson.

> The smallest living thing has five cells. (F)
> All plants and animals have cells. (T)
> A piece of metal is made up of cells. (F)
> Animal cells have a tough cell wall. (F)
> The food plants make is called glucose. (T)

Vocabulary: Write on the board the words shown in bold print throughout the lesson. After reading the first paragraph aloud as a group, split the class into groups of two or three and have students take turns reading the rest of the lesson aloud in small groups. Then reconvene and discuss the following questions while pointing to the relevant vocabulary word on the board: How is a *cell* like a factory? (The parts work together; each part performs a separate life function.) What are *microscopic organisms*? (tiny living things with only one or a few cells) What does the *cell membrane* do? (allows substances to pass into and out of the cell) Why is the *nucleus* important? (It tells the other parts of the cell what to do.) What is in the *cytoplasm* of a cell? (This is the watery material around the nucleus that contains the cells, other structures, including vacuoles for storing food and mitochondria for getting energy from food.) What happens during *photosynthesis*? (plants make food) What is

glucose? (the food made by plants from carbon dioxide and water in the presence of sunlight)

Have students keep a section in their notebooks for new vocabulary words (those in bold print plus any others in the text with which students are unfamiliar). Students should provide the definition for each term, in their own words, along with a sentence using the term and a picture or symbol that will help them remember what the term means. For further reinforcement of word meanings, students might play "Concentration" in pairs. (Two cards are made up for each word, one with the term and the other with the definition. All cards are turned over. The player who is up turns over two cards at a time, attempting to match the term with its definition.)

Application: Ask students the following questions, which link the lesson's content with their daily lives: What do you call someone who works in a hospital or lab, looking at and analyzing cells from various parts of the body? (medical technicians) What do you call someone who uses microscopes and other lab equipment to look for a cure for cancer? (cancer researchers) What do you call the person who checks your cat or dog and looks at specimens of their blood or stool under a microscope? (veterinarian or vet assistant) Have you ever seen a cell? Has anyone ever examined cells from your body? Why might a doctor look at some cells from your throat? (looking for strep-causing germ cells) What is the name of the test recommended that women take annually, and what is its purpose? (Pap smear; cells from the vagina/cervix are examined for cancer.) What is cancer? (a disease in which cells multiply and grow out of control, destroying healthy cells)

Graphics: Help students draw connections between graphics and text by asking questions. What is shown in the picture on page 223? (animal cell and plant cell) What instrument would you need to be able to see what is shown? (microscope) Suppose that one of these cells is taken from a human cheek. Which one is it? (the one on the left) Here, as with other graphics in the book, students might be asked to provide a one- or two-sentence caption that summarizes what is shown in the graphic (For example, "The plant cell is similar to the animal cell, but contains two additional parts: the cell wall and the chloroplasts.")

Role Playing: Discuss with students what "good hygiene" (brushing your teeth, taking a daily bath, etc.) has to do with cells (gets rid of dead surface cells, removes substances that can damage body cells, kills cells that can attack body cells). Have students act out the following situation:

• A parent or public health nurse tries to explain why cleanliness is important.

Reading Strategies Instruction: Read aloud the section "Applying Information in Categories" on page 224. Emphasize that it is not necessary or desirable to spend time memorizing each category in this type of question (here, what each type of cell does). Instead, keep referring back to the general descriptions until you find the one that matches the situation described in the specific case (that you have an infection).

Lesson Wrap-Up

Exercise Discussion: Before students complete the Lesson 1 Exercise on page 225, remind them that they will have a limited amount of time to answer questions on the GED exam, so they will need to work as efficiently as possible. Give them the following instructions:

1. Read the question(s) before you look at the passage.
2. Read the passage for the purpose of answering the question(s).
3. Apply the process of elimination to get rid of obviously wrong choices first.

(You might want to post these steps on a wall for easy reference.)

Encourage students to discuss different opinions on which choices to eliminate until a consensus is reached. Have each student complete the exercises on page 225. Then discuss each question with the class, eliciting opinions about what the correct answers are, and why. Encourage students to explain why each incorrect response is incorrect, giving reasons for their opinions.

Answer Key Discussion: After a consensus is reached, go over the answers and explanations on page A-19. If students need more instruction/practice on applying information in categories, refer them to the Cambridge Pre-GED volume *On Your Own: Reading* , Unit 5, Chapter 20, and the *Threshold* science text, Unit 3, Lesson 27. For more GED-level work, see *The New Revised Cambridge GED Program* the science text, Chapter 2, Lesson 11, and the social studies text, Chapter 2, Lesson 12.

Lesson 2:   Reproduction and Heredity

Lesson Warm-Up

Brainstorming: After reading and discussing the Pre-reading Prompt, preview the lesson with students and ask for predictions about questions the lesson will answer. Then write the words "Reproduction" and "Heredity" on the board, with "spokes" extending around each. As students brainstorm what they know about each term, jot down the ideas around the term. Ask these questions to elicit background knowledge about reproduction and heredity from students: How do human beings reproduce? What organs are

involved? How do new tulips or trees form? What parts are involved? Where do you think the female part of a tulip plant would be? How does a one-celled organism reproduce? What traits did you inherit from your parents? How? What are some problems or illnesses that a parent can pass on to his or her child?

Vocabulary: Write the Key Words (*asexual reproduction*, *sexual reproduction*, *heredity*) on the board, read them aloud, and discuss them with the class. As you read the definitions, point out that "offspring" are children. Draw a Venn diagram on the board (two overlapping circles) and have students describe similarities and differences between the two types of reproduction.

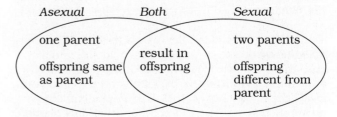

Asexual   *Both*   *Sexual*

one parent   two parents

offspring same   offspring
as parent   result in   different from
                   offspring   parent

Supply a sample sentence using the word *heredity*. ("The book on heredity explains why curly-haired parents often have curly-haired children.") Have students supply other sentences using the word *heredity*.

Lesson Activities

Brainstorming: Have students predict whether the following statements are true (T) or false (F) and discuss all that comes to mind when they hear each statement. Then tell them to check their predictions as they read the lesson.

Reproduction means "the way we get new living things from living things that are already here." (T)

Asexual means "with both male and female parts." (F)

You need a male and female skin cell to produce new skin cells. (F)

Some small living things reproduce just by splitting.(T)

The only way for people to reproduce is sexually.(T)

All plants reproduce asexually. (F)

Human reproduction is similar to reproduction in tulips. (T)

The female part of a plant is in the root. (F)

In sexual reproduction, a sperm cell from the female combines with an egg cell from the male. (F)

Vocabulary: Write on the board the words that appear in bold print throughout the lesson. Read the first two paragraphs aloud and ask students if they have any questions. Then ask the following questions, pointing to the relevant phrases on the board as they come up in your questions and students' answers:

What example of *asexual reproduction* does the textbook give? (formation of human body cells) How do human beings reproduce? (*sexual reproduction*) What other familiar plants and animals do you suppose reproduce that way? When you cut your finger, how do identical new skin cells form? (*mitosis*)

Have student volunteers read the next five paragraphs (the rest of page 227 and the first two paragraphs of page 228) and then ask these questions as you refer to the vocabulary words on the board: How do one-celled organisms reproduce? (*fission*, splitting in half) Why is an amoeba exactly like its one parent? (It gets all the same chromosomes through *asexual reproduction*.) How does something like the yeast plant used to make bread reproduce? (asexually, from *buds* that split off the parent) What is *fertilization*? (uniting of *egg* and sperm during *sexual reproduction*)

Graphics: Refer to the diagram on page 227 and ask these questions: How are mitosis and meiosis alike? (Both involve cell division.) How are they different? (*Mitosis* produces two identical daughter cells; *meiosis* produces 4 different gametes.) How many *chromosomes* does the cell undergoing mitosis on the left have? (4) How many chromosomes does each daughter cell have? (4) How many chromosomes does the cell undergoing meiosis on the right start out with? (6) In what way do the chromosomes look different during the second step? (They split in two.) How many chromosomes does each resulting *gamete* have? (2) Why are these chromosomes important? (They contain the *genes* that provide instructions that determine what the organism will be like.) Where in your body could you find cells undergoing mitosis? (any of the cells in the body) Where in your body could you find cells undergoing meiosis? (Only sex cells form in this way.)

Read the third paragraph on page 228 and refer students to the accompanying diagram of a flower. Ask these questions: Which of these parts of the flower are the female parts? (*stigma, style, ovary*) Which are male parts? (the *stamen*, which includes the *anther* with its *pollen* and the *filament*) How would you use your finger to trace the path taken by pollen during fertilization? (start at the top of the anther, move to the top of the stigma, go down the pollen tube to the ovules in the ovary) Read the final paragraph on page 228, refer students to the diagrams on page 229, and ask these questions: Where does the sperm develop? (in the man's *testes*) Where does the egg start out? (in the woman's *ovary*) How would you use your finger to trace the route taken by the egg during fertilization? (starts in the *ovary*; moves down the *fallopian tube*, where it joins the man's sperm; travels to the *uterus*, where the baby forms).

Summary Discussion: Read aloud the final section, "Genetics and Heredity" and ask these questions: What is genetics? (the study of how parents give traits to their offspring) Who was Gregor Mendel, and why was he important? (a nineteenth-century monk whose

study of pea plants led him to hypothesize the laws of genetics) How does this section "Genetics and Heredity" tie in with the first section, "Asexual and Sexual Reproduction"? Why are they in the same lesson? (During *sexual reproduction*, offspring *inherit* traits from both parents when the sperm and the egg combine.)

Application: The lesson mentions that "even complex plants can sometimes reproduce asexually."

1. Ask students for specific examples of plants they have grown this way. (An ivy plant can be grown by putting a leaf in water until it sprouts roots; a spider plant can be started by rooting one of the "spiders" that grows on the stem; a sweet potato plant can be started by putting a section of the root in water.)
2. Ask students how various forms of birth control work.
3. Have students explain how a child is born.
4. Ask students to suppose that they are being paid to figure out whether a rare plant that might hold the cure for cancer reproduces sexually or asexually. How would you go about finding the answer?

Role Playing: Have students act out one of the following situations:

- Two parents talk with their nine-year-old about the mother's pregnancy (explaining the process and answering the child's questions).
- A parent talks with a daughter or son about the various methods of birth control and how they work.

Narrative: Many people can remember the first time as a child they watched a seed grow. Write about that experience. Where did you get the seed? How did you prepare it? What did you notice? What do you know now about what you were noticing then?

Reading Strategies Instruction: Read aloud the section "Applying Information in Graphics" on pages 229–230. As an activity, have students do drawings that show how a trait, such as eye color or hair color, is inherited. Also, see if students can think up questions based on their own drawings. Point out that students need to use their imaginations to picture each choice and think about whether it resembles the original situation. Using the process of elimination, students then should get rid of obviously wrong choices each so that they have more time to consider the more likely choices.

Lesson Wrap-Up

Exercise Discussion: Before students complete the Lesson 2 Exercise on page 231, review the concepts *dominant* and *recessive*. Ask for student volunteers who wouldn't mind displaying or demonstrating particular dominant or recessive traits (such as widow's peaks or the ability to roll one's tongue). Ask students to look at the chart and predict whether the child will have a particular trait if he or she inherits only one gene for that trait (clockwise hair whorl? yes; dark hair? yes; red hair? yes; widow's peak? yes; short eyelashes? no; dimples? yes; turned-down nose? no)

Remind students to:

1. Read the questions first. (All ask how the artists might have shown traits not shown on the chart.)
2. Look at the graphic for the main idea. (Don't get too distracted by specifics such as whether red hair is dominant or recessive. Instead, notice the way the chart is set up, with the dominant trait captioned and shown by the person on the left in each picture.)
3. Eliminate wrong answers and choose the best one.

Have each student complete the exercises on page 232. Then discuss each question with the class, eliciting opinions about what the correct answers are, and why. Encourage students to explain why each incorrect response is incorrect, giving reasons for their opinions.

Answer Key Discussion: After a consensus is reached, go over the answers and explanations on page A-19. If students need more instruction/practice on applying information in graphics, refer them to the Cambridge Pre-GED volume *On Your Own: Reading,* Unit 5, Chapter 22, the *Threshold* social studies text, Unit 2, Chapter 2, Lesson 16, and the *Threshold* science text, Unit 3, Lesson 29. For more GED-level work, see *The New Revised Cambridge GED Program:* the science text, Chapter 2, Lesson 13, and the social studies text, Chapter 2, Lesson 13.

Lesson 3: The Systems of the Human Body

Lesson Warm-Up

Brainstorming: Have students make a K-W-L chart (see Lesson 1 of this teaching guide). After reading and discussing the Prereading Prompt, take a minute or two to preview the lesson with students (pointing out Key Words, headings, words in bold print, and diagrams). In the left-hand column of their charts, students should list what they already know about the following systems: nervous, digestive, circulatory, and respiratory. To prompt students regarding their background knowledge of various systems, ask these questions:

• **Nervous system :** What does your brain do? Have you ever known anyone with a brain injury? What happens to boxers who are continually hit in the head? What are the signs of a stroke? Have you ever heard of someone having a brain aneurysm? Why

do you need nerves? What may happen to a victim of a motorcycle accident who has a spinal injury?

• **Digestive system:** Can you name the main parts of the body involved in digesting food? Can you describe how the small intestine works to digest food? How does the body absorb digested food? How does the body get rid of the two kinds of waste material left over from digestion?

• **Circulatory system :** Have you ever known anyone with heart or circulatory problems? What are the signs of a heart attack? What should you do if someone seems to be having a heart attack?

• **Respiratory system :** What do your lungs do? Why is smoking bad for your health? Have you ever known anyone with asthma, emphysema or bronchitis?

Model a few "What I Want to Learn" questions: What job does saliva do? Why is it so important for the heart to keep pumping? Have students complete the "What I Learned" column after they finish the Summary Discussion (below).

Graphics: Have students fold a paper twice to form four squares. In each, they should draw the rough outline of a human being. Next, they should position and label as many parts as they can for each of the following four body systems: nervous, digestive, circulatory, and respiratory.

Vocabulary: Write the Key Words (*central nervous system, digestion, respiration, circulation*) on the board, then read and discuss their meanings. Point out that the diagram of the brain and nerves on page 234 shows the *nervous system*. The system that handles *digestion*, the breakdown of food into usable parts and waste, is shown on page 235. The heart, pictured on page 236, pumps blood throughout the *circulatory system* to the lungs and other body parts. The diagram of the lungs and other organs on page 237 shows the system responsible for *respiration*, taking in oxygen and letting off carbon dioxide.

Lesson Activities

Brainstorming: Have students predict whether the following statements are true (T) or false (F) and discuss all that comes to mind when they hear each statement. Then tell them to check their predictions as they read the lesson.

Nerves in your spinal cord send messages to your brain and your muscles. (T)

You can't have digestion without food. (T)

Food goes from the small intestine to the stomach. (F)

Food goes from the small intestine to the stomach. (F)

Arteries carry blood to your heart. (F)

Veins carry blood to the lungs. (F)

Respiration has to do with breathing. (T)

Vocabulary: Write the following words on the board: central nervous system, spinal cord, peripheral nervous system. Read aloud the section on the nervous system, and ask these questions (pointing to the relevant vocabulary words as they come up in your questions or in student answers): What are the parts of the *central nervous system*? (brain and spinal cord) What is the *brain* made of? (nerve cells) When you smell something burning, how does the information get from your nose to your brain? (a message travels up the *spinal cord*) What is the *peripheral nervous system*? (nerves that connect the brain with the outer parts of the body and the inner organs) How does the *heart* get the information to keep beating? (Chemical and electrical messages travel from the brain through the *peripheral nervous system* to the heart.)

Write the following words on the board and pronounce them: *digestion, saliva, esophagus, acids, enzymes, villi.* Have students use each word in a sentence based on what they predict that each word means. Then put students into pairs and have them read to each other the two paragraphs of the section "Digestive System." Afterward, students use what they learned about the vocabulary words to help each other revise any sentences that are inaccurate or unclear.

Write the following words on the board and pronounce them: *capillaries, heart, veins, arteries.* Read the three paragraphs on the circulatory system aloud and ask these questions while pointing to the words on the board: What are *capillaries*, and why do you need them? (very small vessels that allow food to pass easily from the blood to the body cells) What two main jobs does the *heart* perform? (The heart pumps oxygen-poor blood to the lungs and pumps oxygen-rich blood throughout the body.) How are *veins* different from *arteries*? (Veins carry blood to the heart and arteries carry blood from the heart.)

Write the following words on the board and pronounce them: *lungs, respiratory system.* Have a student volunteer read the paragraph on the respiratory system. Ask students to look at the diagram of the respiratory system on page 237 and tell you in their own words how oxygen gets taken into the lungs and how carbon dioxide gets released.

Summary Discussion: Have students reread the chapter silently and write brief (two- to three-sentence) summaries of each section. Then have several student volunteers share these summaries with the class.

Application: Ask students to identify which body system is mainly involved in each situation.

- A lifelong smoker who coughs constantly and has trouble breathing is told that she has chronic emphysema. (respiratory)

- The Secretary of Defense is told that he needs a pacemaker to make his heart beat more regularly. (circulatory)

- A woman's doctor tells her that the stomach pains she is having are due to ulcers. (digestive system)

- A typist develops numbness and soreness in his lower arms; his doctor tells him that the constant typing motion has damaged nerves in his wrists. (nervous system)

Have students discuss what they can do to keep each of the body systems healthy (for example, for the circulatory system—get more aerobic exercise, eat a diet lower in salt and cholesterol).

Debate: Have students debate the idea of whether cigarettes/cigarette advertising should be banned and whether families of lung cancer victims should be able to sue tobacco companies. Use the effects of smoking on different organs of the body to tie the debate to the lesson content.

Role-Playing: Have students role-play a school nurse, a police officer, and a health class. The nurse and police officer are trying to convince the class how important it is to protect the brain and spinal cord by avoiding drugs, using a bike helmet, and so on.

Reading Strategies Instruction: Read aloud the section "Recognizing Facts, Opinions, and Hypotheses" on pages 237–238. Emphasize that facts can be proven and hypotheses can be tested, while opinions are personal beliefs that cannot be proven right or wrong by measurement. (Once a hypothesis has held up under enough testing, it becomes a fact.) Help students make a list of key words that often indicate opinions: *good/bad, desirable/undesirable, delicious/tasteless, beautiful/ugly*, and so on. Bring in a current issue of a newspaper such as *USA Today* and read statements from various sections (news articles, editorials, science briefs) so that students can label the statements (fact, opinion, hypothesis) and discuss their choices. Also, have students write down their own fact, opinion, and hypothesis statements.

Lesson Wrap-Up

Exercise Discussion: Before students complete the Lesson 3 Exercise on pages 238–239, remind them to read the questions before reading the passage. Have student volunteers paraphrase each question so that students know that they are reading for the central hypothesis, for a fact, and for an opinion.

Have students complete the exercises on page 232 individually. Then have students break into small groups to discuss what the correct answers are, and why. Encourage students to explain why each incorrect response is incorrect, giving reasons for their opinions.

Answer Key Discussion: After students have discussed their reasoning, have them read the answers and explanations on page A-19. If students need more instruction/practice with the Pre-GED level on recognizing facts and opinions, refer them to *On Your Own Reading*, Unit 6, Chapter 24, the *Threshold* social studies text, Unit 3, Chapter 25, and the *Threshold* science text, Unit 4, Chapter 2, Lessons 32 and 33. For more GED-level work, see *The New Revised Cambridge GED Program:* the science text, Chapter 2, Lesson 14, and the social studies text, Chapter 2, Lesson 14.

Lesson 4   The Kingdoms and Systems of Nature

Lesson Warm-Up

Brainstorming: After reading and discussing the Pre-reading Prompt, preview the lesson with students and ask what sort of information they expect to find in the lesson. Write the title of this lesson, "Kingdoms and Systems of Nature," on the board and have students say what comes to mind. What do you know about the kingdoms into which scientists divide all living things? What is the purpose of classifying living things, anyway? How do scientists decide which group an organism belongs in? In which kingdom are human beings? What is a *system*, such as a stereo system or the digestive system? Can you name some "systems of nature?" What systems are human beings a part of? How do we depend on plants and other animals? To elicit ideas about living things that depend on each other, offer a couple of examples: human beings and wheat (we eat wheat and plant it); bees and clover (bees need clover for honey and pollinate clover).

Vocabulary: Write the Key Words (*ecosystem, ecology, food chain*) on the board and read them aloud. Write the following sentences on the board and have students predict the meanings of the underlined words from their context:

1. Trees, birds, and soil are all part of a forest ecosystem. (area where living and nonliving things interact)
2. The ecology book explains how the birds and trees in the forest depend on each other. (how organisms in an ecosystem depend on each other)
3. Wheat plants, cows, and human beings are part of the same food chain. (system where each organism feeds on another)

Then have students provide the definitions in their own words and write other sentences containing each term.

Lesson Activities

Brainstorming: Have students predict whether the following statements are true (T) or false (F) and discuss

all that comes to mind when they hear each statement. Then tell them to check their predictions as they read the lesson.

> Scientists have grouped all living things into one of five kingdoms. (T)
>
> All living things in the animal kingdom can use sunlight to make food. (F)
>
> Mushrooms, yeasts, and molds are all fungi. (T)
>
> Animals depend on plants for survival, but plants do not depend on animals. (F)
>
> Salt water, crabs, seagulls, and seaweed might all be part of the same ecosystem.(T)
>
> Cutting down forests can damage ecosystems. (T)
>
> By using pesticides to kill insects, farmers keep the ecosystem in balance. (F)

Vocabulary: Write on the board the words shown in bold print throughout the lesson. Read aloud the section on "The Five Kingdoms of Living Things" and ask students if they have any questions. Then ask the following questions, pointing to the relevant words on the board as they come up in your questions and in students' answers: Why do scientists try to *classify* each living thing? (Grouping similar organisms together makes it easier to study them, to talk about them, and to figure out how they evolved from earlier forms.) How does a scientist decide to put many-celled organism *X* into the kingdom *Plantae* and organism *Y* into the kingdom *Animalia*? (Plants can make food; animals cannot.) What are some *fungi* and what do they have in common? (Fungi, which include mushrooms and molds, have cells walls but cannot make food.) How do scientists decide to put one-celled organism *X* into the kingdom *Monera* and one-celled organism *Y* into the kingdom *Protista*? (Monera have no nuclei, but Protista do.)

Have students read the rest of the lesson (through page 242) silently or in small groups. Then reconvene and ask these questions: In a forest *ecosystem*, what do the bacteria in the soil do for the plants? (The bacteria break down dead matter into soil, which plants use) What is the difference between the *producers* and *consumers* in a *food chain*? (Producers are plants that make food; consumers are animals that eat plants or other animals.) What is *ecological balance*? (If one organism in an ecosystem is threatened, the survival of all others in the system is also threatened.)

Summary Discussion: After reading the lesson together, break students into three groups and assign each group one section of the lesson. Members of each group take turns reading that section aloud, then collaborate on a written summary to be shared with the entire class.

Applications: Encourage students to bring an article about ecology from a news magazine or newspaper. Possible topics include: controversies surrounding lumbering in the Pacific Northwest, attempts to protect endangered animals. Ask students to think of examples in their community of how human beings have upset the balance of an ecosystem—by building or killing or polluting, perhaps.

Talk with students about their personal experiences with how water in an ecosystem can become polluted. Why are so many beaches polluted today? How does some wellwater become polluted? What do you know about acid rain? Why can't you eat the fish caught in many rivers?

Talk with students about other firsthand experiences they have had with pollution and how it affects all living things. How do you and other living things in this area suffer from the air pollution caused by cars and nearby factory *Y*? How has "noise pollution" from airport *Z* upset the balance in which people, animals, and plants lived before the airport was built?

Graphics: Have students create their own illustrated food chains, with a human being at the end of the chain.

Role Playing: Have pairs of students role-play the part of a grandparent and young grandchild. The child asks about changes the grandparent has seen in the neighborhood where he grew up, and the adult tells how the environment in his hometown—the plants, animals, appearance—is different now.

Reading Strategies Instruction: Review with students the difference between facts (can be proven), opinions (personal feelings), and hypotheses (educated guesses). Read aloud the section "Distinguishing Facts and Hypotheses in Graphics" on pages 243–244. Stress how helpful asking yourself questions about a graphic—and then "putting the picture into words"—can be in understanding it. For Pre-GED practice, see the *Threshold* Social Studies text, Unit 3, Chapter 2, Lesson 25. For more GED-level work, see *The New Revised Cambridge GED Program* science text, Chapter 3, Lesson 1, and the social studies text, Chapter 2, Lesson 15.

Lesson Wrap-Up

Exercise Discussion: Before students complete the Lesson 4 Exercise on pages 244–245, have them read the questions (but not the choices) before examining the graphic carefully. Ask students to summarize what things they will be asked to find in the diagram. (They are being asked to look for a fact, a hypothesis, and an opinion supported by the diagram.) Review the steps they should follow (or simply refer students to a chart on the wall where you have listed the steps):

1. Always read the questions first. This will help you focus on the information you need to look for.
2. Look for the main idea of the passage or graphic; don't get too distracted by details.
3. Use the process of elimination to discard answers that are obviously incorrect first.

Have each student complete the exercises on page 245. Then discuss each question with the class, eliciting opinions about what the correct answers are, and why. Encourage students to explain why each incorrect response is incorrect, giving reasons for their opinions.

Answer Key Discussion: After a consensus is reached, go over the answers and explanations on page A-19.

Lesson 5: Behavior and Evolution

Lesson Warm-Up

Brainstorming: Read and discuss the Prereading Prompt. Write the word "Behavior" on the board and ask students what they know about behavior. Prompt students with these questions: What are some of the behaviors—actions—you do in a day? As students suggest examples of different behaviors, make a list on the board (eating, walking, talking, sleeping, etc.). How do you eat breakfast? How do you dress? Why do you jump back on the curb when a car speeds around the corner? Have you ever noticed how a plant acts? Why does a plant in a sunny window bend toward the light? What behaviors of your spouse/boyfriend/girlfriend/parent do you dislike? Which of your own behaviors would you like to change? Then preview the lesson with students and have them write a question about behavior which they think the lesson may answer. Next, write the word "Evolution" on the board and have students say whatever comes to mind as you jot down their ideas around the word. To elicit ideas, ask these questions: How do scientists think human beings got here? What are fossils? What have scientists learned from fossils? Why are some people against teaching the theory of evolution in schools? What does *extinct* mean? Why do you think the dinosaur became extinct? What are some other animals that have become extinct? Why is it that some plants and animals become extinct, whereas others survive?

Vocabulary: Write the Key Words (*behaviors, theory of evolution*) on the board and read the definitions. Have students write sentences using these words and read the sentences to a partner.

Lesson Activities

Brainstorming: Have students predict whether the following statements are true (T) or false (F) and discuss all that comes to mind when they hear each statement. Then tell them to check their predictions as they read the lesson.

Unlike people, one-celled animals cannot react to changes in their environment. (F)

A spider's webbuilding is a reflex action. (F)

Plants can move. (T)

Trying several different ways of getting the top off a pickle jar until you finally hit on the right way is *trial-and-error learning.*(T)

According to the theory of evolution, simple living things developed from more complex forms. (F)

An example of "natural selection" is that a squirrel would prefer to eat a nut rather than a piece of hamburger. (F)

Grizzly bears have become extinct. (F)

Vocabulary: Write the following words on the board: *stimulus, tropisms, behaviors, reflex, instinct, habit, trial and error, insight.* Read aloud the first paragraph on page 246 and have students read in small groups or silently, the rest of the section on behavior. During group discussion, ask these questions (pointing to the relevant vocabulary words as they come up in your questions or in student answers): Do you have any questions about what you read? What is a *stimulus?* (anything that makes a living thing act) What are some examples of stimuli? (heat, light) What are tropisms? Have you ever seen evidence of *tropisms?* (plant responses, such as bending toward light) What is one *behavior* we see in one-celled animals? (moving away when touched with a needle). What example of a human *reflex* does the book give? (shivering when it's cold) Can you think of another? (blinking when something flies near your eye) How are *instincts* different from *habits?* (Instincts such as nest-building are inborn automatic reflexes; habits such as nailbiting are learned.) How does *trial-and-error learning* differ from *insight learning?* Can you think of an example of each that is not mentioned in the book? (Trial-and-error learning involves learning from mistakes; insight learning involves solving a problem with success on the first trial.)

Next, write these words on the board: *theory of evolution, natural selection, mutations, species,* and *extinct.* Read aloud the first paragraph of the section "Evolution" and have students read the rest of the section silently or in small groups. Then discuss these questions as a class: What is Charles Darwin famous for? (He came up with the *theory of evolution,* the idea that all life forms develop slowly from simpler forms.) What is another way of saying *natural selection* (survival of the fittest)? Have you ever seen natural selection at work—in real life or on film? (probably; for example, slower birds tend to be caught by cats) How does natural selection relate to evolution? (Change occurs slowly as the more "fit" survive and multiply; future generations are more likely to have the favorable trait.) What are *mutations* and what do they have to do with evolution? (sudden chance changes in the genes, which if they happen to be favorable, tend to be passed on to future generations) What is a species, and what species are we? (organisms that can interbreed; *Homo sapiens*) What happens when a plant or animal becomes *extinct,* and why does this happen? (All of the organisms of a species die out because they cannot adapt quickly enough to changes in their surroundings.) How many animals can you name that are extinct—or endangered? Which ones do you think we should be working hardest to save? How? Why?

Summary Discussion: Break students up into groups of five or so. Have each group discuss one of the following two questions: What are some examples of different types of behavior (reflex, instinct, habit, trial and error, insight) that a person might show during a typical day? Using specific examples, how do you explain why some living things adapt and change whereas others become extinct? A scribe is chosen to record the group's ideas. The entire group reconvenes and the spokesperson from each group summarizes the group's discussion.

Applications: Have students apply what they have learned in the chapter to each of the following situations.

- You notice that the tiger lilies growing in the park face one way at sunset and another way at sunrise. How do you explain this? (tropism; bending toward the sun).
- What are some ways you regulate your behavior when the weather changes? (putting on a raincoat, taking off an extra sweater)
- Your knee jerks when the doctor taps it with a rubber hammer. How do you explain this? (reflex)
- Your cat meows or your dog comes running every time you open the refrigerator. Why? (conditioned reflex)
- You figure out the answer to an exercise question. What kind of learning is that? (insight learning)
- Early horses were tiny. By what process did the large horse we know come to be? (evolution)
- Suppose that an orange grasshopper suddenly appears. How do you explain the sudden change in the usual color from green to orange? (mutation)
- Now suppose that the grasshopper is quickly spotted and eaten by birds, whereas most of his green brothers and sisters survive and reproduce. What does this demonstrate? (survival of the fittest)
- Passenger pigeons used to be numerous in the United States before they were slaughtered for meat. The last bird died in 1914. In 1913, what word described the species? (endangered). In 1914, what word described the species? (extinct)
- How do you suppose the destruction of rain forests is speeding up extinction of species? (Plants and animals that live only in the rain forest are dying out as their homes and food sources are destroyed.)

Debate: Discuss why environmentalists and businesses do not always see eye to eye on what should be done about endangered species. Then debate the following statements:

- Human beings have the right to build; when development threatens a plant or animal's survival, it is the people's rights that should come first.

Reading Strategies Instruction: Read aloud the section "Identifying Unstated Assumptions in Passages" on pages 248–249. Stress that a good reader does not accept everything in print as true. Unstated assumptions may or may not be accurate. In any case, a good reader needs to recognize what these assumptions are before accepting the argument that a writer makes.

Advertisements are full of unstated assumptions. Have students help you collect various ads and jingles (those for cars and medical remedies are ideal) and discuss the unstated assumptions the advertisers want us to accept.

While going over the practice item about giraffes on page 248, point out the usefulness of reading the question first and then putting it into one's own words. The key phrase, *scientific theory*, tells readers to ask themselves this question as they read the passage: What assumption is this writer making about the way in which scientists should explain things? By keeping this idea in mind, the student avoids distraction by details about the giraffe.

Lesson Wrap-Up

For helpful practice and instruction at a Pre-GED level, see *On Your Own: Reading*, Unit 6, Chapter 25 (on "Identifying the Writer's Tone"), and the *Threshold* social studies text, Unit 3, Chapter 3, Lesson 29. For more GED-level work, see *The New Revised Cambridge GED Program* the science text, Chapter 3, Lesson 2, and the social studies text, Chapter 2, Lesson 16.

Exercise Discussion: Before students complete the Lesson 5 Exercise on page 249, ask one student to summarize the steps to be taken when answering any GED question. Remind students how important it is to read the question carefully; some, like item 1, ask students to identify a statement that is *not* true. Have students complete the exercises on page 250 individually. Then discuss each question with the class, eliciting opinions about what the correct answers are, and why. Encourage students to explain why each incorrect response is incorrect, giving reasons for their opinions.

Answer Key Discussion: After a consensus is reached, go over the answers and explanations on page A-20.

Lesson 6: The Earth: Its Structure, Origin, and Place in the Universe

Lesson Warm-Up

Brainstorming: After reading and discussing the Pre-reading Prompt, take a minute or two to preview the lesson with students (pointing out Key Words, headings, words in dark print, and diagrams). Then have students make a K-W-L chart (See Lesson 1 of this teaching guide).

In the left-hand column of their charts, students should list what they already know about the structure of the Earth. (What is earth science? What do you know about volcanoes? Does anyone collect rocks as a hobby? What do you know about the different kinds of rocks? What do we know about what's inside the Earth? Why are different money-making companies interested?) Also: list what they know about the origin of the Earth. (Have you ever heard of the big-bang theory? What do you know about how the Earth formed, and when? What do you know about earthquakes? What else is happening to change the Earth?) Also: list what they know about the position of the Earth in the universe. (Are any of you "star gazers"? What do you know about the night sky? Do you know a memory game for remembering the order and names of the nine planets? What do you know about space travel? How far have we gone? What is beyond our galaxy?) Also: list what they know about the motions of Earth in space. (What do you know about why we have day and night? summer and winter?).

Have students list in the middle column some things they would like to learn from the lesson. (Provide some sample questions you would like answered: How do scientists have any idea how the Earth formed so long ago? Why does the Earth spin?) Remind students that they will be summarizing the lesson (in the "What I Learned" column of the chart) after reading and discussing it.

Vocabulary: Write the Key Words (*crust, core, mantle, universe*) on the board. Demonstrate the first three terms by cutting through a hard-boiled egg. Point out that the shell is like the crust of the Earth, the mantle is like the white, and the core is like the yoke. Have students make "maps" of each word, using this format:

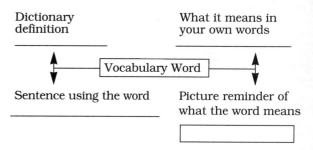

Dictionary definition	What it means in your own words
Sentence using the word	Picture reminder of what the word means

Lesson Activities

Brainstorming: Have students predict whether the following statements are true (T) or false (F) and discuss all that comes to mind when they hear each statement. Then tell them to check their predictions as they read the lesson.

Our galaxy is bigger than our solar system. (T)

The moon is 93 million miles away from us. (F)

The Earth rotates during summer and revolves during the winter. (F)

The big-bang theory says the Earth formed when our sun exploded. (F)

Igneous rock was once lava. (T)

One type of rock can sometimes change into another. (T)

The Earth is still changing. (T)

Weathering is the study of what causes various types of weather. (F)

Vocabulary: Write the following words on the board: *crust, lava, volcanoes, igneous rock, sedimentary rock, metamorphic rock, mantle, core.* Read the first paragraph on pages 251–252 aloud and ask these questions. Can you point to the *crust, mantle,* and *core* of the Earth in the diagram on page 252? What is the core made of? (The outer core is liquid iron and nickel; the inner core is solid nickel.) How far down through the crust would you have to dig before you got to the mantle? (8 to 32 Kilometers). What do you call the liquid rock that comes from volcanoes? (*lava*) What is this called when it cools to form rock? (*igneous rock*) Where would you have to go to see the closest volcano? Is there igneous rock in that area? How is *sedimentary* rock formed? (layers of soil get compressed under water) Do we have any of this around here? (Yes, it is the most common kind of rock.) How is *metamorphic* rock formed? (by pressure and heat on rocks deep within the crust) Use the word map again if you wish.

Write these words on the board: *big-bang theory, plates, continents, weathering, light-years, galaxies, Milky Way, solar system, axis, rotates, revolves.* Have students take turns reading the remaining three sections with a partner. Instruct the pairs to ask each other questions about what they have read after each section is completed, referring to the words on the board if they wish.

Use these questions for whole-class discussion: How would you explain the *big bang theory* in your own words? (Fifteen to twenty billion years ago a clump of matter exploded; swirling particles began sticking together and eventually one of these spinning balls of metal and gas formed the Earth.) What is *plate* movement? (Our continents are rooted in moving plates that make up the crust.) How does soil form? (Rocks undergo *weathering;* they break down into tiny pieces due to wind, changing temperatures, and so on.) What are *light-years*? (the number of years it takes light to travel from one point to another) What's the difference between a solar system and a galaxy? (A galaxy like our Milky Way is made up of many solar systems.) What is shown on page 253? (the nine planets that circle around the sun in our solar system) Can you stand up with a partner and demonstrate what it means to *rotate* (spin in place) and to *revolve* (circle around another body)? Provide a flashlight and an orange and ask, "How would you demonstrate day/night? the reason for seasons?" (The student should rotate the orange while shining the light on it to show how a point goes into the light—

day— and then moves out of it—night; to show the seasons, the student should tilt the orange and move it around the flashlight, to show how direct the rays are on a given point during summer but how diffuse the rays are on the same point when the orange is revolved, still tilted, to the winter position—halfway around the sun.)

Summary Discussion: Have students summarize what they have read by completing and discussing the following statements:

The Earth is composed of four layers,
_____.

The Earth was probably formed
_____.

The Earth is located
_____.

The Earth moves
_____.

Applications: Present the students with the following examples and encourage them to explain the example using words and ideas they learned in the lesson. What season is it in Australia when we are having our cold season? (warm season) Why? (Australia is in that half of the globe that is tilted toward the sun, getting its most direct rays, when we are tilted away.) Stories are told about how the sun was extinguished for awhile when the gods grew angry with human beings. What natural event do you think might be the basis for these stories? (eclipse of the sun). What do you think your Aunt Matilda in California will say if you call her from New York at 7 A.M. to talk with her about the beautiful sunrise? (It is still dark in California, so she'll still be asleep; the earth rotates from west to east.)

You are given a rock and asked to determine which type it is. What would you look for? (Layers would probably indicate sedimentary; veins might indicate metamorphic.) You go to a quarry and find a clamshell-like fossil stuck in a rock. Which type of rock is this probably? (sedimentary) What can you guess about the area? (It was once under a sea.)

You are a farmer. What can you do to reduce erosion? (block wind by planting trees, walls) You love the sand dunes. What can you do to prevent their being destroyed? (encourage people not to walk on them, destroying plants that hold them down; build fences around them)

Role Playing: Have students role-play the following situation:

• A parent is trying to explain to a frightened child how he knows that day will come again tomorrow.

Reading Strategies Instruction: Read aloud the section "Distinguishing Conclusions from Supporting Details in Passages" on pages 254–255. Tell students to think of a written passage as a house. The supporting details are like the building blocks of the house; all help hold it together. The conclusion is like the purpose of putting the house together—to provide shelter. In the passage on the bottom of page 254, the first three sentences provide details about fit between continents and minerals that help build a case for the idea that the continents were once joined. Stress that the conclusion is sometimes—but not always—the final sentence of a passage. Point out how important it is to read questions of this sort carefully; the question asks students to identify the conclusion, not to identify which of five statements is true. (Choices 4 and 5 are accurate statements, but they don't answer the question.) For further instruction and practice at a Pre-GED level, see *On Your Own: Reading*, Unit 3, Chapter 15, as well as the *Threshold* science text, Unit 4, Chapter 3. For more GED-level work, see *The New Revised Cambridge GED Program* science text, Chapter 3, Lesson 4, and the social studies text, Chapter 3, Lesson 2.

Lesson Wrap-Up

Exercise Discussion: Have students complete the Lesson 6 Exercise on pages 255–256 independently. Then discuss each question with the class, eliciting opinions about what the correct answers are, and why. Encourage students to explain why each incorrect response is incorrect, giving reasons for their opinions.

Answer Key Discussion: After a consensus is reached, go over the answers and explanations on page A-21.

Lesson 7: The Earth: Its Atmosphere, Weather, and Climate

Lesson Warm-Up

Brainstorming: Preview the lesson (by having students flip through it and glance at key words, headings, and illustrations) and read the Prereading Prompt aloud. Write the phrases "Greenhouse effect," "Ozone Layer," and "Weather" on the board and jot down what students know about each. Use these questions as prompts:

- **Greenhouse effect:** Have you ever been inside a plant nursery's greenhouse? Why is it so hot and damp there? What gas do the plants need for photosynthesis? This gas is also thrown into Earth's atmosphere when we pollute it by burning many fuels. Why is that a problem? What is happening to the temperature of the Earth compared to what it used to be?

- **Ozone layer:** What would happen to the Earth if we had no atmosphere? How does the atmosphere protect us? What difference does it make if there is a hole in one layer? Why are people who care about the

environment telling us not to use aerosol cans? Why is it more important than ever to use sunscreen?

- **Weather:** How do you follow the weather? Do you watch for certain weather signs, such as the way the wind is blowing? Do you listen to the weather report on TV? How is the weather in your part of the country different from the weather in other parts (or in the country you are from)? Why isn't the weather the same everywhere? Do you know why it rains and snows? Have you ever seen water droplets on your bathroom mirror? How did they get there? Why don't we ever run out of rain? What causes winds?

Lesson Activities

Brainstorming: Have students predict whether the following statements are true (T) or false (F) and discuss all that comes to mind when they hear each statement. Then tell them to check their predictions as they read the lesson.

> The atmosphere is all the air from Earth to the moon. (F)
> The Earth's atmosphere is about 8000 miles thick. (F)
> About one-fifth of the atmosphere is oxygen. (T)
> The ozone in the atmosphere filters out harmful ultraviolet rays from the sun. (T)
> Winds flow because air heated by the sun rises. (T)
> The weather is what the atmosphere is like right here and now. (T)
> Climate is the weather that we usually have at this time of year. (F)
> Cool air rises. (F)
> The winds high over the United States usually blow from west to east. (T)

Vocabulary: Write the following lists on the board as you read the words aloud:

- *Group 1:* atmosphere, gravity, troposphere, stratosphere, ozone, mesosphere, ionosphere, thermosphere.
- *Group 2:* meteoroids, ultraviolet rays, radiation.
- *Group 3:* weather, climate, humidity, evaporates, water cycle, condense, precipitation, convection currents, prevailing winds.

Ask students what they mean as the lesson is read aloud by volunteers.

Summary Discussion: Divide the class into three groups and assign one of the three sections of the lesson to each group. Tell the group to take turns reading the section aloud. Then each person writes a two- or three-sentence summary of the section, using the vocabulary words in the summary. Each person reads the summary to the group and the group selects one summary to read to the class.

Sample summaries:

- *Group 1:* Our atmosphere is the layer of gas, dust, and water held to the Earth by the force of gravity. The layers as you move out from the surface are the troposphere, where clouds form; the stratosphere, where ozone filters out harmful rays from the sun; the mesosphere, where temperatures are very cold; the ionosphere, where radio waves are bounced back to Earth; and the thermosphere, which is the first layer hit by the sun's rays.

- *Group 2:* The atmosphere contains the oxygen and other gases that living things need. It also protects us from meteoroids, rocks from outer space, and from radiation known as the sun's ultraviolet (UV) rays.

- *Group 3:* *Weather* is what the atmosphere is like at a particular place and time; *climate* is the general weather at a place over a long period. During the water cycle, water evaporates from the land and enters the air, making it humid, then condenses back to liquid and falls as precipitation. When air heated by the sun rises, airstreams called convection currents form and these cause prevailing winds to blow over the Earth.

Graphics: Ask students to explain the diagram on page 258. Which layer of the atmosphere is closest to the Earth's surface? (troposphere) Does the temperature get steadily lower as you go higher in the atmosphere? (It goes down, up, down, then up very high in the thermosphere.) Have students redraw and label the layers as concentric circles around a circular Earth.

Have students explain the water cycle shown on page 259. What is the difference between the blue dots and the black arrows? (Blue shows precipitation falling and black arrows show water evaporating.) Why isn't water shown evaporating from the ice cap? (Ice caps on mountaintops usually stay frozen year round because of the low temperature.) What will happen to the levels of the lake and ocean if the temperature rises high enough to melt the ice cap? (They will rise.)

Applications: People are cheering about the fact that information gathered on various space missions shows that the hole in the ozone may be getting smaller. Why are they cheering? (The smaller the hole in the ozone, the fewer UV rays get in and the lower skin cancer rates probably will go.)

Why is our atmosphere more polluted than ever? Why is that such a problem? (There are more cars and factories than ever. Air pollution damages the human health—from increasing rates of asthma to cancer—as well as the health of other living things.)

Debate: Have students argue for or against one of the following statements.

- I personally cause air pollution.

- It would be hard to get by with less water than I use now.

- Air or water pollution is a problem in this community.

- We have the best (or worst) climate in the world right here.

Reading Strategies Instruction: Read aloud the section "Identifying Cause-and-Effect Relationships in Passages" on pages 260–261. Emphasize that while a cause always comes before an effect, not every preceding event causes the one that comes later. Point out that you can sometimes find a cause or effect in a piece of writing by looking for certain signal words. With the class, brainstorm a list of these signal words:

- **Words that signal cause:** because, because of, if, since, for, so that

- **Words that signal effect:** as a result, therefore, thus, consequently, so, then. For further work at a Pre-GED level, see *On Your Own: Reading*, Unit 2, Chapter 9, the *Threshold* science text, Unit 1, Chapter 5, Lesson 14, and the *Threshold* social studies text, Unit 3, Chapter 2, Lesson 23. For more GED-level work, see *The New Revised Cambridge GED Program:* the science text, Chapter 3, Lesson 6, and the social studies text, Chapter 3, Lesson 4.

Lesson Wrap-Up

Exercise Discussion: Before students complete the Lesson 7 Exercise on page 262, review the steps they should follow in answering any multiple-choice item. Remind them that they will have a limited amount of time to answer questions on the GED exam, so they will need to work as efficiently as possible. By reading the questions first, they can save time by knowing what to look for in the passage: two causes (why moist air rises, why the air on the far side of the mountain is dry) and one effect (the final effect of the moist air's movement over the mountains). Have each student complete the exercises on page 262. Then discuss each question with the class, eliciting opinions about what the correct answers are, and why. Encourage students to explain why each incorrect response is incorrect, giving reasons for their opinions.

Answer Key Discussion: After a consensus is reached, go over the answers and explanations on page A-21.

Lesson 8:   The Structure of Matter

Lesson Warm-Up

Brainstorming: After previewing the lesson, read and discuss the Prereading Prompt. Ask these questions to elicit students' background knowledge about matter: What do you know about atoms and molecules? If they're so tiny, how do we know they exist? The diagram of the atom on page 265 looks a little like the diagram of the solar system on page 253. Do you know how the atom and the solar system are alike? What do you know about elements and compounds? Can you name three metals? How are they alike? What metals do you have in the country of your birth? Have you ever seen a periodic table like the one on page 267 before? Have you ever turned a liquid into a solid? How? How do you turn it back into a liquid? Where have you seen liquid water turn into a gas? Jot student responses on the board and suggest that students later refer to the board to see how much of what they already knew came up in the lesson.

Vocabulary: Write the Key Words (*atom, nucleus, protons, neutrons, electrons, molecule, element, compound, mixture, solution*) on the board and read the definitions. To provide students with context clues, present these sentences:

> Every <u>molecule</u> is made up of tiny particles called <u>atoms</u>.
> The <u>electrons</u> of the atom swirl around the <u>nucleus</u>, which contains the <u>protons</u> and <u>neutrons</u>.
> Water is a <u>compound</u> made of the <u>elements</u> hydrogen and oxygen.
> A saltwater <u>solution</u> is a <u>mixture</u> of salt and water.

Have students write the definitions for these terms in their own words and draw simple pictures or symbols that will help them to remember what each term means.

Lesson Activities

Brainstorming: Have students predict whether the following statements are true (T) or false (F) and discuss all that comes to mind when they hear each statement. Then tell them to check their predictions as they read the lesson.

> If something is real, no matter what it is—a cloud, a pickle, a flea—it's made up of matter. (T)
> When a box of ice cream melts, the ice cream takes up less volume. (T)
> When ice cream melts, it loses some of its mass. (F)
> When ice cream melts, it changes state. (T)
> When ice cream melts, it undergoes a chemical change. (F)
> The three states of matter are: large, medium, and small. (F)
> As a car door rusts, it undergoes a chemical change. (T)
> Everything is made of atoms. (T)
> The smallest particle of water is a water atom. (F)

> Hydrogen is an element. (T)
> Water is a compound. (T)
> There are millions of elements. (F)
> If an element is shiny, it is often a metal. (T)
> A mixture is a special type of solution. (F)
> Everything is soluble in water. (F)
> A chemical change is often easy to reverse. (F)
> Cooking an egg is an example of a physical change. (F)
> The water you drink and the hydrogen peroxide you use to clean out a cut have the same two elements. (T)

Vocabulary: Before you or a student volunteer reads each section, write on the board the words that appear in bold print and pronounce them. Point to the words as they come up in discussion of each section. Ask the following questions.

Characteristics of Matter: What is the difference between an object's mass and its volume? (Mass is the amount of material; volume is the amount of space.) Can you think of two objects, one of which has greater mass while the other has a greater volume? (a lead brick and a big bag of feathers) Which types of matter are made of atoms? (all)

The Three States of Matter: What are the three states of matter and what are some examples of each? (solid—ice cube, liquid—milk, gas—oxygen in the air)

Physical and Chemical Properties of Matter: What's the difference between an object's physical and chemical properties? (its size, shape, color, mass, texture, volume, taste, and smell versus its ability to combine with other substances) How would you describe the physical properties of your hair? (six inches long, shaped like an extremely thin barrel, black, thick)

Physical and Chemical Changes in Matter: What's the difference between the two types? (physical changes are reversible and don't change what the material is; chemical changes produce new kinds of matter) What are some examples of each? (physical changes—you cut your hair; chemical changes—you dye your hair)

Atoms and Molecules: What are the parts of an atom? (nucleus at the center containing protons and neutrons, electrons whirling around the nucleus) What are molecules made of? (atoms combined by chemical bonding)

Elements and Compounds: How are elements different from compounds? (Elements combine to form compounds.) What are some examples of each? (hydrogen and oxygen are elements, water is a compound)

The Periodic Table: What is it, and how is it arranged? (a table showing all the elements organized across by atomic number and down by group) What is the difference between the atomic number and atomic weight? (the number of protons versus the number of protons plus neutrons) How are metals different from nonmetals? (shiny, good conductors of electricity versus poor conductors)

Mixtures and Solutions: What are they, and how do they differ? (combinations of substances that don't change physically; a solution is a mixture that is liquid) What is an example of each? (solid mixture—salt and pepper; solution—sugar water) If you make iced tea, what do you call the sugar that dissolves? (solute) the liquid in which it dissolves? (solvent) the drop of oil on the side of the glass which will not dissolve? (insoluble)

Summary Discussion: Divide the class into several groups, each responsible for summarizing one section of the lesson in a "chart talk." (Each group chooses a spokesperson to summarize the section by explaining what is shown in the picture or chart that the group has drawn or cut out from a magazine.)

Applications: Present students with a list of changes you noticed prior to your arrival at class (bread getting toasted, traffic light turning red, paper getting folded, etc.) and have them organize the list into two categories: physical changes and chemical changes

Have students play "Twenty Questions." One student silently chooses an object in the room and other students ask up to twenty questions about the physical and chemical properties of the object. (The questions must all be answerable by "yes" or "no.") The goal is to be the first to guess what the object is.

Have students apply what they have learned in the lesson to each of the following questions.

- How have we put to "practical" use what we know about charges and bonds? (lightning rods, atomic bombs, electricity)

- Suppose that you study mystery element *X*. You observe that it is shiny and conducts electricity. What can you conclude about it? (It may be a metal.)

- Suppose that you analyze a can of soda in a lab. Is it a pure substance? (No) How can you tell? (There are different sorts of molecules in it.) Is it a mixture? (Yes) A solution? (Yes; sugar and flavoring and carbon dioxide are dissolved in water.)

- Suppose you shake two substances together in a laboratory. How would you figure out whether a chemical change had occurred—or just a physical change? (Test and see if the new substance contains the old ones; see if you can reverse the change somehow, as by waiting for the two substances to "settle out." If they do, the change is physical.)

Role Playing: Have students act out the following situations.

- A scientist who worked on the atom bomb explains to his grandchild whether he would do it all again.

- Plastics are compounds that have many advantages (they can be made into many things) and disadvantages (when they are thrown away they do not break down easily). An inventor and an environmentalist talk about the pros and cons of plastics.

- You are giving on-the-job training to someone, stating the steps necessary to make a particular mixture (giving someone instructions about how to make a milkshake, how to mix paint to obtain a particular color, how to mix salt and water for a sore throat, how to mix flour and salt for playdough, etc.).

- You are Julia Child, telling your television audience what changes to look for in deciding whether particular foods (cakes, meats, Jell-O molds, etc.) are done.

- You are on a television show such as *This Old House*, telling your audience about safety precautions to take against dangerous chemical reactions while cleaning/fixing your home (not mixing ammonia and bleach, wearing a mask so as not to inhale corrosive fumes while wallpapering, etc.)

- (For photography buffs) You are a photographer, explaining to a student how to develop film and what chemical reactions to watch for.

Reading Strategies Instruction: Read aloud the section "Evaluating the Adequacy of Information in Passages" on pages 268–269. Compare questions of this sort to the task of a house inspector who is asked to judge whether a building's foundation is strong enough to support the rest of the house. Advertisements are full of claims that are not supported by adequate information. Like many of the incorrect choices on GED test items of this sort, the ads make "broad leaps" from the facts they present to the conclusions they reach (for example, "This car looks snazzy, so it is worth $15,000). Suggest that students collect some conclusions of these ads for discussion of how the support provided by the advertisers is inadequate for their claims. Refer students having difficulty to the Pre-GED *Threshold* social studies text, Unit 3, Chapter 3, Lesson 26, and the *Threshold* science text, Unit 4, Chapter 3, Lesson 35. For more GED-level work, see *The New Revised Cambridge GED Program:* the science text, Chapter 3, Lesson 8, and the social studies text, Chapter 3, Lesson 7.

Lesson Wrap-Up

Exercise Discussion: Before students complete the Lesson 8 Exercise on page 270, review the steps to follow in answering a multiple-choice question. Remind students that in questions of this type (such as "Which statement is best supported...?") they must eliminate not only choices that are false statements and those that have no support, but also those that have *too little* support. To determine if the support is too little, students should ask themselves: Could conclusions other than this choice also be drawn from the same evidence? Have each student complete the exercises on page 270. Then discuss each question with the class, eliciting opinions about what the correct answers are, and why. Encourage students to explain why each incorrect response is incorrect, giving reasons for their opinions.

Answer Key Discussion: After a consensus is reached, go over the answers and explanations on page A-21.

Lesson 9: Chemical Reactions and Energy

Lesson Warm-Up

Brainstorming: After previewing the lesson, read and discuss the Prereading Prompt. Ask these questions to elicit examples of one substance changing into another: How do certain foods (eggs and meat for example) change as you cook them? Do you notice any objects around your house changing color as they get older? Have you ever noticed a color change when you mixed two things—as you were cleaning or doing a hobby, perhaps? Jot student ideas on the board. Ask these questions to elicit examples of acids, bases, or salts: What are some of the acids and bases that you are not supposed to flush down your toilet or put in your regular trash? What are some of the acids and bases that you are advised to lock up to childproof your house? What do you throw on an icy sidewalk to melt the ice?

Vocabulary: Write the Key Words (*chemical reaction*, *reactants*, *products*) on the board and read the definitions. Present the words in context by writing these sentences on the board: When the scientist mixed the two reactants, there was a chemical reaction. Two products of the reaction were salt and water. Have students write the definitions for these terms in their own words and write one sentence for each term.

Lesson Activities

Brainstorming: Have students predict whether the following statements are true (T) or false (F) and discuss all that comes to mind when they hear each statement. Then tell them to check their predictions as they read the lesson.

During a chemical reaction, matter is destroyed and energy is created. (F)
Ammonia cleanser and eggs both contain bases. (T)

If something tastes sour and turns litmus paper red, it is probably an acid. (T)
Soil with a pH of 7 is very acidic. (F)
Add a base to an acid and you get a salt. (T)
Diluting an acid with water is called neutralization. (F)
All acids are harmful to your body. (F)

Vocabulary: Write on the board the words shown in bold print throughout the lesson and pronounce them. Divide students into small groups and have them take turns reading and discussing the lesson. (Each student asks the group at least one question based on the reading.) Reconvene as a whole group and discuss the two sections, using these questions to guide the discussion.

Chemical Changes: What was the *Hindenberg*? (an airship that exploded in 1937) What reactants combined to produce what *products* when that chemical reaction took place? (Hydrogen gas combined with oxygen to form water, with the release of energy.) What is the *law of conservation of matter*? (Matter is neither created nor destroyed during a chemical reaction.) How does that law affect the way we write equations such as the one on page 272? (The number of atoms in the reactants always equals the number of atoms in the product, in this case, six.) What's the difference between an *exothermic* reaction and an *endothermic* reaction? What is an example of each? (During an exothermic reaction such as the *Hindenberg* explosion, energy is given off; during an endothermic reaction such as photosynthesis, energy is absorbed.)

Acids, Bases, and Salts: How are acids and bases different? What are some examples of each? (Acids—such as vinegar and orange juice—are sour and turn litmus paper red; bases—such as seawater and soap— are bitter and turn litmus paper blue.) What is pH? (On this scale, used to measure how acidic or basic something is, 7 is neutral, below 7 is acidic, and above 7 is basic.) What happens when you mix an acid and a base? (*Neutralization* occurs, producing a *salt* plus water.)

Summary Discussion: Each student writes a two-sentence summary of each section. Provide these frames:

When a chemical reaction occurs,_____.
Two types of chemical reactions are _____.
While acids are _____, bases are _____.
When acids and bases are mixed, _____.

Application: In the laboratory, you mix chemicals *A* and *B* and see a flash of light. You test the resulting substance and find that it has properties different from those of *A* and *B*. Was this a chemical or a physical change? (chemical) Do you think it was an exothermic or an endothermic reaction? (exothermic) Suppose that you had two compounds, *X* and *Y*, in the laboratory. You are told that they are either two acids or an acid and a base. How might you find out which is which? (Litmus paper turning red indicates acid; if one is shown in this way to be acid, try mixing it with the other. If salt plus water is produced, the other is a base.)

Provide students with some litmus paper and some "mystery liquids" (soap solution, orange juice, lemon juice) Have them test the substances to see which are acids. Remind them that although "taste" can sometimes be used to distinguish acids from bases (sour versus bitter), the taste test should not be used on mystery substances.

Graphics: Have students illustrate the equation on page 272 by drawing the explosion of the *Hindenberg*.

Have students create group posters (with drawings/magazine cutouts) that demonstrate chemical reactions (a firecracker or flashbulb going off, a cake in the oven)

Have students form small groups to create posters showing useful acids, bases, and salts. (Each group divides a large piece of paper into thirds, labeled "Acids," "Bases," and "Salts." One part of the group is responsible for drawing/pasting up examples of useful acids, such as tomato juice and battery acid; one group is responsible for illustrating useful bases, such as ammonia and milk of magnesia; one group is responsible for showing useful salts, such as Epsom salts and rock salt.

Role Playing: Have students act out one of the following situations.

- A nutritionist gives instruction about all the ways in which you can get the citric acid (vitamin C) you need.
- "Heloise" gives some hints for using common household acids (vinegar to whiten porcelain in the bathroom), bases (baking soda to freshen the refrigerator), and salts (rock salt to melt ice on the driveway).
- A recycling representative talks about the corrosive (acid- and base-containing) substances people may want to discard (car batteries, for example), and what they need to do rather than just dump them in the trash.
- You are a representative of the local Poison Control Center. Talk to your audience about the dangers of many acids and bases (mentioning precautions as well as steps to take if an accident occurs, importance of reading warning labels). (For this role-play, you might have students bring in warning labels, such as those from oven cleaner or a vitamin C bottle.)

Reading Strategies Instruction: Read aloud the section "Identifying Faulty Logic in Graphics" on pages

273–274. Review some of the common types of "faulty logic" (circular reasoning—"People with blue eyes are stuck-up, and that's because blue-eyed people are conceited"; proof by selected instances—"My sister is a nurse and she is neat, so nurses are neat"; avoiding the question—"Do you plan to raise taxes?" "No one wants taxes to be raised"; special pleading—"Don't drink and drive, although it's okay for me to drink and drive"; faking a connection—"A dandelion is a plant. A tulip is a plant. So a dandelion is a tulip."). Look together for examples in political speeches and product advertisements. Refer students having difficulty to the Pre-GED *Threshold* social studies text, Unit 3, Chapter 3, Lesson 28, and also the *Threshold* science text, Unit 4, Chapter 3, Lesson 35. For more GED-level work, see *The New Revised Cambridge GED Program*: the science text, Chapter 4, Lesson 4, and the social studies text, Chapter 4, Lesson 2.

Lesson Wrap-Up

Exercise Discussion: Before students complete the Lesson 9 Exercise on pages 275–276, have a volunteer summarize the steps in answering a multiple-choice item. Review with students how to read a line graph like the one shown on the top of page 275. Have students complete the exercise individually. Then discuss each question with the class, eliciting opinions about what the correct answers are, and why. Encourage students to explain why each incorrect response is incorrect, giving reasons for their opinions.

Answer Key Discussion: After a consensus is reached, go over the answers and explanations on page A-22.

Lesson 10:   The World of Physics

Lesson Warm-Up

Brainstorming: Read aloud the Prereading Prompt and have students share their ideas. Then take a minute or two to preview the lesson with students (pointing out key words, headings, words in bold print, and diagrams). Next, ask what they already know about motion and energy, the topics of Part 1. (To prompt students, ask: Have you ever gone ice skating or roller skating? Which way do you go when you push back on your skates? What happens when you stop pushing? Which way do you have to push when you come to a turn in the rink if you don't want to bang into the wall? What happens to the amount of work you do if you have to push a child in front of you? Have you ever gone to an amusement park? Which way does your neck snap as the ride moves forward? Which way does your body tilt as the ride zooms around a corner?)

Who was Newton? Remind students that they will be summarizing the lesson (in the "What I Learned" column of the chart) after reading and discussing it. Then have students jot down what they know and would like to know about the Part 2 topic—waves, sound, and light (*Ask:* Have you ever watched waves at the beach? How do they act? How do they sound? Why are some bigger than others? What happens when two big ones meet? How do we hear sounds? Why are some people unable to hear? Why do we hear thunder after we see lightning? What do you know about light? What causes a rainbow?) as well as what they know about the topic of Part 3—electricity and magnetism (*Ask:* What do you think of when you hear the word "electricity"? What do you know about how light bulbs or batteries work? You've probably noticed that "voltage" is often marked on appliances such as dryers. Do you know what voltage is? Do you know anything about the circuits or circuit breakers in a home or car? Do you use any magnets in your house? on your refrigerator? in your vacuum cleaner? What do you know about how magnets work? Have you ever used a compass? How does it help people figure out where they are?)

Vocabulary: Write the Key Words (*energy*, *wave*) on the board, read their definitions, and provide these two sentences: A baseball player's bat has *energy* that is used to do the work of moving a ball. An ocean *wave* transfers energy from one place to another as it passes through the water.

Lesson Activities

Brainstorming: Have students predict whether the following statements are true (T) or false (F) and discuss all that comes to mind when they hear each statement. Then tell them to check their predictions as they read the lesson.

This is an example of inertia: Without a seat belt, a passenger might be thrown through the windshield if the car stops suddenly. (T)

Newton was an English scientist who studied how and why things move. (T)

Energy is the same as work. (F)

The more work you need to do, the more energy you need to do it. (T)

There is only one form of energy. (F)

A holiday ornament spinning above a lighted candle is an example of energy conversion; heat energy changes into mechanical energy. (T)

Energy can be created, but it can never be destroyed. (F)

Heat energy is created by the movement of molecules. (T)

Thermodynamics is the study of how light and electricity are related. (F)

Heat flows from a colder object to a warmer one. (F)

A wave transfers energy from one place to another. (T)

The number of waves that pass by in a second tells you the frequency. (T)

The amplitude of an ocean wave is how high it rises above the surface of the ocean. (T)

Radio waves have shorter wavelengths than those of x-rays. (F)

Light waves travel faster than sound waves. (T)

A scream is a sound with high frequency that has a high pitch. (T)

As light passes from air to water it is bent, or refracted. (T)

Radio waves, visible light, and ultraviolet waves all have the same frequency. (F)

Radio waves, visible light, and ultraviolet waves are all part of the electromagnetic spectrum. (T)

A rainbow develops when the various frequencies of white light are separated. (T)

Radio waves have a lower frequency than gamma rays. (F)

Electricity is the flow of protons around the nucleus of an atom. (F)

If you want to slow down the flow of electricity to prevent shock, use a conductor. (F)

Static electricity results from the buildup of charges on an object, such as a rug. (T)

All substances possess magnetism. (T)

The push and pull of a magnet is strongest at the poles. (T)

In a magnet, opposite poles repel or push each other. (F)

Vocabulary: Write on the board the words that appear in bold print throughout the lesson, and pronounce them. As a class, have students take turns reading and discussing the lesson. (Each student asks the group at least one question based on the reading.) Reconvene as a group and discuss the three parts, using these questions to guide the discussion.

Motion and Energy: What are the *three laws of motion*, and what is an example of each? (An object in motion—such as a passenger on a roller coaster—will tend to continue in motion along a straight line; the force needed to move an object is directly proportional to the object's mass, so it is harder to push a heavy box than a light one; for every force there is an equal and opposite force—as when a gun is fired.) What is the difference between *kinetic energy* and *potential energy*? (The first is the energy of motion, such as that of a baseball bat being swung, and the second is stored energy, such as that of a bat at rest.) What is an example of *heat energy* being converted into *mechanical energy*? (Hot gases in a car move the car's pistons.) What are the two laws of thermodynamics? (The *law of conservation of energy* states that energy is neither created nor destroyed; the *second law of thermodynamics* states that heat will always move from a hotter object to a cooler one.)

Waves, Sound, and Light: How would you explain the diagram on page 279? (The *amplitude* is how high the wave rises; the *crest* is the high point of the wave and the *trough* is the low point; the *wavelength* is the distance between crests, and the *frequency* is how many waves pass by a point per second.) How would you explain the diagram on page 280? (Light and other *electromagnetic* waves are arranged by increasing frequency on a scale called the *electromagnetic spectrum*. Some waves, including *radio waves, infrared rays, ultraviolet rays,* and *X-rays*, cannot be seen and are part of the *invisible spectrum*. The light waves we see are part of the *visible spectrum* and owe their colors to their frequency. What is the difference between *reflection and refraction?* (Both describe light's behavior; sometimes light bounces or *reflects* off objects; other times it bends or *refracts* as it passes through an object, like a *prism.*)

Electricity and Magnetism: What is the difference between *static electricity and current electricity?* (Static electricity results from the buildup of stationary charges; while current electricity is the flow of electrons, as in an electric circuit.) What is *magnetism?* (An area of pull and push called the *magnetic field* extends from one end or *pole* of a magnet to the other.)

Applications: Have students demonstrate potential and kinetic energy using objects in the classroom (such as a book raised over a desk, then dropped).

Present students with a list of everyday phenomena that illustrate Newton's three laws and have them identify which law is at work. (In a game of tug-of-war, it is harder to pull over a man than to pull over a child—second law; a gymnast pushes down on a trampoline and springs up into the air—third law; water on a head of lettuce flies out into the air when the lettuce is spun in a spinner—first law.) After modeling these examples, have student pairs come up with examples of their own.

Have students think of everyday examples of the conversion of heat to mechanical energy. (Lighting a firecracker causes it to move, for example.) To elicit examples of the conversion of mechanical energy to heat energy, say, "Think of examples of machines that became hot as you used them." (A drill bit is still hot after use; bicycle tires feel warm after hard riding.)

For a class quiz, provide a few problem situations created by waves and ask for solutions.

1. If you wanted to reduce noise from a neighbor's TV set coming through the wall of your living room, what could you do and why would that work? (Put foam rubber behind a bookcase; foam rubber absorbs noise. It is dense, meaning that its molecules are tightly packed together and don't bounce around much; therefore, sound—which passes by making the molecules of a medium vibrate—is not transmitted well through it. *Note:* Just because a medium is hard or solid does not mean that it is dense iron, for example.)

2. Residents of a neighborhood near the highway complain of the noise. What could be done? (Erect sound barriers along the side of the road made of a material that does not transmit sound well, such as lead.)

Have students experiment making waves of different wavelengths and frequencies (by pushing down on water in a pan or by shaking the end of a rope attached to a chair). Have students observe refraction by putting a pencil in a clear glass of water, creating a "rainbow" with a prism. Ask students why we are reminded to block UV rays, and how. (UV rays can cause skin cancer; use a sunscreen.) Describe a type of ray and see if students can figure out which one it probably is (I try to block out this kind of ray when I put on sunscreen—ultraviolet; these waves have higher frequency than ultraviolet rays but lower frequency than gamma rays—x-rays; the lead walls in nuclear reactors are meant to keep these rays from escaping—gamma rays.)

Have students distinguish between real-life examples of static and current electricity (building up a charge on a balloon by rubbing it against your hair, then sticking it to the wall—static electricity; the electricity that flows through the overhead lights—current electricity).

Have students distinguish between substances that are probably good conductors/insulators. (an aluminum can—conductor; rubber-soled sneakers—insulator)

Talk with students about electrical safety and have them apply what they learned in the lesson.

What should you have on your feet whenever you use a washer or dryer? (shoes, preferably rubber-soled, as good insulators) Why shouldn't you use a hair dryer around bathwater? (Appliances dropped into water can give a severe shock, as water is a good conductor.)

Have students use small magnets to confirm that "opposites attract; likes repel." Have partners test objects in the classroom to discover which contain iron (attract magnets).

Place two magnets, ends an inch or two apart, under a piece of paper and sprinkle iron filings on the paper. See if students can figure out from the pattern of filings whether you have put like or unlike poles together.

Ask students who have compasses to bring them in and demonstrate how they work.

Debate: Write the following debate topic on the board and read it aloud.

• Every state should have a law making it illegal to drive without a seat belt.

Tell students to decide whether they agree or disagree with the idea. Then ask them to give specific examples and reasons for their opinion.

Discuss with students the fact that some protest groups in the 1960s argued for a "return to nature," rejecting modern technology. Have students brainstorm a list of electric-powered devices. (electric can openers, air conditioners, TV, electric lights, etc.) Which would you be willing to give up? What would you use instead? If you could only keep three, what would they be?

Discuss the fact that some people feel that schools and homes should not be built near power lines. Builders and power companies argue, however, that there is no proof that these lines raise cancer risks. Debate whether the government should place stricter controls on where power lines are placed.

Have students help generate debate topics using the following framework:

The worst thing about when the electricity goes out is going without _____.

Choose one of the responses and tell students to decide whether they agree or disagree with the idea, and why.

Reading Strategies Instruction: Read aloud the section "Evaluating the Effect of Values on Information in Passages" on pages 283–284. Have students brainstorm a list of values (fame, achievement, helping humankind, earning money, preserving the environment, education, etc.) Discuss various ads, editorials, speeches, etc. (like those you might find in *Time*, *USA Today*, or on TV) and talk about how the writer's values affect the information that he or she chooses to present. Point out that "listening" to "hear" the writer's "tone of voice" as you read often helps you become aware of the values the writer is promoting. Refer students having difficulty to the Pre-GED *Threshold* social studies text, Unit 3, Chapter 3, Lesson 29, and to the Pre-GED *On Your Own: Reading*, Unit 6, Chapter 27 ("Detecting Propaganda"). For more GED-level work, see *The New Revised Cambridge GED Program* the science text, Chapter 4, Lesson 2, and the social studies text, Chapter 3, Lesson 8.

Lesson Wrap-Up

Exercise Discussion: Before students complete the Lesson 10 Exercise on page 285, have a volunteer summarize the steps in answering a multiple-choice item. Have students complete the exercise individually. Then discuss each question with the class, eliciting opinions about what the correct answers are, and why. Encourage students to explain why each incorrect response is incorrect, giving reasons for their opinions.

Answer Key Discussion: After a consensus is reached, go over the answers and explanations on page A-22.

Refer students who still need more practice evaluating the effect of values to the Cambridge Pre-GED Series, *On Your Own: Reading*, Unit 6, Chapters 25 through 27.

Chapter 1 Nonfiction

Vocabulary: Write the word "Nonfiction" on the board and ask what it means. Point out that *non* means *not* and *fiction* refers to stories about imaginary people and events. Nonfiction is writing about real people and events.

Brainstorming: Ask students to preview the chapter opener on pages 288–289 to get an idea of what the chapter will be about. What do they see when they glance at the picture? (TV coverage of a real-life event such as a sports event); the headings? (Nonfiction, What Is Nonfiction?); the words in bold print? (biography, autobiography, article, or essay) What will the chapter probably be about? (writing about real-life events such as news and life stories)

Read page 288 aloud and discuss the Prereading Prompt. As students offer examples of nonfiction, quickly jot them down on the board around the word "Nonfiction." To elicit ideas, ask, "Who are some actors, musicians, or politicians who have had books written about them? Can you name some famous people who have written their life stories? Have you seen any TV shows or read stories about real events in history? If you were to flip through some hobby or how-to magazines, what sorts of articles would you find? Can you name some of the types of articles that you find in various sections of the newspaper?

Vocabulary: Read page 289 aloud. Then provide each of the Key Words in context:

- She wanted to read about the life of Malcolm X, so she bought the *biography* written by John Smith.
- The college application asks you to summarize your life in a short *autobiography*.
- In today's paper there are two *essays* on the death penalty: one for it and the other against it.

Divide students into small groups and tell them to work together on definitions and sentences for the Key Words. A spokesperson from each group shares the group's definitions and sentences with the entire group.

Lesson 1: Literal Comprehension of Nonfiction

Lesson Warm-Up

Vocabulary: Write the Key Words (*literal, topic, main idea, topic sentence, supporting details*) on the board, pronounce them, and discuss their meanings. Reinforce their meanings by having students fill in the following blanks:

- He read the article about volcanoes because he is interested in that _____ (topic).
- He can tell you the _____ (main idea) of the article on volcanoes if you don't have time to read the entire thing.
- The _____ (topic sentence), which states the main idea, happens to be the first sentence of the article.
- The second, third, and fourth sentences provide _____(supporting details) that explain why volcanoes erupt.
- The quiz tests your _____ (literal comprehension) of what the author tells you directly about volcanoes; you don't have to read between the lines for the answers.

Brainstorming: Read the Prereading Prompt aloud and ask students to say whatever comes to mind when they hear the words *main idea*. Elicit ideas by asking: What are some other ways of saying "main idea"? (key point, central or most important idea, gist) What are some times in real life when you are asked to figure out the main idea? (You try to understand the punch line of a joke, the main point a politician is making in a speech, the main reason a telephone solicitor is calling.) In real life, what steps do you take to figure out the main idea? (Listen for the speaker to state it directly, try to figure out what all the pieces of information build up to)

Lesson Activities

Vocabulary: Read aloud together the top of page 291 ("What is Literal Comprehension?"). Check to make sure that students understand what literal comprehension is by having them reread the Pre-reading Prompt paragraph. Which of these questions about that paragraph tests a reader's literal understanding?

- For students preparing to take the GED, what is it important to know how to find?
- What is an example of a hot political issue?

Explain that literal questions ask the reader to look for information that is *right on the page.*

The paragraph states directly that it is important for students taking the GED to know how to find the main idea of a passage.

Before students read the next two sections ("Finding the Topic and the Main Idea of a Paragraph," "Finding the Topic and Main Idea of a Passage"), have them discuss briefly their ideas on why craft hobbies are good. (What are some craft hobbies that students pursue? Why do they enjoy these hobbies?)

Break students into small groups and have them take turns reading each of the two sections that follow. Encourage groups to discuss what the section is about, to ask each other questions about the section, and to help each other understand words that may be difficult (such as *wares, craft fairs, profitable, passage, stagehands, dedicated, perceptive*).

Summary Discussion: Have small groups reconvene and lead an oral, section-by-section review. Some questions to guide discussion follow.

- What is the topic of any paragraph? How do you find it? What is the topic of the paragraph "What Is Good about Craft Hobbies"? How do you know?
- What is the main idea of any paragraph? How do you find it? What is the main idea of the paragraph about craft hobbies? How do you know?
- What is the difference between a paragraph and a passage? How is finding the main idea of a paragraph different from finding the main idea of a passage?

Reading Strategies Instruction: Have student volunteers take turns reading aloud the instructions and model passage on page 293. (Stop them after they read the purpose question—"What attitude do the dancers have toward the stagehands?"—and have them spend a few minutes predicting what the dancers' attitude toward stagehands might be. (What do stagehands do? When do they speak or work with dancers? What kind of personality does a "typical dancer" supposedly have? Improvise what a ballerina might have to say about stagehands.) After students have finished the entire section, ask them to state in

their own words what the passage is about. What is the topic? What is the main idea? Do the model question together. Before students read the text explanation on page 294, ask them to explain in their own words why the right answer is right and why the other choices are wrong. Discuss differences among their answers.

Review with students the steps in answering a question about the main idea of a passage. (Read the passage with the purpose question in mind; identify the topic; look for the topic sentence of each paragraph; think of a general idea that covers all the topic sentences.)

For additional practice in finding the main idea, have students reread the passage on page 289, "What Is Nonfiction?" Have students identify the topic (nonfiction) and the main idea about the topic (that nonfiction literature is skillful writing about real people and events that has lasting value). Point out that the entire passage is about *nonfiction,* a word that is repeated throughout the passage. Emphasize that all the supporting details—what nonfiction is about, examples of nonfiction writing, how some writers blend fact and fiction, what is special about nonfiction literature—describe and explain the topic (nonfiction). Have students test the idea that the main idea they have come up with is a general statement that covers all the details and explains the main point the author is trying to make with them.

Narrative: After students have read the passage about dancers and stagehands, have students discuss the following three ideas with a partner, then write about one for 10 minutes:

1. State why your hobby is a good one.
2. Describe a complainer or group of complainers that you have known.
3. Tell about a time when you felt as if you were "part of the scenery" (or treated someone else that way).

Partners share what they have written and practice identifying the topic and main idea of each other's writing.

Lesson Wrap-Up

Exercise Discussion: The first lesson exercise (pages 294–295) should be done together as a class. Teach students the following strategy for approaching multiple-choice items:

1. Read the purpose question (in capitals) and the test question(s) before you look at the passage.
2. Read the passage for the purpose of answering the questions. Don't waste time reading things twice.
3. Apply the process of elimination.
4. Read the question + the remaining, best choice to make sure that it sounds like the best answer.

(Post these steps on a wall for easy reference.) Encourage students to discuss different opinions on which choices to eliminate, until a consensus is reached.

Answer Key Discussion: Students should compare their reasoning carefully with that outlined in the answer key and discuss what they find. Stress that they should study the answer keys carefully. Emphasize that understanding *why* answers are correct is much more important than simply getting the right answer. What is vital to success on the GED overall is understanding the strategy for finding correct answers and eliminating incorrect ones. (If students need more instruction/practice on finding the main idea at a Pre-GED level, refer them to *On Your Own: Reading* , Unit 2, Chapters 7 and 10, the *Threshold* volume on interpreting literature and the arts, Unit 1, Chapter 2, the *Threshold* science text, Unit 1, Chapter 4, and the *Threshold* social studies text, Unit 1, Chapter 2.

Lesson 2:   Inferential Comprehension of Nonfiction

Lesson Warm-Up

Role Playing: Write the following words on the board: *angry, sad, surprised, bored, nervous, happy, puzzled.* Have student volunteers secretly choose one of these emotions and pantomime it. Tell the other students to write down what they see. Explain that they—like authors—are writing down information from which inferences can be drawn. Students then read their writing out loud and discuss what inferences can be drawn about the actors' feelings by putting the clues together.

Vocabulary: Write the Key Words (*inference, imply, point of view*) on the board, then read the words and their definitions aloud. Provide each of the key words in context:

- Isabel stops smiling, and screams. What *inference* can you draw about how she feels?
- Does the author mean to *imply* that Isabel is frightened, without saying so directly?
- What does the author's essay on the death penalty tell you about his *point of view*? Personally, I am against it.

Ask students these questions to make sure that they understand the meanings: Suppose you read a description about an apartment house owned by a rich landlord. The passage contains several details about the broken windows, the holes in the roof, the six children who are forced to live in the run-down apartment. What inference can be drawn about the rich landlord? (He does not bother to fix problems.) Who draws the inference—the reader or the author? (the reader) Who implies that the landlord is uncar-

ing? (the author) What is the author's point of view on rich, uncaring landlords? (The author doesn't think much of them.)

Brainstorming: Write the following statements on the board:

- Cigarettes should be illegal.
- The drinking age should be 18.
- Motorcycle helmets should be required by law.
- The death penalty should be outlawed.
- Parents should never spank children.

Have students brainstorm other controversial topics and add them to the list. Then have students split up into pairs. Each pair chooses a topic from the list and discusses both sides of the issue for 10 minutes or so. Then the partners take opposing viewpoints and write a paragraph *without coming out and stating what that viewpoint is.* Finally, each student reads his or her paragraph to the class. As the class guesses what opinion is being supported, explain that a reader often does the same thing–infers the author's "point of view" on a particular topic.

Lesson Activities

Vocabulary: Read aloud the Prereading Prompt on page 296. Ask how this lesson is different from the last one. (Both cover finding the main idea in nonfiction; Lesson 1 teaches finding main ideas that are stated directly and this lesson teaches finding main ideas that are not stated.)

Read the first section, "Making Inferences," aloud together. Stop after the purpose question and ask students what they already know about why a climate change probably made dinosaurs extinct; have a volunteer read to the end of the section. Ask these questions to make sure that students understand difficult vocabulary words:

What is a more common way of saying *inferential comprehension*? (reading between the lines) Can you think of an example? What does *extinct* mean? (all of these living things are dead) Can you use the word in a sentence? What are vegetarians? (those who eat no meat) Can you use the word in a sentence? In your own words, what is the main idea of the paragraph about dinosaurs? How can you tell? What clues did you find? How did you "read between the lines"?

Break students into pairs and have them take turns reading each of the two sections that follow out loud. As the reader finishes reading a section, he or she puts the book down and the partner asks the questions of his or her choice about that section. (You might first model some questions that range in difficulty: What does "scan" mean? What is the "purpose question"? How can you tell whether a test question requires you to make an inference—or whether the answer is found in the passage? What steps do you take if you need to infer the main idea?)

Summary Discussion: Together, partners write a one-sentence summary of each section and share with the entire group.

Reading Strategies Instruction: Have student volunteers take turns reading aloud the instructions and model passage on page 299. (Stop them after they read the purpose question, "What do he and his girlfriend feel about each other?" and have them put the question in their own words. Remind students to keep that question in mind, looking for clues to the answer as they read the passage.) After students have finished the passage, ask them to state in their own words what happens. (If necessary, elicit a plot summary by asking these questions: Who is speaking? What does he remember about the time he met his girlfriend in Cleveland after the trip to Europe? What does he remember about the time he visited her house the year before? What is the speaker like? What is his "girl" like? What is her family like? Do the model question together. Before students read the text explanation on page 300, ask them to explain in their own words why they have chosen a particular answer and why the other choices are wrong. Discuss any differences among their answers.

Review with students the steps in answering a question about the main idea of a passage. (Read the passage with the purpose question in mind; identify the topic; look for the topic sentence of each paragraph; think of a general idea that covers all the topic sentences.)

For additional practice in inferring the main idea, have students reread the Predictor Test passage on page 28, "What can be done about unemployment?" Have students identify the topic (looking for work), state the main idea of each paragraph (The number of want ads gave the author confidence at first; he soon lost confidence; he eliminated many of the ads; later he got discouraged; he wonders why there is unemployment; he proposes a solution to the problem), and infer the main idea of the entire passage (The author's experience with being out of work convinces him that help wanted ads don't help much—not that unemployment is unsolvable). Have students discuss the main ideas proposed by individual students by asking: Is this a general statement about the topic of all the paragraphs that includes each main idea?

Role Playing: After students have read the passage on page 299, discuss how an actor would probably read the passage. Explain that "listening" to how the speaker in a piece of literature "sounds" often helps in determining that speaker's point of view.

What tone of voice do they imagine the speaker to have as he starts telling about the trip to Cleveland— and why do you think so? Would he sound bored? Sarcastic? Unhappy? Pleased with himself? What is his attitude toward his girlfriend? How does he sound when he describes how nervous she was to be driving her brother's car? Amused? Irritated? What about his attitude toward her mother? How does he sound when

he describes her head popping through the window? Pleased at the memory? Annoyed by it? How might his voice change as he remembers the visit he made the year before? Sentimental? Matter-of-fact? How does he seem to feel about her parents making the "Grand Tour of Europe" and her brother putting up his Dartmouth pennants? Affectionate? Envious? Sarcastic?

Application: Have students apply what they have learned by splitting into small groups and reading from a magazine such as *People* or a newspaper such as *USA Today*. Each group writes one sentence summarizing the main idea of the article.

Mindmap: Draw the following graphic on the board.

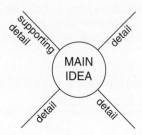

Explain that this chart is a handy way to take notes on written information—or to organize the student's own writing.

Narrative: Have students discuss the following three topics with a partner, then choose one to write about. Suggest that they use the main idea graphic above to organize their thoughts before writing.

• The greatest problem faced by this country today
• A favorite book or movie
• An important invention

Partners share what they have written and practice figuring out (1) whether the main idea of the partner's writing is stated or implied and (2) what that main idea is.

Lesson Wrap-Up

Brainstorming: Write on the board the lesson title, "Inferential Comprehension of Nonfiction," and have students brainstorm all that they have learned about that topic from this lesson—as well as a list of questions that they still have. (Model three or four questions, such as: Do all nonfiction passages have a main idea? Do you find the main idea of a science article the same way that you find the main idea of a movie review? I still don't understand what it says on page ___. Which parts of this lesson are the most important to remember?)

Exercise Discussion: Give students five minutes to complete the Lesson 2 Exercise on pages 300–301.

Before students look at the answer key, discuss each question with the class, eliciting opinions about what the correct answers are, what the wrong choices are, and why. Encourage students to defend different opinions, referring to the passage for supportive evidence, until a consensus is reached.

Answer Key Discussion: Students should compare their reasoning carefully with that outlined in the answer key and discuss what they find. If students need more instruction/practice on inferring the main idea, refer them to the Cambridge Pre-GED volumes *On Your Own: Reading*, Unit 3, Chapters 12 and 13, the *Threshold* text on interpreting literature and the arts, Unit 2, the *Threshold* social studies text, Unit 2, Chapters 2 and 3, and science text, Unit 2.

Lesson 3:   Applying Ideas in Nonfiction

Lesson Warm-Up

Brainstorming: Help students make connections between how one thinks in one situation to how that person might react in a new situation by presenting these facts about someone: Carol is shy and afraid of many things. She likes to read to her younger brother, draw, and cook. Best of all, she enjoys knitting sweaters for her family.

Ask the following questions about the person described above: "Do you think Carol will participate in the following activities, or not?"

Attend a football game (no)

Play soccer (no)

Read in the backyard (yes)

Take a walk by herself (yes)

Look for various kinds of birds in the park (yes)

Take tap dancing lessons (no)

Point out that being able to apply information is one important test of whether you have learned it. Stress that on the GED, students will be asked to apply what they read to new situations. Emphasize that students already apply information to new situations many times in a typical day. Offer some examples:

- Listening to the weather report, then getting out an umbrella
- Reading about the harmfulness of chewing tobacco, then breaking your habit
- Watching a home repair show, then fixing your leaky faucet
- Hearing a friend say that she likes country music, then buying her a ticket to a Willie Nelson concert

Have students brainstorm other examples and jot their ideas on the board.

Vocabulary: Write the Key Word (apply) on the board and read the definition. Point out that many words have more than one meaning. In this lesson, the word *apply* means "use"—not "sign up" (I will apply for the job) or "rub in" (apply the sunscreen). Have students write sentences in which *apply* means "to use" (I will apply what I learn in my review class when I actually take the GED.)

Lesson Activities

Vocabulary: Write the following words and phrases on the board: *principles, strategy, national health care system, epidemic, fixed purpose.* Discuss the meanings, then have students provide examples of how the terms might be used in sentences.

Read aloud the Prereading Prompt on page 302, then have students read the first section, "Applying Details and Main Ideas" (aloud in small groups; silently only if readers are high level). Encourage students to discuss any vocabulary words they do not understand.

Ask these questions: What are two examples of GED-type questions that ask you to apply details and main ideas from your reading? (bottom of page 302)

How do you read for the answer to this type of question? (top of page 303) Then have students read the section "Applying the Author's Attitudes." Prod students into becoming aware of words they might not understand by asking them to paraphrase ("put into your own words") difficult sections ("When you answer application questions, the key is understanding the principle behind the author's attitudes about the subject at hand.") The teacher models paraphrasing by "translating" this into: You have to understand how the author feels about what he or she is saying before you can figure out what he or she would say about something else.)

To check for comprehension, ask these questions: Why does this section mention an AIDS health care worker? (as an example of how you might be asked to apply information about someone's attitude from one situation to another) What are some examples of GED-type questions that ask you to apply an author's attitude? (end of the section) Can you make up some of your own questions of this sort? Does this section raise any questions in your mind?

Application: Have students describe a person they know well (spouse, lover, parent, friend). They should describe in detail as many of the person's traits as possible. When the person has been described fully so that the entire class feels that they are "familiar" with the person, ask the class to say what they think that person might say or do in the following situations. (*Note:* If any of these situations are not appropriate for the person who has been described, omit it and ask the class to come up with other situations.)

The person has just won the lottery.

The person has just been accused of murder.

The person is mugged on the street.

The person has just been proposed to.

The person learns that he or she is adopted.

Now have the class work in pairs. Each pair should try to describe a person's traits fully. The person can be based on one they have seen on television or in a movie or the person could be one who comes from their imaginations. Each pair should then come up with three different situations that a person might find himself or herself in. The situations can be ones that they've seen or ones they come up with: a person is fired from a job; a person has just received a raise; a person is accused of murder; a person learns that his or her spouse has been cheating on him or her; and so on. When everyone has finished, each pair should pass its list of situations to another pair of students. That pair should say what its person would probably say or do in each of these three situations. When everyone has finished, each pair should read aloud its sketches and relate each of the three situations and what they felt their particular person would do or say in each. Others should feel free to agree or disagree.

Reading Strategies Instruction: Have student volunteers take turns reading aloud the instructions and model passage on pages 303–304. (Stop them after they read the purpose question, "What does this slave learn about the pathway from slavery to freedom?" and have them put the question in their own words. Remind students to pay close attention to details in the passage that will help them answer that question as they read.) After students have finished the passage, ask them to say in their own words how Mrs. Auld changed Frederick Douglass's life. (If necessary, elicit a plot summary by asking these questions: Who were Mr. and Mrs. Auld? Who was the speaker? What did Mrs. Auld start to teach the speaker? How did her husband react? What did the speaker learn from the husband? What goal did the speaker set for himself? Have you ever had an experience like the speaker's?)

Do the model question together. Before students read the text explanation on page 304, ask them to explain in their own words why they have chosen a particular answer and why the other choices are wrong. Discuss any differences between their answers.

For additional practice in applying the author's attitude, have students reread the Lesson 2 Exercise passage on page 300. Ask students how the author seems to feel about the Great Plains. (He has many memories of their beauty, spaciousness, and richness.) Have students speculate on other areas of the world that the writer would or would not have similar positive feelings about. (He would, for example, probably enjoy the unfenced parts of Canada more

than crowded inner-city Washington, DC or New Delhi, India.)

Narrative: Have students discuss the following topic with a partner, then write about it for 10 minutes:

• A time when you, like Frederick Douglass, became more set than ever on doing something after someone told you you could not do it.

Lesson Wrap-Up

Exercise Discussion: Give students 5 minutes to complete the Lesson 3 Exercise on pages 300–301. Before students look at the answer key, discuss each question with the class, eliciting opinions about what the correct answers are, what the wrong choices are, and why. Encourage students to defend different opinions, referring to the passage for supportive evidence, until a consensus is reached.

Answer Key Discussion: Students should compare their reasoning carefully with that outlined in the answer key and discuss what they find. If students need more instruction/practice on applying information, refer them to the Cambridge Pre-GED volumes *On Your Own: Reading*, Unit 5, Chapters 21 and 22, the *Threshold* text on interpreting literature and the arts, Unit 3, Chapter 1, the *Threshold* social studies text, Unit 3, Chapter 1, and the *Threshold* science text, Unit 3.

Lesson 4:   Analyzing Nonfiction

Lesson Warm-Up

Brainstorming: Draw on the board a chart like the following:

Cause	Effect
1. You forget to buy your mother a Mother's Day present, so	_____
2. You oversleep and as a result	_____
3. Because you fail a test	_____
4. You win the lottery and the effect is	_____
5. _____	so you celebrate.
6. _____	so you cry.
7. _____	so you get the job.

Have students brainstorm as many causes and effects as they can think of as you jot down their ideas on the chart. Point out that another word for *cause* is *reason* and that another word for *effect* is *result*. Refer students to the chart and have them brainstorm words that are often used by speakers and writers to indicate cause/effect (*so, as a result, because, thus, since*). Write these words on the board: *angry, playful, sarcastic, proud, affectionate.* Have students brainstorm as many other words as they can think of that can be used to describe a person's tone of voice.

Role Playing: Have students demonstrate what various tones of voice (see the list above) sound like (by saying something such as "Did you close the door?" in varying tones). Remind students that writers, too, use a particular *tone of voice.* Write the sentence, "I want to help you" on the board and have students read it in several different tones of voice (sincere, angry, sarcastic, condescending). Stress that understanding an author's tone is essential to understanding what the author really means.

Vocabulary: Write the Key Words (*analysis, tone, cause and effect*), on the board, then read the words and their definitions aloud. Ask students these questions to reinforce their understanding of each word.

- When you have a blood <u>analysis</u>, does the lab worker look at your blood as a whole or at the separate parts? (parts)
- What <u>tone</u> of voice would you probably use if you received a call from the U.S. President? (surprised, respectful)
- What might be the <u>cause and effect</u> of failure to pay your phone bill?

Lesson Activities

Vocabulary: Write the following words and phrases on the board and pronounce them: *structure, technique, style, formal, persuade, motive, import, objective, wretched, resignation.* Ask students to share what they *think* the words mean and to use the words in sentences. (Explain that after they are finished reading the entire lesson, they will work with a partner on revising/changing the sentences based on what they learned.)

After reading aloud the Prereading Prompt, have students read the first section, "What is Analysis?" and ask these questions: What are two things an analysis question on the "Literature and the Arts" section might ask you to think about? (why a writer uses a certain structure or style) What does it mean to dress in a certain *style* (unique way) or use a certain *technique* (method) for starting a conversation? How is this like the style, or technique, that a writer uses? (A writer's style is the particular way in which he or she writes.) What are some words you might use to describe a person's style of dress? (formal, informal, showy) Can you guess what words might be used to describe a writer's style? (similar words—*formal, conversational, simple*)

What three or four purposes might a writer have for writing a piece? (report, explain, persuade, describe) How is writing to persuade different from writing to explain or describe? (To *persuade* means to try to convince someone that your opinion is the right one.) (For homework, you might have students look through a newspaper for an example of each of these types of nonfiction writing.)

Then have students read the section "Analyzing Cause-and-Effect Relationships." Stop them after they read the purpose question and ask whether that question asks for a cause or an effect. (effect) Should they read to find a reason for the war—something that happened before the war—or a result of the war—something that happened after the war? (result) Have students discuss their reasoning as they eliminate wrong choices and choose the right one before reading the text explanation on page 308.

Finally, have students take turns reading the section, "Analyzing Tone." Ask these questions: What is the difference between writing that has an objective tone and writing that has a subjective tone? (An objective tone is neutral, whereas a subjective tone reveals the writer's feelings about the subject.) In a newspaper, where would you be likely to find an example of writing in each type of tone? (objective—news story; subjective—letter to the editor or editorial or cartoon)

Summary Discussion: Have individual students write two- to three-sentence summaries of each of the three sections, then discuss with the teacher or with a partner.

Application: Ask students about causes and effects described in earlier passages. For example, refer them to the passage on page 299 and ask, "What was the reason for the girl's nervousness about driving the car?" (She knew how upset her brother would be if she had an accident with a car that he was still paying for.) What effect did seeing the girl's house have on the speaker the first time he saw it? (He admired the house and thought how lucky she was to have such a quiet, stable life.) How was the effect on him different the next year? (He realizes now that she wasn't so lucky—that there is something to be said for seeing the world.)

Refer students to the brainstormed list of words that can be used to describe tone. Then have them reread various passages from previous lessons (such as the ones on pages 300, 303, and 304) and pick out the word that best describes the tone of each.

Reading Strategies Instruction: Have student volunteers take turns reading the instructions and model passage on page 309. Stop them after they read the purpose question,"What is most troubling to Beethoven about his deafness?" Ask who Beethoven was. Have students put the question in their own words and predict a possible answer. After students have finished the passage, ask them to put Beethoven's thoughts into their own words. If necessary, elicit a summary by asking these questions: What is his deafness like? How has he changed his activities as a result? Why? What is he afraid of? What does his attitude about hearing loss seem to be? What words clue you in to that attitude? At the end, how does he seem to feel about the future? Have you ever felt that way?

Do the model question together. Before students read the text explanation on the bottom of page 309, ask them to explain in their own words why they have chosen a particular answer and why the other choices are wrong. Discuss differences among their answers.

Graphics: Discuss the fact that a cause may have several effects (Acid rain kills plants, fish, harms buildings), an effect may have several causes (The U.S. President's popularity goes down because he breaks promises, comes up with unpopular ideas, gets involved in personal scandals), and there may be a "chain" of cause and effect in which cause becomes effect (a mother receives poor prenatal care so her child is sickly; because the child is sickly, he has problems learning; because he has problems learning, he has poor self-esteem; because of his lack of self-confidence and skills, he gets into trouble). Draw each of these graphics on the board and explain that they can be useful in taking notes (to better understand and remember what a piece of writing is about) and in organizing the student's own ideas before writing.

One cause has several effects

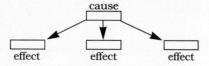

One effect has several causes

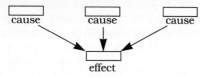

A cause-and-effect chain

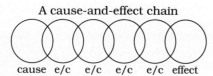

Narrative: Have students discuss the following topics with a partner, then write about one for 10 min-utes. (Suggest that students use the graphics above to organize their thoughts—and also, if appropriate, some of the signal words listed during the initial pre-reading brainstorming activity.)

- A time when the way you dressed had a definite effect on people
- Some of your reasons for deciding to take the GED test

Lesson Wrap-Up

Vocabulary: Have students apply their new under-standing of the vocabulary words listed during the Lesson Activity (vocabulary) by revising or rewriting the sentences they wrote.

Brainstorming: Have students brainstorm a list of questions they would use to test a reader's under-standing of this lesson.

Exercise Discussion: Give students five minutes to complete the Lesson 4 Exercise on pages 310–311. Before students look at the answer key, discuss each question with the class, eliciting opinions about what the correct answers are, what the wrong choices are, and why. Encourage students to defend different opinions, referring to the passage for supportive evidence, until a consensus is reached.

Answer Key Discussion: Students should compare their reasoning carefully with that outlined in the answer key and discuss what they find. If students need more instruction/practice on analyzing cause and effect and tone, refer them to the Cambridge Pre-GED volume, *On Your Own: Reading*, Unit 2, Chapter 9 and Unit 6, Chapter 25 as well as *On Your Own: Writing Process*, Unit 2, Chapter 10, the *Threshold* social studies text, Unit 1, Chapter 3, Lesson 7, and the *Threshold* science text, Unit 1, Chapter 5, Lesson 14.

Chapter

2

Fiction

Vocabulary: Create the following "T chart" on the board:

Fiction	Nonfiction

Have students compare what they know about fiction with what they know about nonfiction as you jot down their ideas on the chart. The completed chart might look like this:

Fiction	Nonfiction
Imaginary people, events Short stories, novels	Real people and events Biographies, auto- biographies, essays
Examples: *The Tell-Tale Heart, Jurassic Park*	Examples: *The Auto-biography of Malcolm X, My Summer Vacation*

Brainstorming: Tell students to preview the chapter opener on pages 312–313 to get an idea of what the chapter will be about. What do they see when they glance at the picture? (a photo of an American fiction writer); the headings? (Fiction, What Is Fiction?); the words in bold print? (fiction, novels, short stories) What will the chapter probably be about? (fiction writing—such as novels and short stories—about imaginary events)

Read page 312 aloud and discuss the Prereading Prompt. (Some questions to elicit further discussion: What kinds of imaginary stories do you enjoy most? Mysteries? Adventures? What sorts of characters do you like to read about? People like yourself? travelers? What titles come to mind when you think of "fiction"? What is memorable about these stories?) Have students suggest some fiction titles and jot them quickly down on the board around the word "Fiction."

Vocabulary: Read page 313 aloud. Then provide each of the Key Words in context:

- I enjoy reading *fiction* because I can escape into an imaginary world.
- She read a *short story* on the bus ride between her apartment and work.
- It took him two years to write the 300-page *novel*.

Divide students into small groups and tell them to work together on definitions and sentences for the Key Words. A spokesperson from each group shares the group's definitions and sentences with the entire group.

Lesson 1:   Literal Comprehension of Fiction

Lesson Warm-Up

Brainstorming: Make the following chart on the board:

TV Show	Setting

Ask students to name some of their favorite TV series and to state when and where the stories take place. Put the ideas on the chart, then ask students what they think *setting* is (the time and place of the story). Next ask them to state briefly what happened on one show they watched recently. Ask if they know another word that describes the *storyline* they have just given (plot). Ask if they can think of shows that are told by one of the characters (such as Parker Lewis, *Wonder Years*). Explain that these stories are told from the first-person point of view. Many other stories are told by a storyteller who isn't part of the story. These are told from the third-person point of view.

Vocabulary: Write the Key Words (*action, setting, narrative point of view*) on the board, pronounce them, and read the definitions. Have students offer sentences containing the words.

Lesson Activities

Vocabulary: Read the first section ("Action, Plot, and Setting") aloud together and have students paraphrase it (How would you put this into your own words?) Encourage students to become aware of words in this section that they may not understand, by asking: What are sequences? (events put in order, such as a list of everything that happened between morning and night) What are two different ways in which authors might arrange a sequence of events? (the order in which they happened, the order in which they come up in a character's mind) Describe a pleasant childhood memory you have—first, stating events in the order in which they happened, then in the order in which you happen to remember them. What do "complex" and "simple" mean? (complicated versus plain) Can you think of a story that has a complex plot? one that has a simple plot? What is the difference between "major" and "minor" events? (important versus less important) What are the major events in a story such as "Little Red Riding Hood"? (Little Red Riding Hood walks through the woods, talks to the Wolf, almost gets eaten when she gets to Grandma's.) What is a minor event in that story? (Little Red Riding Hood knocks on her grandmother's door.)

Lesson Activities

Narrative Activity 1: Ask students to work in pairs and come up with a narrative based on one of the topics listed below or on any topic of their choice. When they are finished, one person from each pair should read the written narrative aloud. Other students volunteer to summarize the action in one sentence. Other students can respond, pointing out details left out, inaccuracies, and better choices of words to name the elements.

> A rock concert
> An arrest
> Arriving in this country
> A trip
> A fire
> A fight with a lover or spouse
> A job interview
> Trouble with parents
> A gang war
> The World Series

Narrative Activity 2: Have students volunteer accounts of real-life experiences in which they responded intensely. (For example: A woman has a blind date she does not like; later, he keeps showing up where she is and she begins to feel he is stalking her.) Then have another student summarize this first-person account—that is, retell it from a third-person point of view. The teacher can then ask: How are the two accounts different? Probably the first-person account will be more intense; the third-person account may comment on the alleged "stalker" so that he is more understandable (maybe he's just shy but wants to know the woman). *Ask:* What two narrative points of view are used in these two accounts? Point out that personal letters and journals are first-person, factual news stories are third-person, narratives. To elicit more topics for this activity, teacher can ask students to recall emotional events about which they wrote letters to friends or family (or wrote about in journals, or just talked about to friends).

Role Playing: The purpose of the following activities is to show that an account by any one of the characters in a scene would be a first-person account of the action; that an account of the action that summarized all the character's attitudes would be a third-person account. Set up a situation and cast three students as characters in it with three distinctly different attitudes toward the situation.

- Three young men argue about how to respond to an attack on one of them by a local bully; one argues for group counterattack, another for "forgetting it" and avoiding the bully, another for having one of them challenge the bully.
- Three women advise a fourth woman with a violent, abusive husband what to do about her situation: the woman wants to get her family and his family together to help save her marriage. The three women argue against this: one argues for divorce; another argues for going to a counselor with him; the third argues for leaving town and hiding from him.
- Three people, men and women, argue over how to bring up a complaint about a supervisor of theirs who is harassing them.
- A grown sister and brother argue about how to care for their old father or mother; the old parent can disagree with either or both of them.

After a short scene had been acted out, have students summarize dialogue. Ask students to describe the attitude toward the situation they detect in each character's remarks. Point out that only a third-person narrator could describe all three characters' attitudes.

Reading Strategies Instruction: Have student volunteers take turns reading aloud the instructions and model passage on page 316. (After they have read the purpose question, "When does the speaker begin to feel Chinese?" ask them what questions they should ask themselves as they read.) Clarify the meanings of words that may be unfamiliar to students (Caucasian—white; genetics—study of how we inherit traits such as eye color; werewolf—half man/half wolf; mutant tag of DNA—a piece of genetic material that has somehow been altered; replicating—repeating, reproducing). After students have finished the passage, ask them to state in their own words what it is about. (If necessary, elicit a plot summary by asking these questions: What do you know about the speaker? What does she remember about her mother from when she was a teenager? How old is the speaker now? Where is she going? With whom? Why? How is she feeling?) Do the model questions together. Begin by having students paraphrase what the questions ask. Point out that "main action" (item 1) refers to what is happening now, not what the speaker remembers from the past. Before students read the text explanation on page 317, ask them to explain in their own words why they have chosen a particular answer and why the other choices are wrong. Discuss any differences among their answers.

For additional practice in literal comprehension of fiction, have students reread the excerpt from "The Fellowship of the Rings" on page 27 of the Predictor Test. Refer students having difficulty to the Pre-GED *Threshold* text on interpreting literature and the arts, Unit 1.

Draw the following graphic on the board. Explain that the plot of most stories follows this form.

STORY MAP
THE SETTING
   Place:
   Time:
CHARACTER(S)
THE PROBLEM
THE GOAL
   EVENT 1
   EVENT 2
   EVENT 3
THE RESOLUTION

Model how to use the map by mapping the passage on page 27.

STORY MAP
THE SETTING
   Place: a riverbank
   Time: day, time indefinite
CHARACTER(S): Sam and Mr. Frodo
THE PROBLEM:
   Sam falls into the water while trying to catch up with Mr. Frodo.

THE GOAL:
   Sam needs to be rescued
   EVENT 1: Mr. Frodo paddles the boat to Sam.
   EVENT 2: Mr. Frodo holds out his hand.
   EVENT 3: Mr. Frodo paddles the boat to the bank.
THE RESOLUTION
   Sam scrambles out of the water and gets Mr. Frodo's permission to go along to Mordor.

Lesson Wrap-Up

Exercise Discussion: After students read the passage on pages 317—318 ("Is This Man a Thief?"), ask them 1) to retell the story in their own words, and 2) how they figured out the meanings of the following words: *revolting, contempt, offensively, incredulously, urbanely, appalling.* [If students have difficulty using context clues, you might give a mini-lesson based on *On Your Own: Reading,* Unit 1, Chapter 2: "Using Context Clues to Unlock Word Meaning."

Give students five minutes to complete the Lesson 1 Exercise on pages 317–318. Before students look at the answer key, discuss each question with the class, eliciting opinions about what the correct answers are, what the wrong choices are, and why. Encourage students to defend different opinions, referring to the passage for supportive evidence, until a consensus is reached.

Answer Key Discussion: Students should compare their reasoning carefully with that outlined in the answer key and discuss what they find.

Lesson 2: Inferential Comprehension of Fiction

Lesson Warm-Up

Vocabulary: Review with students what they learned about the meaning of *inference* in Chapter 1, Lesson 2. (The writer gives the reader certain clues, which the reader uses to *infer* information that is not directly stated—"to read between the lines.")

Brainstorming: Write these sentences on the board and ask students what they can infer:

1. About the setting
   - The leaves were beginning to change from green to orange, red, and yellow. (autumn)
   - The people looked like ants from where he stood at the top of the Empire State Building. (New York)

- Tom was a Union soldier, but his brother John joined the Confederate Army. (Civil War time, 1860s)
- The conductor woke her and asked her for her ticket. (train)

2. About the character
- Her hands were wrinkled and crisscrossed with veins. (She is old.)
- His knees shook as he stood at the microphone. (He is nervous.)
- She shared the winnings with her friends and family. (She is generous.)

Point out that whenever they read or listen to stories, students are continually putting clues together to find hidden meanings.

Vocabulary: Write the Key Words (*theme, conflict, characterization*) on the board, then read the words and their definitions aloud. Provide each of the Key Words in context:

- The difficulty of growing up is a common *theme* in her writing.
- In *A Raisin in the Sun*, there is a *conflict* between a black family and the residents of a white neighborhood.
- Through the author's *characterization* of Mama, we see her as a strong, loving, hard-working woman.

To make sure that students understand the meaning of each of the Key Words ask them which word describes each of the following:

- The description of a character's beautiful eyes, her crippled leg, her love for a minister, her kindness toward everyone. (characterization)
- A writer's main message, such as "There are no winners in war" or "Beauty is only skin deep" or "Children are our future" or "Prejudice is wrong." (theme)
- A fist fight between two characters, a character's struggle to make a decision, a character's efforts to stay alive during a blizzard. (conflicts)

Lesson Activities

Vocabulary: Read aloud the Prereading Prompt on page 319. Ask how this lesson is different from Chapter 1, Lesson 2. (That lesson covered inferential comprehension of nonfiction, whereas this covers inferential comprehension of fiction.)

Read the first section, "Inferring Character and Setting," aloud together. Ask these questions to make sure that students understand difficult vocabulary words: What does people-watching have to do with characterization? (Just as we form impressions of real people by watching them, we form ideas

about characters from what the author lets us "see" of them.) How can you infer the setting of a story? Can you think of examples? (from details that clue you in to the time or place such as details about the weather, references to historical events, landmarks)

Separate students into pairs and have them take turns reading aloud the second section, "Inferring the Theme." As the reader finishes reading a section, he or she puts the book down and the partner asks the questions of his or her choice about that section. (First model some questions that range in difficulty: What does *harshly* mean? What are *insights about life*? If you were going to write a story about an insight you have had, what would it be about? What are three typical inference questions you might find after a piece of fiction writing on the GED? What is the difference between "internal" and "external" conflict?)

Application: Read several fables to students, leaving out the final "moral." Have students summarize the theme.

Write several conflict situations on the board and have students identify whether they are internal or external (between characters, between character and society, between character and nature). For example:

- An unemployed father grows increasingly depressed. (internal)
- A black doctor dedicates his life to the fight against racial oppression by whites. (between character and society)
- A doctor argues with his son, who has been arrested. (between characters)
- A doctor is chilled while making his rounds in a rainstorm and gets sick. (character versus nature)

Summary Discussion: As a group, review the first two sections by writing these sentence starters on the board and having students suggest how to complete them.

- To infer character, pay attention to _____. (how characters look, what they do, what they say, what others say about them)
- To infer setting, pay attention to _____. (clues about when and where the action is happening)
- To infer theme, pay attention to_____. (what the conflict in the story tells you about the author's basic beliefs about life)

Reading Strategies Instruction: Have student volunteers take turns reading aloud the instructions and model passage on page 321. (After they have read the purpose question, "What does the boy feel about his father?" ask them to put the question into their own words:) Elicit or clarify the meanings of words that may be unfamiliar to students (*khaki, cobbles,* musty, *Gurkha knives*, *wardrobe*, *magpie*). After students have finished the passage, ask them to say in their own words what it is about. (If necessary, elicit a plot summary by asking these questions: What do you know about the speaker? How far back is he remembering? What does he remember about his father's appearance? the sounds his father made? the way his father smelled and felt? Why does he call his father a "bit of a magpie"? How did the speaker and his mother feel about the father's collections? Are these memories more pleasant or unpleasant? Does the father remind you of anyone you know?)

Do the model question together. Begin by having students paraphrase what the question asks. Point out that you can infer a character's attitude toward his father in the same way that you would infer a real son's attitude—by what he says about his father and how he says it. Point out also that this is the type of question where students should try to predict the answer before looking at the choices. Before students read the text explanation on page 322, ask them to explain in their own words why they have chosen a particular answer and why the other choices are wrong. Emphasize that some answers are wrong because they are incorrect statements according to the story, such as choices 2 and 5, whereas others are wrong simply because there is no evidence to support them, such as choices 3 and 4. Discuss differences among students' answers.

For further practice in inferring character and setting, you might have students reread the excerpt from "The Fellowship of the Ring" on page 27 and ask: What is your impression of Sam? (impulsive, clumsy, loyal) What does Mr. Frodo seem to be like? (irritable but kindly) What is the author saying about loyalty and courage? (Both are admirable; you find loyalty and courage in some unlikely people.) How can you tell that this isn't set in a real-life place? (Mordor sounds like a fantasyland—isn't a real place.)

Students having special difficulties with inferencing in literature can be referred to the Pre-GED instruction and for practice can be referred to the *Threshold* literature and arts text, Unit 2, and to its Unit 3, Chapter 2, Lessons 16 and 17 for characterization and setting in fiction.

Role Playing: Have students discuss and then improvise conflict situations that might arise between any of the following pairs of characters:

A parent and a teenager
A police officer and a suspect
A boyfriend and a girlfriend
A brother and a sister
A boss and an employee
A teacher and a student

Application: Have students apply what they have learned about inferring character, setting, and theme to a short story or to a magazine or newspaper account of your choice or one that they bring in.

Graphics: Draw the following "character attribute web" on the board and explain that it is a helpful way to organize information about what a character is like. (Students might use webs to help understand and remember what a character is like or to help organize information about a character they are creating for a story.)

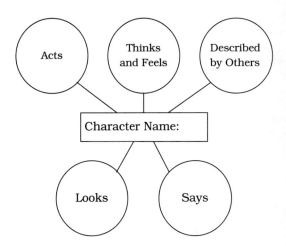

Narrative: Have students brainstorm ideas with a partner about what each of the following three characters might be like and what problems they might run up against. Then choose one character and one problem. Write a short story about how the character deals with the problem. Suggest that they use the attribute web above to organize their thoughts before writing.

- A recent immigrant to this country
- A middle-aged man preparing for the GED
- A teenager who doesn't get along with her or his parents

Partners share what they have written and practice inferring character and setting of each other's writing.

Role Playing: Tell students that in fiction, as in nonfiction, "listening" to the speaker's tone of voice helps the reader infer what that speaker is like. Have students discuss their impressions of the son in the Frank O'Connor story (page 321). What tone of voice would he have as he remembers his father? angry? matter-of-fact? "smiling"? Then have students assume the role of the son and read the piece in several possible tones of voice. Afterward, students should choose which rendition is most appropriate and discuss why.

Lesson Wrap-Up

Exercise Discussion: Give students five minutes to complete the Lesson 2 Exercise on pages 322–323. Before students look at the answer key, discuss each question with the class, eliciting opinions about what the correct answers are, what the wrong choices are, and why. Encourage students to defend different opinions, referring to the passage for supportive evidence, until a consensus is reached.

Answer Key Discussion: Students should compare their reasoning carefully with that outlined in the answer key and discuss what they find. Emphasize how important it is to read the questions carefully. All three questions ask the reader to infer the *speaker's* attitude toward Don Anselmo—not the *reader's*. Whether or not the *reader* feels that Don Anselmo's refusal is honorable is irrelevant.

Lesson 3:   Applying Ideas in Fiction

Lesson Warm-Up

Brainstorming: Write the following problems on the board as well as a list of characters from novels, movies, or television. Have students brainstorm additions to the list. Then have them brainstorm predictions about what the characters would say and do if asked for advice about the problems listed.

- Your boyfriend/girlfriend "dumps" you.
- You are in love with a much younger man/woman.
- You suspect your friend of stealing.
- You are flunking a class.
- You want to lose weight.

After students explain the reasons for their predictions, ask whether the exercise made them think hard about what the character is like. Point out that applying what you know about a character to a new situation is one way of getting to "know" the character better—and to understand a piece of fiction better. An active reader should go beyond the page and ask himself or herself what the character would do in other situations. This will help students answer certain GED questions, and will make better readers out of them, overall.

Lesson Activity

Vocabulary: Write the following words and phrases on the board: *hostess, hat rack, festive, infused, freshman executive job.* Discuss the meanings and have student pairs look the words up in a dictionary and put them into sentences. For additional reinforcement, have students put the correct word in each blank:

- In the days when more people wore hats, you saw more _____ (hat racks) in restaurants and entertainment halls.
- The balloons and crepe paper made the kitchen look _____ (festive).
- The _____ (hostess) showed the customers to their table and introduced the waitress.
- After the new coach gave his pep talk, the team was _____ (infused) with enthusiasm.
- Someday I want to be head of the company, but right now I am happy with my _____ (freshman executive job).

Read aloud the Prereading Prompt on page 3, then read "Applying the Attitude of an Author or of a Character" together.

Summary Discussion: Ask these questions: What will this lesson teach you how to do? (figure out how a writer or character might act in another situation) How can you predict that Don Anselmo (see page 322) would tell his neighbors he could not break his word if they told him he had been foolish? (Figure out what his attitude in the story is—that it is important to be a man of one's word—and figure out how that attitude would make him act in a new situation— proud, with head held high.)

Narrative: Have a student tell a narrative about dealing with someone in authority; doctors and/or nurses in a hospital, authorities in a government office; or authorities in a school. The narrator-student could spell out his or her attitude in specifics: "I told this nurse I had to see my girlfriend now because I couldn't come during regular visiting hours. So when she left, I sneaked in and saw my girlfriend." Ask students to:

1. Describe or name the narrator's attitude.
2. Describe another situation in which the narrator's attitude would come out: any other situation in which a rule is set forth and if it frustrates the person, he or she gets around it.
3. Write another narrative, identifying the narrator's attitude and then see if the attitudes of the narrators in the two narratives can be transposed. Ask, "How would the first narrator act in situation 2?"
4. Once any attitude-of-narrator is identified, say how one of them—one of the students—might

have acted differently or ask, "What do you think the opposite or very contrasting attitude might be?" (such as a man at hospital: by contrast, he might have just gone home; or appealed to a higher authority and gotten in; or gone home but written a letter of protest; or gotten off work early so that he could make the visiting hours)

Lesson Activity

Write the following on the board: Have students volunteer their individual attitudes in the following situations. Then follow the four steps just described to generate an activity.

- Disciplining a child (What is the right thing to do with a child in a certain situation?)
- Having an argument with a parent (either with parent as authority figure or parent you give care to)
- Having a disagreement about money (the best way to use it, "what it's for")
- Having a disagreement with the people you live with (what each person's rights and responsibilities are; questions of "personal space" and "consideration of others")
- Having a disagreement with a lover (What does one person owe the other in the relationship? Issues of faithfulness versus freedom; sensitivity to each other's feelings versus acceptance of different lifestyles and interests)

Reading Strategies Instruction: Have student volunteers take turns reading the instructions and model passage on page 325. (Stop them after they read the purpose question, "What kind of person is Joan?" and have them put the question in their own words. Remind students to pay close attention to details in the passage, which will help them answer that question as they read.) After students have finished the passage, ask them to put the speaker's description of Joan into their own words. (If necessary, elicit a summary by asking these questions: Where did Joan move? What did she want to be at first? Why did she change her mind? What did she do for the rest of the summer? What did she look like? What was her personality like? What new job did she take in the fall? What was her relationship with Jack like? Does she remind you of anyone? Would she be a friend of yours?)

Do the model question together. Before students read the text explanation on page 325, ask them to explain in their own words why they have chosen a particular answer and why the other choices are wrong. Discuss any differences between their answers.

For additional practice in applying the character's attitude, have students reread the passage on page 27. Ask, "What if Mr. Frodo and Sam get lost on the way to Mordor? How will they act? What if Mr. Frodo and Sam are attacked by savage beasts? How will each react? Refer students having difficulty to the Pre-GED *Threshold* text on interpreting literature and the arts, Unit 3, Lesson 13.

Lesson Wrap-Up

Brainstorming: Have students list what they remember about the lesson—the most important points it makes, the descriptions that remain most vivid in their minds.

Exercise Discussion: Give students five minutes to complete the Lesson 3 Exercise on pages 326–327. Before students look at the answer key, discuss each question with the class, eliciting opinions about what the correct answers are, what the wrong choices are, and why. Encourage students to defend different opinions, referring to the passage for supportive evidence, until a consensus is reached. Emphasize how useful it is to try to link the purpose question with the test question. (For example, item 2: If the student understands what the narrator's attitude toward thinking is, it is easier to understand what his attitude toward college might be.)

Answer Key Discussion: Students should compare their reasoning carefully with that outlined in the answer key and discuss what they find.

Lesson 4:   Analyzing Fiction

Lesson Warm-Up

Brainstorming: Display ads showing a variety of styles of clothing. As students examine these, have them brainstorm a list of words that describe clothing styles (*elegant, simple, romantic, sporty*). Point out that writing, like clothing, comes in many styles.

Then hold up a grocery ad showing a piece of fruit and write a simple sentence describing it on the board. For example:

The apple is green.

Give students five minutes to work independently on one sentence describing the food. Tell students that they can describe the food in any way they wish—in a sentence that is as long or short as they wish. Then have students read their sentences aloud and discuss the variability among them—variability in both the words chosen and the ideas expressed. Elicit from students the observation that some sentences, for example, are short and direct, whereas others are complex and full of detail. Some may be serious, others may be humorous. Some may be more scientific, focusing on the nutritional value of the food, others are more poetic, describing the beauty of the food's appearance.

Remark that each student writes in a unique way—in his or her own "style." Style is the way in which writers say whatever they say. A writer's personality and the idea that he or she wants to express both affect the style the writer chooses.

Present students with the following situation: Suppose that a young woman wears a flaming red dress to her grandfather's funeral. Ask students why she might have done it. (Did she do it because she likes to be the center of attention? Was she showing deliberate disrespect for a man she never got along with? Did she wear red because she knows that her grandfather loved that color? Was she trying to show that she wanted to celebrate her grandfather's life rather than mourn his death?) Point out that interpreting the young woman's dressing style and personal style helps you understand what the young woman is trying to "say."

Similarly, recognizing a writer's style—on the GED and elsewhere—is important in understanding the author's meaning and purpose for writing.

Vocabulary: Write the Key Words (*mood, irony, sarcasm*) on the board, then read aloud the words and their definitions. Ask students questions to reinforce their understanding of each word.

After reading the Prereading Prompt aloud, have students read the section "How Does an Author's Style Create a Tone or Mood?" and ask these questions: What is the tone of a story? (the author's attitude toward the subject) What is the mood of a story? (the feeling the story creates in the reader) What is irony? (situation or statement that is different from what it appears to be) What is sarcasm? (an extreme form of irony in which a person means the opposite of what he says) Can you think of an example of an ironic situation—one that is different from what you would expect? Can you say something in a sarcastic tone? What do your words really mean?

What sort of *mood* does a description of a "dark and stormy night" create? (gloomy, threatening) A drug enforcement officer's son is a drug dealer. What is the *irony* in this situation? (You would expect him to teach his son to stay away from drugs.)

Why might a mother's comment to her daughter, "I can see you've worked hard on cleaning up your room," be loaded with *sarcasm*? (Maybe the mess makes it clear that the daughter didn't work at all on cleaning up her room.)

Lesson Activities

Vocabulary: Write the following words and phrases on the board and pronounce them: *appropriate, communicate, tone, fundamental, valise, mileage, outskirts, organdy, sachet.* Ask students to share what they *think* the words mean and to use the words in sentences. (Explain that after they are finished reading the entire lesson, they will work with a partner on revising/changing the sentences based on what they learned.)

Lesson Activity 1 on Tone: Read aloud the following two short narratives. As you read, tell students to think about the following questions, which you might want to write on the board:

- What is the author's tone?
- What is the author's purpose?
- Which details contribute to creating the tone?

1. Marcy took Fido to the park as she did every afternoon after school. Fido was Marcy's best friend, even though Fido was a dog. Fido was always there to listen to Marcy, to be faithful, to be kind—not like the other people in Marcy's life, who tended to be angry, mean, and often cruel.

On this afternoon, as soon as Marcy got to the park and let Fido off the leash to walk beside her, Fido raced away after a squirrel. Marcy yelled and yelled, but Fido kept going. There were acres and acres of rolling hills, bushes and trees. Marcy raced after him, but he was nowhere to be found. After an hour of searching and yelling and crying, Marcy admitted to herself that Fido was lost. Marcy was lost, too. She didn't know what to do.

2. As soon as we got to the meeting we knew it wasn't going to be easy to express our views. The room was small. The people were jammed in, many standing in the aisle. Many had banners. Some were already yelling.

We knew we had to keep the sports program and music program in our schools, even though there weren't enough funds. We just had to have the parents chip in, even if it meant making some sacrifices. After all, if these programs were eliminated, many kids would be on the streets in the afternoon, probably getting into lots of trouble.

After everyone was seated, we said what we thought. Others screamed at us. "Get out of here!" The room seemed to get smaller and smaller. The voices got louder and louder. We kept on, calmly stating our point of view. We never lost our tempers but kept trying to show people how important sports and music are to kids.

Finally, after three hours, we won.

Lesson activity 2 on Tone: After students have answered the questions from above, have students work in pairs and come up with similar stories to present to the class. Below is a list of possible topics for the students to choose from. When everyone has finished, have the groups say their stories aloud. The class should describe the tone of each.

- The events that lead up to my marriage (or new job)
- The story of how my family came to this country
- My best/worst recent experience
- What happened at the community meeting
- The events that led up to an accident
- The way the population of the neighborhood has changed over the years

Summary Discussion: Have students write a two-sentence summary of the section and share with a partner or with the whole group. (For example: An author's style is how he or she says what is said, and is created by the words that he or she chooses and the way those words are arranged. Style helps create a particular feeling in the reader, as when the writer uses an ironic tone to let the reader know that things are not what one would expect.)

Application: Ask students to identify the style and tone used by authors in earlier passages. For example, refer students to the model passage on page 321 and ask them which of these words they would use to describe the style—and why: conversational (yes); formal; bare; eloquent; flowery; economical; concrete (yes). Also ask which of these words they would use to describe the tone—and why: ironic (yes, at the end); objective; thoughtful (yes); pleased (yes); bitter; sarcastic; ironic (yes, at the end); reflective (yes).

Reading Strategies Instruction: Have student volunteers take turns reading the instructions and model passage on page 329. (Stop them after they read the purpose question, "How does the grandmother prepare herself for a car trip?" Have students put the question in their own words and predict a possible answer. After students have fin-

ished the passage, ask them to say what images— "pictures"—come to mind when they think about the passage. (If necessary, elicit a summary by asking these questions: What do you imagine the grandmother to look like? Where is she? What does she do? What do you know about her thoughts about others? How does she contrast with the children's mother?)

Do the model question together. Point out how useful it is to read the question first. In this case, the question points out the importance of paying attention to one sentence in particular—the last one. Before students read the text explanation on the bottom of page 330, ask them to explain in their own words why they have chosen a particular answer and why the other choices are wrong. Discuss any differences between their answers.

Students having difficulty with the subject of tone can be referred to the extensive Pre-GED instruction and practice on tone in *On Your Own: Reading*, Chapter 25, and in the Pre-GED *Threshold* text on interpreting literature and the arts, Unit 3, Chapter 2, Lesson 18.

Narrative:

1) Discuss Flannery O'Connor's style with students, pointing out the wealth of small details about the scene, the details about the grandmother's inner world, the humor (the valise "looked like the head of a hippopotamus"), the irony. Then have students rewrite the passage, using a different style (perhaps one that is more objective, less detailed, devoid of humor). In small-group discussion, have students compare their version with the original and explain why one or the other is more effective.

2) Have students write a description of someone (a friend, relative, co-worker) that conveys what that person is like—by showing, not telling. (Using the passage on pages 330–331 as a model, students should describe clothing, bearing, actions—but no dialogue.)

Lesson Wrap-Up

Vocabulary: Have students apply their new understanding of the vocabulary words listed during the Lesson Activity (vocabulary) by revising or rewriting the sentences they wrote.

Brainstorming: Have students brainstorm answers to this question: How does the material in this lesson relate to the material you have studied in earlier lessons in Unit 4, Interpreting Literature and the Arts?

Exercise Discussion: Give students five minutes to complete the Lesson 4 Exercise on page 331. Remind students to read the questions before reading the passage, and point out that on the GED, as in the Lesson 4 Exercise, there may well be questions that focus on the first or last sentence in a passage. It is important, therefore, to pay special attention to how the author says what he says in these sentences—and why. Have students explain how they figured out the meanings of some of the more difficult words in the passage, such as *vegetation, rioted, impenetrable, sluggish, nob, shoals, vengeful.* Before students look at the answer key, discuss each question with the class, eliciting opinions about what the correct answers are, what the wrong choices are, and why. Encourage students to defend different opinions, referring to the passage for supportive evidence, until a consensus is reached.

Answer Key Discussion: Students should compare their reasoning carefully with that outlined in the answer key and discuss what they find.

Chapter 3   Drama

Vocabulary: Write the word "Drama" on the board and ask students what they think of when they hear the word. Jot down their answers on a "map" like the following:

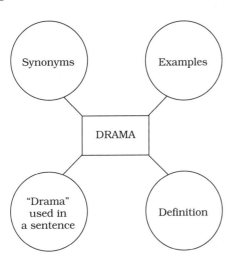

Point out that unlike the forms of literature discussed in earlier chapters, drama is written to be performed by actors and actresses.

Brainstorming: Tell students to preview the chapter opener on pages 332–333 to get an idea of what the chapter will be about. What do they see when they glance at the picture? (dancers performing)—the headings? (Drama, What is Drama?)—the words in dark print? (drama, playwrights, play, script) What will the chapter probably be about? (literature, such as the play, that is written to be performed)

Read page 332 aloud and discuss the Prereading Prompt. As students offer ways that writers help play audiences experience what they are watching, jot ideas on the board. To elicit ideas, ask, "How do good actors and actresses portray emotions realistically? What kinds of realistic props have you seen? How can lighting be used to set the mood, suggest the time of day, etc?)

Vocabulary: Read page 333 aloud. Then have student pairs write sentences using the four key words—

putting all four words into one sentence, if possible (e.g. After studying drama for several years, the playwright wrote his first play and sold the script for $5,000.)

Mindmap: Draw these graphics on the board:

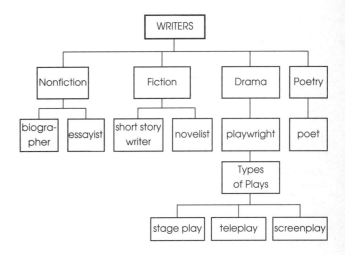

Ask these questions to check for comprehension: How is a playwright different from a novelist? (Playwright writes plays; novelist writes novels.)

How is a stage play different from a teleplay or a screenplay? (Stage play is performed on stage; teleplay is for television; screenplay is for film.)

Lesson 1: Literal Comprehension of Drama

Lesson Warm-Up

Role Playing: Tell students to think about what they did during the few minutes before class began. How did they enter the classroom? With whom did they chat? What did they say? How were they feeling? Would that have been evident to anyone watching them?

Have pairs of volunteers reenact those few minutes before class. Tell the "audience" to note not only what the "actors" say, but how they say it, and what they do. Jot down what is said, in dialogue form:

NAME:
OTHER NAME:

Have "audience" members help you fill in some stage directions. (Ask these questions: What does the room look like? How did he enter the room? Where did he go? What tone of voice did he use? What gestures did he make? Model for students how stage directions are put in parentheses.)

Vocabulary: Write the Key Words (*dialogue, stage directions*) on the board, pronounce them, and discuss their meanings. Reinforce their meanings by having students complete the following sentences:

- The dialogue between the husband and wife at the beginning of the play tells what they _____ (*sample:* argue about after a party)
- The stage directions at the beginning of the play tell that the story _____ (*sample:* takes place in a living room)

Brainstorming: Read the Prereading Prompt aloud and have students share memories of taking part in plays as you jot down what they say on the board.

Lesson Activities

Vocabulary: Read aloud together the section, "Dialogue and Stage Directions." As you come across difficult vocabulary words, check for understanding. For example, ask: What are italics? What are parentheses? How are descriptive passages different from lines of dialogue? (Dialogue is direct conversation; descriptive passages contain a narrator's explanation of what was said, done, etc.) What does an unassuming voice sound like? How do you look if you step, then falter?

Check to make sure that students understand what dialogue and stage directions are by having them reread the excerpt on pages 29–30 of the Predictor Test and asking questions about the dialogue and stage directions. For instance, how can students identify stage directions? (parentheses and italics) What do they learn from the stage directions about where Eddie is? (sitting at the table) What do the stage directions show about Eddie's reaction on hearing how much money Beatrice would make? (He is surprised.) What does Eddie's line, "You'll never get nowheres unless you finish school" show you about him? (He values education; his grammar indicates that he himself may not have had a lot of education.)

Summary Discussion: Lead an oral, whole-group discussion of each section. Ask, What can you learn from dialogue? What might some literal questions about dialogue ask? (What characters say helps you under-stand past and present events as well as hopes for the future. Some sample questions might be: What line tells you *X*? What does character *X* say about *Y*?) What can you learn from stage directions? What might some literal questions about stage directions ask? (Stage directions often tell you where the play is set, and when; how a character gestures or speaks. Some sample questions might be: What does the character do after she says *X*? Where does the scene take place?)

Reading Strategies Instruction: Ask students what question they should be asking themselves as they read the scene from the play—in their own words. (For example, What does Martin think he has done wrong?) Have student pairs take turns reading aloud the instructions and model passage on page 336. After students have finished the passage, ask them to state in their own words what the passage is about. (If necessary, elicit a summary by asking these questions: What time of day is it? Where are Richie and Martin? How can you tell that they are friends? What is wrong with Martin? Why is he bandaged? Why does he vomit every morning? What does Martin mean by the last line, "I don't care. I'd be out"?) Before students try to answer the question, point out how important it is to understand key words in the question—and to try to predict the answer before reading the passage. They are looking for lines that tell how Martin reacts "physically." Ask what it means to react physically (to have a body response, such as getting a headache, blushing, breaking out in a rash, vomiting).

Before students read the text explanation on page 337, ask them to explain in their own words why the right answer is right and why the other choices are wrong. Discuss any differences between their answers.

Further GED instruction and practice about literal comprehension of dialogue and stage directions can be found in *The New Revised Cambridge GED: Interpreting Literature and the Arts*, Chapter 3, Lessons 1 and 2. Pre-GED work on dramatic dialogue can be found in the *Threshold* text on literature and the arts, Unit 1, Chapter 3, Lesson 6.

Role Playing: Have partners assume the roles of Martin and Richie. First, partners discuss these questions: What story Martin and Richie might come up with? Who might be the first person to ask about Martin's wrist? How and why is he or she asking? What might both Richie and Martin say and do, in response? Would the questioner believe them? Then partners write the dialogue, add stage directions, and act out the scene.

Narrative: Have students discuss the following three ideas with a partner, then write a dialogue based on one of the ideas.

- Describe the argument you and someone else had over how to arrange the furniture after moving into a new place.

- Describe an argument you had with a friend over something he didn't think you should have done.
- Describe a conversation you had with a friend who was worried about you.

Partners share what they have written and help each other improve the dialogue (to sound more natural), and the stage directions (to make the actors' gestures more clear).

Lesson Wrap-Up

Exercise Discussion: Give students five minutes to complete the Lesson 1 Exercise on page 337. Remind students to read the questions before reading the passage and to try looking in the passage for key words from the question (for example, try looking for something that sounds like "a bad day to make candy" when answering Exercise 2). Point out also that questions that ask about the setting or the actors' motions (such as Exercise 3) probably can be answered by looking at stage directions—words in parentheses—rather than dialogue.

Before students look at the answer key, discuss each question with the class, eliciting opinions about what the correct answers are, what the wrong choices are, and why. Encourage students to defend different opinions, referring to the passage for supportive evidence, until a consensus is reached.

Answer Key Discussion: Students should compare their reasoning carefully with that outlined in the answer key and discuss what they find.

Lesson 2:   Inferential Comprehension of Drama

Lesson Warm-Up

Vocabulary: Review with students what they learned about the meaning of *inference* in Chapter 1, Lesson 2. (The writer gives the reader certain clues, which the reader uses to *infer* information that is not directly stated—"read between the lines.")

Role Playing: Have partners do a "Reader's Theater" performance of the excerpt from *You Can't Take It with You*, on page 337. (Readers are seated facing each other so that they can see each other's expressions. Both remain seated and read their lines with feeling, while gesturing.) Ask these questions: What can you infer about the season during which this scene is set? (It's hot, so it is probably summer.) How can you infer that the story probably takes place sometime before the present day? (Essie is typing, not using a word processor.) We aren't told why or how Penny asks, "Do you have to make candy today, Essie?" How can you infer that Penny probably makes the comment to be sympathetic—not to show her

impatience with Essie? (She seems proud of Essie's candy-making; shortly after asking the question, she compliments Essie on the success she and Ed are having in getting candy orders.)

Point out that whenever they read or watch plays—just as when they read or listen to fiction—students are continually putting clues together to find unstated meanings.

Write the Key Word (motivation), on the board, pronounce it, and read the definition aloud.

Discuss this question with students: What is your *motivation* for working toward an equivalency diploma?

Brainstorming: Draw the following graphic on the board.

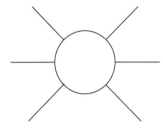

Write this statement in the circle and have students brainstorm ideas about the person's *motivation*. ("Why did the person do what he or she did?")

He told police that he had murdered the shopkeeper, although he hadn't.

Jot down student ideas on the "spokes."

Sample answer:

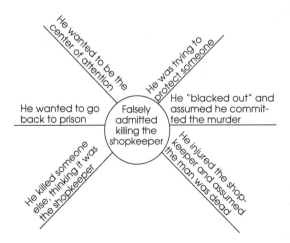

Repeat, using these statements:
1. She packed the hotel towel in her suitcase.
2. He gave away his lunch.
3. She moved to another country.
4. He went on a diet.
5. She pretended not to see him.

6. He ate the last piece of pie.

7. She stayed with him despite the abuse.

8. He cleaned up the apartment.

Write the following words on the board, and have students brainstorm ideas about various actions that might be motivated by each. (*Note:* Teacher should brainstorm *resentment* and *status-conscious* before beginning this activity.

Greed

Love

Fear

Selfishness

Generosity

Desire to please

Frustration

Resentment

Confusion

Being "status conscious"

Sample Answer:

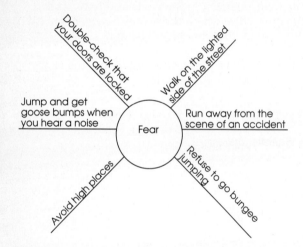

Lesson Activities

Vocabulary: After reading aloud the Prereading Prompt, read together the first section, "Making Inferences in Drama," As you come across difficult vocabulary words, check for understanding. For example, ask: What is a character's motivation? (his reasons for doing what he does) As you watch a play, how can you figure out a character's motivation? (Pay attention to his words and actions and what preceded them.) What are interactions between people? (how people behave toward each other; what they say and do when they are face to face) Can you think of an example of how "Your knowledge of the way people interact gives you an idea of cause and effect in the behavior of people that helps you interpret dramas..."? (For example, as you read the excerpt on

page 29, you can relate what you know about parents and their teenaged children. You know that most parents want their children to finish school and do well in life. Therefore, you can understand Eddie's anger when Catherine proposes taking an office job.) What is a person's "attitude"? What are some different attitudes that one person might have toward another? (Attitude is a person's manner or belief. Some words that describe attitudes are: *affectionate, condescending, annoyed, respectful, tolerant.*)

Before students read the next two sections ("Inferring Setting" and "Inferring Theme") on their own, discuss these words and their meanings:

• **Excerpt:** Portion of a piece of writing, such as a scene from a play.

• **Underlying truth:** Basic fact about life, such as "Everyone has to die sometime, so enjoy life while you can."

• **Conveyed:** Indicated or shown; "The frown on her face conveyed her anger."

• **Dramatic conflict:** Tension between characters; "The play centers around the dramatic conflict between white and black South Africans."

Summary Discussion: Lead an oral, whole-group discussion of each section. *Ask:* "How do you often learn the setting of a play?" (sometimes by statements a character makes directly about the setting, but often by putting clues together from what characters say and do) What are some clues to the theme of a play? (title, plot, dialogue, actions, setting, mood) How is inferring the theme of a play like inferring the main idea of a passage? (You connect details into a general summary; instead of facts, the details describe attitudes and conflicts.)

Application: Have students refer to earlier play excerpts and discuss what they infer about the setting from what the characters say and do. (For example: page 336: As Martin flops on a bunk and talks about enlisting and feeling terribly scared, we gather that this is an army bunkhouse, somewhere close to a battlefield; page 337: By watching Penny type on a typewriter and hearing Essie mention that her mother is a writer, we infer that the scene is set in Penny's study, sometime in the past.)

Reading Strategies Instruction: Ask students what question they should be asking themselves as they read the scene from the play—in their own words (For example: What has come right before this scene?)

Have student pairs take turns reading aloud the instructions and model passage on page 341. After students have finished the passage, ask them to say in their own words what the passage is about. (If necessary, elicit a summary by asking these questions: Why is Edna shaking a book as the scene begins? Why does Mel hope someone will have a car accident and die? What items have been stolen? Why is Mel so upset about having his shaving cream stolen? Where does Mel think Edna should have hidden the money? At the end, what tone of voice do you think Mel uses in talking to Edna? Have you ever been robbed? Was your reaction at all like Mel and Edna's? How did you feel as you read this excerpt? Saddened? Angered? Amused?) Before students try to answer the multiple-choice question, remind them to try to predict what statement about life the author is making, before reading the passage. Help elicit that prediction by asking, "What do all the details—Mel's outrage about the fact that the shaving cream was stolen along with the TV, Edna's disgust that they looked in the medicine chest and even in her book, her anger toward "sick people" who would take dental floss and mouthwash—say about crime today?"

Before students read the text explanation on page 337, ask them to explain in their own words why the right answer is right and why the other choices are wrong. Discuss any differences between their answers. As students read the answer key explanation, point out the importance of reading the question carefully. Students are looking for the author's general statement about life today, not any single statement that one of the characters might make. Therefore, choice 3 is wrong, even though it is a statement made by Edna.

For further GED instruction and practice, see *The New Revised Cambridge GED Program: Interpreting Literature and the Arts*, Chapter 3, Lesson 3 and 4.

Narrative: Have students discuss the following ideas with a partner, then write a dialogue based on one of the ideas. (Students should provide clues to the setting, but not state it directly.)

1. A real memory you have of a time you talked with someone about your feeling that someone else had taken advantage of you.
2. A real memory you have of your reaction to being robbed.

Partners share what they have written and help each other improve the piece (for example, by adding details that show the characters' attitudes more clearly and taking out unnecessary details). The entire group applies concepts from the lesson to draw inferences about the setting and theme of the piece.

Lesson Wrap-Up

Exercise Discussion: Give students five minutes to complete the Lesson 2 Exercise on pages 342–343. Remind students to read the questions before reading the passage, and to try predicting the answer before examining the choices. Point out also that questions about the characters' movements require the student to refer to stage directions. Since Exercise 3 asks about Mary's "reactions" to what she

sees out the window, students should refer to the place where Mary goes to the window and skim all that she says and does afterward.

Before students look at the answer key, discuss each question with the class, eliciting opinions about what the correct answers are, what the wrong choices are, and why. Encourage students to defend different opinions, referring to the passage for supportive evidence, until a consensus is reached.

Answer Key Discussion: Students should compare their reasoning carefully with that outlined in the answer key and discuss what they find.

Lesson 3: Applying Ideas in Drama

Lesson Warm-Up

Brainstorming: After reading and discussing the Prereading Prompt, point out that writers usually try to make characters act in fairly "consistent" predictable ways—as real people with particular personalities usually do. As a character enters a new situation, the writer asks herself, "How would my character react to this problem or this person?" Similarly, readers and audiences constantly apply characters' attitudes to new situations—something the GED asks students to do.

Tap students' real-life experiences with applying ideas in drama by discussing these questions: Have you ever read a novel or story about a lead character you have read about before and noticed that something was "wrong" with the way he or she behaved?—that is, the person's actions or words were out of character?

Have you ever been disappointed by the ending of a movie or by a sequel because the main character didn't do what you expected him to do, knowing his personality?

Lesson Activities

Vocabulary: Separate students into small groups and have them discuss the following words that are found in the lesson: *emotional, rational, philosophies, recruited, motives, exploiting, promotion, sympathize, self-defeating, measly.*

Students should work together to come up with a group definition for each word or phrase (helping each other find the word in the dictionary, if necessary). Students should also use the words in sentences.

Then have students read the lesson aloud in groups, taking turns so that they can spot additional words they do not understand and help each other figure out the meanings. Encourage students to discuss each section after the group has completed it, using the difficult vocabulary words in their own paraphrases and asking fellow group members questions about the section.

Applying the Playwright's and Character's Attitude:
With whom do you side in the conflict between Rose and Troy? With whom does the author side?

Summary Discussion: Instruct each group to agree on a summary of each of the lesson sections (page 344 to top of page 346). Then have the groups share the summaries with the class for discussion.

Lesson Activities

Narrative Activity 1: Have a student tell a narrative about dealing with someone in authority: dealing with police; with a boss; with a parent; with authorities in a government office; or with authorities in a school. The narrator-student could spell out his or her attitude in specifics: "I told the principal that if she didn't provide sex education classes as well as free condoms by the end of the week, I would immediately stage a walkout and get as many students as I could to follow." Ask students to:

1. Describe or name the narrator's attitude.
2. Describe another situation in which the narrator's attitude would come out: any other situation in which the person is frustrated, and how he or she gets around it.
3. Compose another narrative, identifying the narrator's attitude, and see if the attitudes of the narrators in the two narratives can be transposed. Ask, "How would the first narrator act in situation 2?"
4. Once any attitude-of-narrator is identified, say how one of them—one of the students—might have acted differently or ask "What do you think the opposite or very contrasting attitude might be?" (student at school: by contrast, he might have appealed to a higher authority and gotten what he wanted, or he might have gone home and written a letter of protest; he could have requested a meeting with the principal to lay out his ideas)

Narrative Activity 2: Have students recall a situation in which they were uncomfortable or embarrassed. "What values do they have that caused them to feel that way?"

Examples:

• A time when they felt they were being sexually harassed
• A time when they felt they were treated unfairly by someone in authority
• A time when they felt they could not tell someone the truth
• A time when they felt someone they liked was not being honest with them
• A time when they disagreed about money with someone

Have "audience" students predict how the person narrating would react in one of the *other* situations listed here—or in a situation suggested by the teacher or other students.

Reading Strategies Instruction: Have student volunteers take turns reading the instructions and model passage on page 346. (Stop them after they read the purpose question, Why does Biff think his life is mixed up? and have them put the question in their own words. Remind students to keep that question in mind as they read the passage.) After students have finished the passage, ask them to say in their own words what Happy and Biff are talking about. (If necessary, elicit a summary by asking these questions: What sorts of jobs did Biff take during the six or seven years after high school? Why? How did he feel about those jobs? Where is he working now? How does he feel about his current job? Why has he come home? How does Happy react to Biff? What does Biff think might make him happy? What do you think might make you happy? Have you ever had any of the thoughts about the future that Biff is having? Do you agree with him?)

Do the model question together. Before students read the text explanation on page 347, ask them to explain in their own words why they have chosen a particular answer and why the other choices are wrong. Discuss differences among their answers.

For additional practice in applying ideas in drama, ask students these questions:

• Which presidential candidate do you think Biff would have voted for in the last election? Why?
• What kind of reading materials do you think Biff enjoys? Why?
• What movies or TV shows would Biff enjoy?
• What job do you think Biff would be most happy at?
• What do you think Biff would do if he won or inherited a lot of money?

The following two situations could be acted out:

• What do you think Biff would say if Happy suggested that his life would have more meaning if he volunteered to help the needy?
• What do you think Biff would advise Troy to say to the recruiters if Troy were his son? (See the passage on page 345.)

Debate: After reading the first section, students can debate the following statements:

• Troy is right. If you are a black male college student, sports won't get you anywhere. You should put your energy into learning how to make a living.
• Rose is right. It's an honor to be recruited and her son should accept.
• Bitterness is self-defeating.

- Anger can be constructive.
- If Troy had a daughter who was being recruited for the women's basketball team, he would say the same thing.

Role Playing: Have students act out the following situations:

- Troy talks directly to one of the football recruiters about his son's college plans.
- Rose reports back to her son on the conversation she had with Troy.

For further GED instruction and practice, see *The New Revised Cambridge GED Program: Interpreting Literature and the Arts*, Chapter 3, Lesson 6.

Lesson Wrap-Up

Exercise Discussion: Give students five minutes to complete the Lesson 3 Exercise on pages 347–348. Before students look at the answer key, discuss each question with the class, eliciting opinions about what the correct answers are, what the wrong choices are, and why. Encourage students to defend different opinions, referring to the passage for supportive evidence, until a consensus is reached.

Point out that students can try predicting the answer to a question like Exerciese 2 before looking at the choices. Questions such as Exercises 1 and 3, however, require that the student read each choice carefully to test whether it is like or consistent with the situation in the play.

Answer Key Discussion: Students should compare their reasoning carefully with that outlined in the answer key and discuss what they find.

Lesson 4: Analyzing the Effects of Language in Drama

Lesson Warm-Up

Brainstorming: After reading aloud the Prereading Prompt, have students demonstrate as many ways as they can think of to say "hello," varying tone of voice and body language. Students should discuss what feelings are conveyed by each—and how.

Students might try the same exercise, with another short phrase, such as "Don't worry about it," or "Excuse me," or "I'm sorry," or "Really?"

Vocabulary: Write the Key Word (*gestures*) on the board, pronounce it, and read the definition. Talk with students about how actors (and the rest of us) use "body language" to communicate (with—or instead of—words). Demonstrate two or three gestures (such as using a finger to beckon or raising your

shoulders in a questioning shrug). Then have students work in pairs to come up with as many gestures as they can. Have the whole group reconvene and share, with "audience members" suggesting how you should describe the gesture being demonstrated in words on the board.

Next, read the following lines to your students:

> *Speaker 1:* She don't plan to go out that there way.
>
> *Speaker 2:* She doesn't plan to leave by that door.
>
> *Speaker 3:* She does not intend to depart via that exit.

Ask what the different style of language used in each case shows about the speaker. (Elicit the idea that speaker 1 may not be as well-educated, or at least as careful to use proper grammar—as speaker 2; speaker 3 may be well-educated but affected.)

Lesson Activities

Vocabulary: Separate students into small groups and have them discuss the following words that are found in the lesson: *portray, stage directions, techniques, casually, agitation, bodily motions, obscure, gasp, realism, malarkey, illusions, misrepresent, expose, resistance.* Students should work together to come up with a group definition for each word or phrase (helping each other find the word in the dictionary, if necessary). Students should also use the words in sentences.

Then have students read the lesson aloud in groups, taking turns so that they can spot additional words they do not understand and help each other figure out the meanings. Encourage students to discuss each section after the group has completed it, using the difficult vocabulary words in their own paraphrases and asking fellow group members questions about the section. (To elicit some of this discussion, put these questions on the board: What are three techniques playwrights use to convey their ideas? (what characters do, say, and how they gesture) How do you know what tone of voice a character is using? (It might be mentioned in the stage directions.) What can a character's style of language tell you about the character? (something about her background, age, education) How can "creating a movie in your mind" help you answer questions about drama on the GED exam? (Imagining the characters on stage can help answer specific questions about gestures—and help in general comprehension of the story.)

Application: Ask students what emotions are revealed by these gestures (from excerpts in the preceding lesson):

(p.347)   Miss Cooper gently propels Sibyl to the sofa (concern, tenderness)

She pats Sibyl's knee affectionately (affection)

(p.346)   Biff speaks "after a pause"—line 25—(hope-lessness, searching for words)

(p.342)   Mary, evading Edmund's eyes (doesn't want to be honest about her concern, doesn't want to worry him)

Ask students to look again at excerpts in the previous lesson and discuss how the playwright uses language to get across his or her ideas (For example: What do the following lines from page 347 show about Miss Cooper's educational level, age, and attitudes? "I've never met an ordinary person...In a sort of way, it's an insult to our Maker, don't you think, to suppose that He could possibly work to any set pattern?" (Miss Cooper seems to have lived a fairly long time, to be well-spoken, well-educated, religious, with a respect for people's differences.) Page 345: (Rose) "The white man ain't gonna let him get nowhere with that foot-ball. I told him when he first come to me with it." (He is black, angry with whites, rather authoritarian—would rather tell his son what to do than talk with him about it; probably doesn't have the level of educa-tion he wants his son to get.)

Summary Discussion: Lead an oral class review of the lesson. Have students write down one- or two-sen-tence summaries, using the words *playwright*, *stage directions*, *style of language*, and *gestures*. Students then share their summaries with the class.

Reading Strategies Instruction: Have student volun-teers take turns reading the instructions and model passage on pages 350–351. (Stop them after they read the purpose question, "What is Blanche's view of life?"and have them put the question in their own words. Remind students to keep that question in mind as they read the passage.) After students have finished the passage, ask them to state in their own words what Blanche and Mitch are arguing about. (If necessary, elicit a summary by asking these ques-tions: How can you tell that Blanche doesn't like to be in the light? How can you tell that that makes Mitch angry? What is Blanche's explanation? Do you think she understands her own feelings? Does Mitch? How does Mitch make more light in the room? What is Blanche's reaction? Why do you think Mitch does it—because he is angry, or because he wants to help Blanche, or both? What has Blanche done in the past to make Mitch bitter?)

Do the model question together. Before students read the text explanation on pages 351–352, ask them to explain in their own words why they have chosen a particular answer and why the other choices are wrong. Discuss any differences among their answers. *Note:* By a printer's error, the last sentence in the explanation is incomplete. It should conclude: "she does not know that Mitch believes she is not straight."

For additional practice in analyzing the effects of language in drama, ask students these questions:

- Who uses better grammar—Mitch or Blanche? (Blanche)
- Who uses rougher language, including curses? (Mitch uses rougher language; both curse, but Blanche's curse is more literary—"Let me be damned for it" while Mitch's is more crude and direct—"Christ!")
- Whose language is more direct and concrete? (Mitch's) Whose is more flowery and abstract? (Blanche's)

For further GED instruction and practice, see *The New Revised GED Program: Interpreting Literature and the Arts,* Chapter 3, Lessons 6 and 7. For Pre-GED work, see the *Threshold* literature and arts text, Unit 3, Chapter 2, Lesson 19.

Role Playing: Have students act out how Blanche and Mitch celebrate Blanche's birthday (or don't). Have students act out a recent argument they had with someone.

Narrative: Have students form small groups and recount an episode (orally, then in writing) in which they had an argument with someone of a different sex, age, and/or educational background. Then have other group members discuss how the writer's use of language reveals something about how the characters differ, and suggest how the language might be improved to bring the characters more "to life."

Lesson Wrap-Up

Exercise Discussion: Give students five minutes to complete the Lesson 4 Exercise on pages 352–353. Before students look at the answer key, discuss each question with the class, eliciting opinions about what the correct answers are, what the wrong choices are, and why. Point out that students should have tried to predict the answers to all three questions before look-ing at the choices (Although students probably can't predict the correct answer to a negatively phrased questions such as number 2, emphasize that they CAN brainstorm reasons the playwright WOULD end the scene that way. When done before looking at choices, this makes eliminating wrong choices quicker and easier.) Encourage students to defend different opinions, referring to the passage for supportive evi-dence, until a consensus is reached.

Answer Key Discussion: Students should compare their reasoning carefully with that outlined in the answer key and discuss what they find.

Chapter 4   Poetry

Vocabulary: Write the word "Poetry" on the board and ask students what they think of when they hear the word. Some questions to elicit responses might be: What is poetry? What is special about poetry? What can poetry be about? What poems do you remember reading or hearing? Can you think of the names of some poets?

Tell students to preview the chapter opener on pages 354–355 to get an idea of what the chapter will be about. What do they see when they glance at the picture? (a stream in the snow), the headings? (Poetry, What Is Poetry?), the words in bold print? (images, metaphor) Putting all these clues together, what will the chapter probably be about? (how poets use images and metaphors in writing poetry—a special type of literature that may be about nature or other things)

Read page 354 aloud and discuss the Prereading Prompt. Ask for a show of hands to indicate whether students would choose to watch a movie or read poetry. Why?

Brainstorming: Ask students to brainstorm a list of places where poetry can be found. What about song lyrics and advertisements and nursery rhymes? What do students like about poetry? Which kinds do they prefer? What don't they like about some poetry? Did they hear Maya Angelou read her work at President Clinton's inauguration? What did/didn't they like about that poem? Have students ever tried writing poetry themselves?

First, have students express their ideas in the following chart:

Similes	*Image* (Student draws picture)
1. _____ is like _____ because both_____ _____.	
2. _____ is like _____ because both _____ _____.	
3. _____ is like _____ because both _____ _____.	

Ask students to generate a list of similes they have heard.

Read page 355 aloud. Brainstorm the meaning of *metaphor*. Then read students each of the following metaphors. Ask students to describe the image created: "What do you see in your mind as you read those words?" (You might also point out that some imagery describes sounds, smells, sights, feelings, and tastes.) Then have them discuss what two things are being compared in each metaphor, and how those things are alike.

1. Life is a rat race.
2. My home is a three-ring circus.
3. The football player's legs were tree trunks.

Have students write some metaphors of their own, then share in a small group.

War is a _____.
Love is a _____.
Health is a _____.
The GED test is a _____.
Money is a _____.

Lesson 1:   Literal Comprehension of Poetry

Lesson Warm-Up

Brainstorming: Write the following statements on the board (or photocopy them) and have students label each on a scale of 1 to 5.

1	2	3	4	5
____/____/____/____/____/				
agree strongly				disagree strongly

1 (agree) to 5 (disagree):

___ Poems are hard to understand.

___ The language in poems is strange and wishy-washy.

___ Poems are about beautiful things like love and nature.

___ Poems rhyme.

___ A song is a poem.

___ Poems can tell a story.

___ I enjoy reading poetry.

___ I enjoy hearing poetry.

After students have completed the lesson, have them return to the statements to see whether they would change any of their responses.

Lesson Activities

Brainstorming: Read aloud the Prereading Prompt and have students list specific ideas that are expressed *directly* by songs. To get students started, you might put the following graphic on the board and jot down lyrics on the "spokes" as they are suggested.

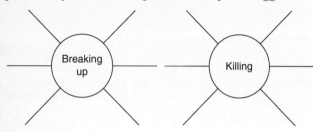

Vocabulary: Write the Key Words (*rhyme, rhythm, narrative poetry, lyric poetry*) on the board, pronounce them, and discuss their meanings. Reinforce their meanings by having students complete the following sentences:

- The _____ (rhythm) of the poem about rain reminds me of the pattern of sounds raindrops make when they fall on a rooftop.

    I think that I shall never see,
    a poem as lovely as a tree.
- The ends of these two lines _____.
- The short poem about the poet's sense of grief following the death of her father is an example of _____. (lyrical poetry)
- The poem that tells the story of lonely old Eben Flood who drinks from a jug by himself is an example of _____. (narrative poetry)

  Read aloud together the section, "The Form of Poetry." Emphasize that students should read poetry *aloud*. Poetry is written to be heard; only by listening to it can the rhythms and rhymes be fully appreciated. As you come across difficult vocabulary words, check for understanding. For example, ask: What is the difference between the form and the content of a poem? (Form is the arrangement of words; content is what the words are about.) How are lines related to stanzas? (Stanzas are groups of lines.) In the poem "Annabel Lee" on page 357, what do the capital letters and underlining show? (Accented, or "heavy" sounds that help set the rhythm.) How would you "clap out"

the rhythm of that poem? (Show students how to clap out stressed syllables while reading the poem aloud.)

  What does the text mean when it says that poems are like "nuggets" of thoughts? (A nugget is a small, rich piece—like a nugget of gold. Poets often use only a few words to capture a special, "rich" meaning.)

Application: For homework, have students remember and write down song lyrics they like and have them read them aloud. Suggest that they clap or use some other way to demonstrate the poem's rhythm. (For example, students might perform a rap piece complete with body motions and sound effects.)

Summary Discussion: After reading "The Form of Poetry" as a group, have students read "Finding Main Ideas and Details in Poems" with a partner. Student pairs should work together on one-sentence summaries of each poem, using the purpose questions ("What does the mill worker think of her life?" "What does the speaker think of sensations") as guides.

Graphics: Draw a Venn diagram on the board and have students discuss similarities and differences between lyrical and narrative poetry. Jot down ideas on the diagram. (A sample diagram follows:)

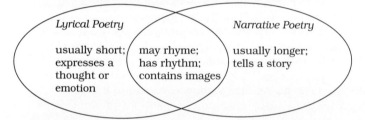

Reading Strategies Instruction: Have students form small groups and take turns reading aloud the James Taylor poem on page 358 and the instructions on page 359. Encourage them to discuss their thoughts, reactions, and questions about the song. Remind students to reword the question and predict the answer before looking at the choices. Make sure that students understand that they are trying to figure out what the millworker thinks about her entire life—not just millwork.

  Before students read the text explanation on page 359, ask them to explain in their own words why the right answer is right and why the other choices are wrong. Discuss differences among their answers.

  For further instruction and practice at the GED level, see *The New Revised GED Program: Interpreting Literature and the Arts*, Chapter 4, Lesson 1. For Pre-GED Work, see the *Threshold* text on literature and the arts, Unit 1 (the poems in it).

Role Playing: Discuss with students what gestures the millworker or the speaker in Rimbaud's poem might make. Encourage students not only to read the poems aloud, but to act them out.

Application: Have students discuss the rhyme, rhythm, and imagery of the James Taylor (only occasional rhyme, but a steady, repetitive rhythm; images of the speaker's grandfather, father, husband, children, mill) and Arthur Rimbaud pieces (no rhyme, uneven wandering rhythm—like the image of the speaker wandering like a gypsy), as well as the literal meaning of the Edgar Allen Poe and Countee Cullen poems on page 357 (Annabel Lee's love for the speaker and his for her; a black man's thoughts about his African heritage). As homework, have students bring in song lyrics or poems that demonstrate use of rhythm, rhyme, and/or imagery.

Lesson Wrap-Up

Exercise Discussion: Review with students the steps in answering a question about the main idea of a passage. (Read the passage with the purpose question in mind; identify the topic; look for the topic sentence of each paragraph; think of a general idea that covers all the topic sentences.) Point out the process for finding the main idea of a poem is similar—except that there is usually no topic sentence. Rather, students have to look for the general idea that covers all the details in the poem.

Give students five minutes to complete the Lesson 1 Exercise on page 360. Before students look at the answer key, discuss each question with the class, eliciting opinions about what the correct answers are, what the wrong choices are, and why. Encourage students to defend different opinions, referring to the passage for supportive evidence, until a consensus is reached.

Answer Key Discussion: Students should compare their reasoning carefully with that outlined in the answer key and discuss what they find.

Lesson 2: Inferring the Meaning of Figurative Language in Poetry

Lesson Warm-up

Vocabulary: Write the phrase *figurative language* on the board and read the text definition ("language that expresses more than just the dictionary definition" of the words). Point out that students have learned about one type of figurative language—the metaphor—in the last lesson, and that they will learn about another type—the simile—in this one. Check that students can identify figurative language by having them tell which sentence in the following pairs is figurative and which is literal.

- His brain is a sponge. (figurative)
- He has a good memory. (literal)

Have a student volunteer explain why the first sentence is figurative, not literal. (The words don't mean exactly what they say. His brain isn't really a sponge.) Ask how a brain and a sponge can be alike. (Both can take in. A sponge absorbs water. A brain can take in facts and ideas.)

Present students with these pairs of statements and have them distinguish the literal from the figurative language.

- He eats sloppily. (literal)
- He eats like a pig. (figurative)

- Talking with him is like walking on eggshells. (figurative)
- I have to be careful what I say when I talk with him. (literal)

- I saw red. (figurative)
- I felt very angry. (literal)

Write the Key Words (*simile, personification, symbol*) on the board, pronounce them, and discuss their meanings. Review also what a metaphor is (comparison without *like* or *as*). Have students work in pairs to create some similes and examples of personification on their own, using the following sentence starters:

For similes:

- Falling in love is like _____.
- My mother is like _____.
- The clouds are like _____.
- My anger is like _____.
- My favorite chair is like _____.

For personification:

- The moon smiles _____.
- The arms of the pines stretched out _____.
- The sun had no sympathy _____.

One partner explains to the other how the two ideas in the simile are alike.

Write the following on the board:

dove   heart   Uncle Sam

Ask students what each symbolizes ("What does each of these stand for?") (dove—peace; heart—love; Uncle Sam—United States)

Have students brainstorm other common symbols.

Lesson Activities

Brainstorming: Read aloud the Prereading Prompt and have students brainstorm a list of other common "figures of speech" (expressions). You might start the list yourself by writing:

You had better toe the line.

The car is a lemon.

What a nut she is.

His memory of the war is like an open wound.

Jot down the student ideas. Discuss what the expressions mean and ask students why figures of speech sometimes give ESL speakers trouble. (The words aren't meant to be taken literally.)

Then have students sort them according to which are similes and which are metaphors. (Your students would probably enjoy seeing and discussing Fred Gwynne's illustrated book of expressions, *Chocolate Moose.*)

Vocabulary: Write the following words (found in this lesson) on the board: *genres, reliance, suited, condensed language, nonhuman, represents, broader in scope.* Before students read the lesson, have them discuss what they know about the meanings of these words and phrases. (One student should look up and read the dictionary definition of words that are unfamiliar to all.) Afterward, ask these questions to test comprehension of the words: What is a genre? (type of literature) What genre is studied in this lesson? (poetry) What other genres were discussed in earlier lessons? (nonfiction, fiction, drama). How is poetry different from other genres? (reliance on figurative language) How are similes and metaphors suited to poetry? (helpful in giving brief descriptions) What is condensed language, and where might you find it? (A few words convey a lot of meaning; in poetry.) What is the nonhuman in this line: The moon holds nothing in her arms. (the moon). How is that nonhuman object like a human being? (The moon is like a woman with empty arms.) What idea does the Star of David represent? (Judaism) How is that idea "broader in scope" than the star itself? (The star is a simple pattern; it stands for a whole religion.)

Application/Graphics: Have students come up with their own simple symbols for the following: crime, drug use, poverty, homelessness, war.

Summary Discussion: Ask students how the point of this lesson was different from the point of the last lesson. (This lesson taught how to understand figurative language in poetry; the last lesson dealt with what the poet's words mean literally.)

Ask students to write two or three sentences in which they recall the important ideas the author has discussed (should include simile, personification, symbol).

Reading Strategies Instruction: Have students form small groups and take turns reading the instructions and model poem on page 363. Suggest that each student in the group read the poem once. Then have students react to the poem, stating what they "saw in

their mind" as it was read, what lines they especially liked, how they felt as they read the last line, whether it reminds them of anyone they know or anything they have experienced, what questions they have about the poem, and so on.

After discussion of the poem, have students try to predict the answer to the question about how the poet presents "day" in the poem. Before students read the text explanation on page 363, ask them to explain in their own words why they have chosen a particular answer and why the other choices are wrong. Discuss any differences between their answers.

For further GED instruction and practice, see *The New Revised Cambridge GED Program: Interpreting Literature and the Arts*, Chapter 4, Lesson 3. For Pre-GED work, see the poems in Unit 2 of the *Threshold* literature and arts text.

Application: Have students look for and discuss examples of simile, personification, and symbol in poems reprinted in the last lesson. (For example, students may note the simile in line 21 of Bob Dylan's song on page 361: "Whose visions in the final end must shatter like the glass.")

Lesson Wrap-Up

Exercise Discussion: Give students five minutes to complete the Lesson 2 Exercise on page 364. Before students look at the answer key, discuss each question with the class, eliciting opinions about what the correct answers are, what the wrong choices are, and why. Point out that students should have tried to predict the answers to all three questions before looking at the choices. Encourage students to defend different opinions, referring to the passage for supportive evidence, until a consensus is reached.

Answer Key Discussion: Students should compare their reasoning carefully with that outlined in the answer key and discuss what they find.

Lesson 3:   Applying Ideas in Poetry

Lesson Warm-up

Brainstorming: Read and discuss the Prereading Prompt. Elicit the ideas that Robin Hood, champion of the poor, would probably be against taxes that seem to hurt the poor more than others: Betsy Ross, who designed the flag, would probably be aghast at the idea of flag burning and might well advocate punishment; in today's world, Romeo and Juliet's family problems might erupt in gang warfare—or might be handled by counseling. Brainstorm Robin Hood, Betsy Ross, Romeo and Juliet in case students do not know about them.

Tap students' real-life experiences with applying ideas in poetry by asking these questions:

- Do you listen to the lyrics of any popular songs today and feel as if the singer is talking about your life?
- Have you ever been surprised by your favorite singer or group's latest song—because it doesn't seem to "fit" the ideas they sang about in earlier songs? (such as, a bitter song by someone who usually takes a positive attitude; a religious song by someone who had never seemed religious).

Lesson Activities

Vocabulary: Break students into small groups and have them discuss the following words that are found in the lesson: *universal, identify with, translate, looking glass, upon reflection, distinguish between, urban scene, pastoral scene, yearning, wretched refuse, teeming, tempest.*

Students should work together to come up with a group definition for each word or phrase (helping each other find the word in the dictionary, if necessary). Students should also use the words in sentences.

Then have students read the lesson aloud in groups, taking turns so that they can spot additional words they do not understand and help each other figure out the meanings. Encourage students to discuss each section after the group has completed it, using the difficult vocabulary words in their own paraphrases and asking fellow group members questions about the section. (To elicit some of this discussion, interject the questions suggested below.)

Applying Themes and Details: What is a "universal theme"? What are some examples? (an idea that many people recognize and experience, such as "Love conquers all"; "War is hell"; "Time heals all wounds".) What are all the things the world would see if it looked in a mirror? (hate, war, sorrow, fear) What do these things have in common? (All are bad; all have to do with our problems getting along together.) Why would the world run away? (in shame at all the bad things it had seen in itself) Why would the TV doze off? (from boredom at all the boring things it had seen) If the poet who wrote the TV poem had included three details about what the TV would see, what might they be? (Details should suggest boredom, directly or indirectly; such as, pointless sitcoms, meaningless violence, endless ads.)

Applying the Poet's Attitude: Have students look at other poems in this book or other poems they might have at home. Have them work in pairs and think up one situation that is different from the situation being described in the poem. Have them suggest how they think the poet/speaker would react in that situation, and state why. Others should comment on whether or not they agree with the pair's ideas by citing specific details from the poem that led them to their conclusion.

Summary Discussion: Instruct each group to agree on a summary of both of the lesson sections (page 365

to the middle of page 366). Then have the groups share the summaries with the class for discussion.

Reading Strategies Instruction: Have a student volunteer read the instructions and model poem on page 366. (Stop them after they read the purpose question and see if they have any ideas about what the poem may say.) After the volunteer has finished the poem, ask students to put into their own words what the words on the Statue of Liberty mean. Whom does the statue welcome?

Do the model question together. Remind students to read the purpose and test questions before reading the poem. Although they cannot predict the answer before looking at the choices, reading the test question ahead of time lets students know that they should be reading to determine the poet's ideas so that they can apply those ideas to the present day.

Before students read the text explanation on page 367, ask them to explain in their own words why they have chosen a particular answer and why the other choices are wrong. Discuss any differences between their answers.

For additional practice in applying the poet's attitude, refer to poems in the preceding lesson and encourage students to tie them in with items in the news today. For example, what would Langston Hughes say about the LA riots after the Rodney King trial? What examples might he point to as problems that have arisen because of "dreams deferred"? (urban crime, racial tensions on various college campuses, etc.) Looking at how minorities reacted to the last election, would he say that their dream "dried up" or "festered" or "crusted over" or "exploded"?

For further instruction and practice, see *The New Revised GED Program: Interpreting Literature and the Arts*, Chapter 4, Lesson 4.

Application: Have students write their own poem, using Vannessa Howard's poem as a model and any of these first lines as starters:
- If _____ looked in a looking glass, (our president, the white man, doctors, the computer, name of a famous athlete)

Lesson Wrap-Up

Brainstorming: Have students brainstorm what they learned about applying ideas from Lesson 3 of Chapters 1, 2, and 3. Then have them brainstorm a list of important ideas from this lesson and discuss how applying ideas in poetry is like/different from applying ideas from other genres. (In all cases, the student must first comprehend what the writer is saying, then build a bridge of ideas to what the author might say about a different situation.)

Exercise Discussion: Before students do the Lesson 3 Exercise, review the steps to take when answering any GED item.

1. Read the poem with its purpose question and then read the questions. (Poems require more careful, focused reading than is required by prose.)
2. After reading the questions, read the poem again to find the answer.
3. Apply the process of elimination.
4. Read the question + the remaining, best choice to make sure that it sounds like the best answer.

Give students five minutes to complete the Lesson 3 Exercise on pages 367–368. Before students look at the answer key, discuss each question with the class, eliciting opinions about what the correct answers are, what the wrong choices are, and why. Encourage students to defend different opinions, referring to the passage for supportive evidence, until a consensus is reached. Point out that students can try predicting the answer to all three questions before looking at the choices.

Answer Key Discussion: Students should compare their reasoning carefully with that outlined in the answer key and discuss what they find.

Lesson 4:   Analyzing Poetry

Lesson Warm-Up

Brainstorming: After reading aloud the Prereading Prompt , have students suggest other sounds that filmmakers use—say, at the opening of a movie, before the first picture has come on the screen—to create certain effects or moods (such as, violin music to create a romantic mood, the "rat-a-tat" of gunfire to suggest violence; seagulls and waves gently slapping the shore to suggest a calm, relaxed feeling). Point out that poets also use "sound effects" and write these lists on the board.

1. big, bragging, bruising bully ("b" sounds to suggest the brutal power, loudness, and size of the bully)
2. "I hear the lake water lapping with low sounds by the shore" (William Butler Yeats, "The Lake Isle of Innisfree": "l" sounds for a gentle, soothing, or lulling effect)
3. "Good things of day begin to droop and drowse" (William Shakespeare, *Macbeth*: "d" sounds to suggest the sinking downward of animals and plants into the sleep and darkness of night
4. Cold, old, bones—"o" sounds to suggest a sense of loneliness and hollow emptiness

Ask: Which repeated sound suggests rapid-fire action, change, explosiveness? (repeated "p") What sounds make you think of smoothness and mildness? (repeated "s", repeated "m") How does the repeated "o" sound make you feel? (sense of emptiness, hollowness)

Discussion: Review with students some of the different moods/tones an author can create (as discussed in Chapter 2, Lesson 4). Point out that many of the words used to describe mood are also used to describe weather (gloomy, threatening, oppressive, cheerful, tranquil). Many words used to describe the tone of a poem or other piece of literature are also used to describe a person's speaking voice (pessimistic, frightened, triumphant, sad, angry)

Vocabulary: Write the Key Words (*alliteration, assonance*) on the board , then read the words and their definitions aloud. Ask students to explain the difference. (*Alliteration* involves repetition of initial consonant sounds, *assonance* involves repetition of internal vowel sounds.) Have students label each of the four word lists as examples of alliteration (the first three) or assonance (the last one). Then have students create sentences using alliteration and assonance (as silly as they like) to share with the group.

Lesson Activities

Vocabulary: Write the following words and phrases on the board and pronounce them: *presentation, patterns of sounds, basic technique, repetition, consonant, raven, melancholy, anguish, drowsily.* Ask students to share what they *think* the words mean and to use the words in sentences. (Explain that after they are finished reading the entire lesson, they will work with a partner on revising/changing the sentences based on what they learned.)

Have students read the section, "Effects of Sound in Poetry" and ask these questions: What are two ways in which a poet can create a mood? (through the images presented and the sounds used). What are three ways a poet can repeat sounds? (rhyme, alliteration, assonance) What are the lines from the Poe poem about? (looking into the dark, thinking frightening thoughts) What sound is repeated? ("d") What is the effect? Why? (The repeated "d" helps create a mysterious, fearful effect—partly because of the dull, cheerless sound of "d" itself. Also, the "d" sound became linked with mysterious ideas in the first line—deep/dark—so we continue to link this sound with a feeling of mystery in the second line—in "doubting," "dreaming," "dared.") What are the lines from the Keats poem about? (someone falling asleep) What sound is repeated? ("ow") What is the effect? Why? (emptiness, heaviness; the sound itself is hollow, and the words containing the sound—"drowsily"/"drown" —both suggest heavy descent)

Summary Discussion: Have students write a summary of the main points of the lesson, using the following frame.

1. Three sound effects used by poets are
   a. _____, which is _____.
   b. _____, which is _____.
   c. _____, which is _____.

2. All three types of repeated sounds help create the _____.

Answers: 1. Rhyme, repeated end sounds; alliteration, repeated beginning consonants; assonance, repeated vowel sounds in words; 2. mood of the poem.

Students share their summaries with the group or with a partner.

Application: Have students identify examples of all three types of repeated sounds in poems found in the previous three lessons. For example, in Herford's poem on page 367, every other line rhymes. There are several examples of alliteration —like the repeated "s" sounds in "suddenly"/"space" (l2) and the repeated "h" sounds in "hissing, headlong"(l3)—and several examples of assonance—such as the repeated long "a" sounds in lines 13 and 15 ("say," "same," "exclaim")

Reading Strategies Instruction: Write these words on the board and discuss their meanings with students: *chipware, flatware, grandeur, foil, rod, generations, trod, toil, shod, spent, brink broods.*

Read the instructions and purpose question on page 370. Tell students to put the purpose question in their own words.(For example: What do the people in the poem keep remembering?) Then read the test question and have students paraphrase it. (For example: Why are lines 12 and 13 a good way to end the poem?) Finally, give students a minute to read the poem silently, then have a student volunteer to read the poem aloud.

Ask students to put down their books and share what they "see" and feel as they listen to the poem. (If necessary, ask these questions to elicit key images: How many people are there in the poem? Why did the poet choose this title? What are the dishes, table, knives, and forks like? Why are the couple "yellow"? How do the two spend most of their time? What do the words "twinklings and twingings" (line 11) show you about how the two feel as they remember? What do you "see" in the backroom, around the couple?

Do the first model question together. Point out that students should try to predict the answer before they look at the choices. However, even if their prediction is not listed, they can eliminate all of the other choices as incorrect because they are false. (Point out how important it is to refer to the lines in question and reread them.

Emphasize that questions of this sort—Why is the first/last line effective?—generally have one true choice and four choices that are incorrect because they are *false*—not just because they are irrelevant to the question. Once the student figures out the lines' meaning and their effect on him or her (how they make the student feel and what they help him or her "see"), choosing the right answer becomes simpler. Before students read the text explanation on page 371, ask them to explain in their own words why they have chosen a particular answer and why the other choices are wrong. Discuss any differences between their answers.

Repeat this process with the second model poem. After the volunteer has completed the poem, ask: As you read this poem, what do you see? hear? smell? feel? How do words like *grandeur, shining, greatness, freshness, springs* make you feel? What are the "last lights off the black West"? Make sure that students understand that the word *contrasts* in the question means "tells or shows the difference between." Have students predict the answer before examining the choices. Then have them compare their answers and reasons with each other's—and with the book's.

For further work at a Pre-GED level, see the *Threshold* text on literature and the art, Unit 3, Lesson 20. For GED work, see *The New Revised Cambridge GED Program: Interpreting Literature and the Arts*, Chapter 4, Lessons 5 and 6.

Lesson Wrap-Up

Vocabulary: Have students apply their new understanding of the vocabulary words listed during the Lesson Activity (vocabulary) by revising or rewriting the sentences they wrote for the vocabulary Lesson Activity.

Brainstorming: Have students brainstorm answers to this question: How does the material in this lesson relate to the material you have studied in earlier lessons in Chapter 4? (Like the previous three lessons, it is about understanding poetry; like all Lesson 4, it focuses on the writer's style—*how* she or he uses words.)

Exercise Discussion: Give students five minutes to complete the Lesson 4 Exercise on page 373. Remind students to reread the line or stanza to which a question refers. Have students explain how they figured out the meanings of some of the more difficult words in the poem, such as *boughs, helms, spurs, meditation.* Before students look at the answer key, discuss each question with the class, eliciting opinions about what the correct answers are, what the wrong choices are, and why. Encourage students to defend different opinions, referring to the passage for supportive evidence, until a consensus is reached.

Answer Key Discussion: Students should compare their reasoning carefully with that outlined in the answer key and discuss what they find.

<table>
<tr><td>Chapter
5</td><td># Commentary
on the Arts</td></tr>
</table>

Vocabulary: Write the sentence, "She wrote a comment on his composition" on the board. Ask what *comment* means (remark, observation, criticism). Write the word "Commentary" on the board and ask students if they know what it is (a type of writing in which the writer describes and evaluates a piece of literature or another form of art). Read two or three short examples of different types, such as a TV/video review from the "Life" section of *USA Today*, the commentary on Disney movies found on page 31 of the Predictor Test, and an art or music or book review from a newspaper (such as your local paper or *Rolling Stone*) or magazine (such as *Time* or *Newsweek*). Ask students what all these examples of commentary have in common and read them the text definition found on the top of page 375: "Commentary is a type of nonfiction prose about literature and other kinds of creative works."

Write the phrase "the arts" and have students brainstorm as many examples as they can. (literature, dance, music, painting, sculpture, film, etc.)

Tell students to preview the chapter opener on pages 374–375 to get an idea of what the chapter will be about. What do they see when they glance at the picture? (skyscrapers, some examples of city architecture); the headings? (Commentary, What Is Commentary on the Arts?); the words in bold print? (commentary, standards, critics, reviewers) Putting all these clues together, what will the chapter probably be about? (How to read commentary on the arts, in which critics and reviewers make judgments about such things as certain types of architecture.)

Read page 374 aloud and discuss the Prereading Prompt. Have students brainstorm a list of things they value in a good movie. (To elicit ideas, ask: What about the actors? How do you feel about violence? What type of ending do you look for?)

Jot down the ideas on the board under the phrase "Standards for a Good Movie."

Brainstorming: Ask students to brainstorm all that they know about commentary as you jot down their ideas on the board using this framework:

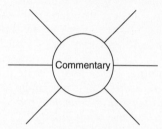

To elicit ideas, ask for a list of places where commentary can be found. What about the daily paper? Is there commentary on TV? on the radio? Have they ever read commentary in a newspaper or magazine? What's good about reading commentary? Have they ever written commentary, themselves—as in a letter to a friend about a recent movie they saw?

Lesson 1:   Literal Comprehension of Commentary

Lesson Warm-Up

Brainstorming: Write the following statements on the board (or photocopy them) and have students write down whether they agree (A) or disagree (D) with the statements, then discuss their reasons. Instruct them to see whether they change their minds about any of the statements as they read the lesson.

- Reviewers state an opinion and try to convince their readers to adopt that opinion, too. (A)
- Reviewers usually imply their opinions without stating them directly. (D)
- Reviewers give only opinions, not facts. (D)

Vocabulary: Write the Key Words (*facts, opinions*) on the board, pronounce them, and discuss their meanings. Have students write sentences using the words. Reinforce their meanings by writing the following statements on the board and having students label them F or O.

- Clint Eastwood's film *Unforgiven*, is favored to give Warner Brothers its sixth best-picture Oscar. (F)

- The Saturday TV special about Warner Brothers hosted by Eastwood is dull and disorganized.(O)
- The show contains several rejected screen tests of stars such as Marlon Brando, Lana Turner, and Paul Newman. (F)
- Paul Newman's audition as James Dean's brother on *East of Eden* is one to treasure. (O)

Lesson Activities

Brainstorming: Read aloud the Prereading Prompt. Tell students to think of a good recent movie, book, or song. Break students into pairs and have each student give his partner as many reasons as he can why he should see the movie (or read the book or listen to the music). Reconvene and discuss the types of reasons that come up (statistics—"It's broken box office records"; quotations—Siskel and Ebert both called it "hilarious").

Vocabulary: Write the following words and phrases from the lesson on the board and pronounce them: *painting exhibition, evaluate, sway, in-depth analysis, trend in music, contrast ideas, statistics.* Have students work in small groups to discuss the words' meanings, look the words up in a dictionary, and write sentences using the words. Read the first section, "Reviews," aloud, and ask these questions to check for general comprehension of the section and specific understanding of the difficult vocabulary words: What is a review, and what are some things that might be reviewed? (a piece of writing giving the author's opinion of a piece of art, such as a concert, show of paintings, play) What is another way of saying that a reviewer "evaluates" artwork? (judges, gives his opinion about) What are the "standards by which a reviewer judges artwork," and why does the reviewer often include them in the review? (The reviewer often gives the "measuring sticks" he uses, in order to sway the reader.)

Have a student volunteer to read the next section, "Essays," aloud. Draw the following graphic on the board:

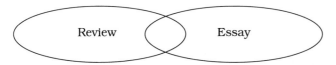

and ask: What is an essay, and how is it like a review? (Jot down in the overlapping area: Essays and reviews are both commentary on the arts.) What are two ways in which an essay is different from a review? (Jot down under "essay": often more detailed, often assumes the readers know something about the topic. Jot down under "review": often shorter, less in-depth; usually addressed to the general reading public.)

Summary Discussion: Have students read the remaining two sections of the lesson, "Stated Main Ideas" and "Supporting Details," with a partner, in a small group, or silently (only if they are high-level readers). Instruct each student to prepare a summary of the sections *in their own words,* using this frame:

Two ways that critics might present their main idea are _____ (as a conclusion based on several general statements) and _____ (by presenting ideas on one side, then their own, different ideas). To find the main idea of a piece of commentary, the first step is to _____. (figure out what the topic is and then decide what the reviewer is saying about it)

In a good review or essay, the writer should back up _____ (opinions) with facts. Four types of facts the critic might use are: _____, _____, _____, _____. (what an expert has said, numbers that have been collected, statements about how the piece is like a similar piece that has already been evaluated, backup statements that point to the storyline or something else specific in the writing)

Have students share and discuss their summaries.

Reading Strategies Instruction: Before students read the model passage, have them discuss what they already know about jazz singers such as Marvin Gaye and Anita Baker. Discuss the meanings of the following words from the review: *contradictions, inquisitive, predictable, flourishes, upscale make-out music, guarantee, aspirations.* Ask what two steps they should take before reading the review itself. (Read the purpose question and the test question.)

Have students form groups of four and take turns reading the four paragraphs of the passage aloud. (Stop them after they read the purpose question, "Why should this album be titled contradictions?") Ask what "contradictions" are and ask for some examples. (inconsistencies; one fact denies another or itself—two ideas don't "add up"; e.g.: "I believe in keeping fit, but I smoke.") Then ask, "In your own words, what question are you going to keep in mind as you read this passage?" (What is it about this collection of songs that doesn't quite "add up"?) Encourage them to put the review in their own words, and discuss their thoughts, reactions, and questions about the review.

After students have finished the entire section in groups, reconvene and ask them to state in their own words what the passage is about. (Ask these questions to check for understanding of difficult vocabulary words and comprehension of the main idea: What album is the writer talking about? What is a "solo" album? What is the writer's general opinion of Anita Baker? What is the writer's opinion of her fourth solo album? What does he mean by saying that she is a "jazz artist masquerading as a pop singer"? How is her singing like Sarah Vaughn's? How is it different? Is the writer complimenting or criticizing Anita Baker when he says that "her no-nonsense style is devoid of the heavy effect that marred much of Vaughn's work"? Which songs does the writer like? Why doesn't he like most of the other songs on the album? Why does the writer say that "Contradictions" would have been a good title for the album?

Review with students the steps in answering a question about the main idea of a passage. (Read the passage with the purpose question in mind; identify the topic; look for the topic sentence of each paragraph; think of a general idea that covers all the topic sentences.)

Ask students to write one sentence about the main idea of the passage, beginning "This album should be titled "Contradictions" because _____." Have students test the idea that the main idea they have come up with is a general statement that covers all the details and explains the main point the author is trying to make with them.

Do the model question together. Before students read the text explanation on pages 378 and 379, ask them to explain in their own words why the right answer is right and why the other choices are wrong. Discuss any differences between their answers.

For further GED instruction and practice, see *The New Revised Cambridge GED Program: Interpreting Literature and the Arts*, Chapter 5, Lesson 1. Students still having difficulty with literal comprehension of nonfiction writing might review the literal comprehension sections of the *Threshold* texts in social studies, science, and literature and the arts, as well as relevant parts of *On Your Own: Reading*, Units 1 and 2.

Debate: Have students brainstorm a list of songs or movies that have come out recently and vote on one to "review." Then have students who give the song or movie "thumbs up" sit on one side of the room and students who give the song or movie "thumbs down" sit on the other. Students who haven't heard the song or seen the movie or are undecided sit in the middle. Students on each side try to convince those in the middle that the song or movie is good/bad.

Application: For additional practice in literal comprehension of commentary, have students reread the essay on page 31 of the Predictor Test. Ask what the writer's opinion of Disney movies today is (not as good as they used to be), whether the writer presents the main idea as a conclusion based on general statements, or as a contrast (contrast—between what the writer remembered of Bambi and the writer's reaction to a recent Disney movie), and what facts the writer uses to support his/her opinion (specific references to the human characters in the recent show).

Lesson Wrap-Up

Exercise Discussion: Before students complete the Lesson 1 Exercise independently, have them discuss the meanings of the following words: *mooning, magpie, seductive hybrid, resistible, sappiness.* Ask who has seen the movie *Ghost,* and what those students thought of it. Encourage students to "weigh" pros and cons of the movie by putting the following graphic on the board and listing student ideas.

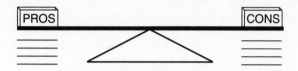

Give students five minutes to complete the Lesson 1 Exercise on pages 379–380. Before students look at the answer key, discuss each question with the class, eliciting opinions about what the correct answers are, what the wrong choices are, and why. Encourage students to defend different opinions, referring to the passage for supportive evidence, until a consensus is reached.

Answer Key Discussion: Students should compare their reasoning carefully with that outlined in the answer key and discuss what they find. Emphasize how important it is to read the questions carefully and how helpful it can be to paraphrase them for better understanding. For example, question 2 asks the student to identify facts *that were used in the review*— not simply to identify true facts. Question 3 asks for the sentence *that supports the critic's main opinion*— not for the sentence that contains the opinion.

Lesson 2: Inferential Comprehension of Commentary

Lesson Warm-Up

Brainstorming: Write the following statements on the board (or photocopy them) and have students write down whether they agree (A) or disagree (D) with the statements, then discuss their reasons. Instruct them to see whether they change their minds about any of the statements as they read the lesson.

- A good critic tries to keep his or her personal taste out of his or her reviews. (D)
- The best reviews are based on recognized standards, not personal opinions. (D)
- Knowing a critic's bias can help you decide whether his or her taste is like your own. (A)
- Knowing a critic's bias can help you decide whether he or she used good reasoning in a review. (A)
- The movie reviews in my local paper tend to be very objective. (Answers will vary.)

Vocabulary: Write the Key Words (*bias, objectivity*), on the board, pronounce them, and discuss their meanings. Have students write sentences using the words. Emphasize that there is a place for both bias (personal opinion) and objectivity (using recognized standards); an objective statement is not always preferable to a biased one. Reinforce their meanings by having students label the following statements as showing "bias" (B) or "objectivity" (O).

* Compared to popular song styles of the past, rap music is more a matter of rhythm than melody. (O)
* Rap music is too violent to have real artistic value. (B)
* I always have thought that romantic ballads were the only authentic kind of American popular song. (B)
* Like all popular music, rap music will make more money for the music producers than for many of its performers. (O)

Lesson Activities

Brainstorming: Read aloud the Prereading Prompt. Write these sentence starters on the board:

A good _____ (movie, book, TV show, play, piece of music, piece of art)_____.

Have students brainstorm questions they ask themselves when deciding how "good" a piece of literature or art is. Explain that these measuring sticks (criteria) form the basis of their opinions. You might add that critics are something like judges who evaluate skaters at the Olympic games. Their ratings depend in part on objective, recognized standards for a particular sport (how accurately a skater performs a figure 8, for example) and in part on their personal opinion (how "artistic" a particular routine is).

Vocabulary: Write the following words and phrases from the lesson on the board and pronounce them: *background, evaluating, recognized standards, colored by personal tastes, valid.* Have students work in small groups to discuss the words' meanings, look the words up in a dictionary, and write sentences using the words.

Read the first section, "Bias," aloud, and ask these questions to check for general comprehension of the section and specific understanding of the difficult vocabulary words: How are writers of commentary different from other writers? (specially trained in evaluating, or judging, the arts; more likely to write about personal taste) What are two reasons it is important to recognize the writer's bias? (to decide if the review is well reasoned and to decide whether his or her taste is like yours)

Have student volunteers read the next section, "Objectivity," aloud. Ask these questions: What is the difference between "recognized standards" and "personal taste"? What are some examples of each? ("Recognized standards" are measuring sticks that are

commonly used to judge art. For instance, it is commonly accepted that a good short story has one central idea, believable characters, and realistic dialogue. Personal taste means one's individual opinion. One person may prefer short stories that involve mystery, while another prefers a story that is humorous.) Can an author make a valid point without being objective? (Yes) Can you think of an example? (A writer may decide that a movie is not worth seeing because it is violent, and he or she is personally opposed to a lot of violence on the screen. If the critic backs up that negative opinion with several facts about the movie, he or she has made a valid point—although not necessarily an objective one.)

Summary Discussion: Have students write one-sentence summaries of each of the first two sections ("Bias" and "Objectivity") and share with the whole class for discussion.

Reading Strategies Instruction: Before students read the model passage, ask who has seen *Dick Tracy* or some other recent movie, what they remember most vividly about it, and what opinion of the film they hold. Discuss the meanings of the following words from the review: *fedora, myth, immense, realism, menacing, grotesque, perspectives, primal, subtlest, lacquered, profusion, Formica, enhanced, stylized.*

Ask what two steps they should take before reading the review itself. (Read the purpose question and the test question.) Have students form pairs and take turns reading the two paragraphs of the passage aloud. (Stop them after they read the purpose question, "What makes Dick Tracy a classic 'comic strip' movie?" Ask what a "classic" movie is and ask for some examples (a movie that meets certain standards and has stood the test of time; *The Phantom of the Opera* is a "classic" horror film). What is a "comic strip" movie? (Movies like *Superman* and *Dennis the Menace* that are based on comic strips.) Then ask, "In your own words, what question are you going to keep in mind as you read this passage?" (What does *Dick Tracy* have in common with other long-lasting comic strip movies?) Encourage them to put the review in their own words, and discuss their thoughts, reactions, and questions about the review. After students have finished the entire section in groups, reconvene and ask them to tell in their own words what the passage is about. (Ask these questions to check for understanding of difficult vocabulary words and comprehension of the main idea: What do you see as the movie opens? When does *Dick Tracy* take place? How does the movie compare with the comic strip? What are the colors in the movie like? What are some examples of how the movie goes "beyond realism"? What are the special effects like?)

Do the model question together. Remind students that when they are answering questions that require "reading between the lines," it helps to (a) look for key words that relate to the question (such as *style*) and (b) try to "hear" the author's tone of voice. (This author's voice "sounds" enthusiastic, as he uses such words as *triumphantly* and *enchanted*.)

Before students read the text explanation on pages 383 and 384, ask them to explain in their own words why the right answer is right and why the other choices are wrong. Discuss any differences between their answers.

Students still having difficulty with inferential comprehension of nonfiction material might review the inferential comprehension sections of the Pre-GED *On Your Own: Reading* (Unit 3) and of the *Threshold* texts in social studies, science, and literature and the arts. For further GED work on inferencing with commentary, see *The New Revised Cambridge GED Program: Interpreting Literature and the Arts*, Chapter 5, Lesson 2.

Application: Have students bring in reviews from magazines and newspapers (the teacher can also do this). Have students reread pieces of commentary from earlier lessons (such as the passages on pages 378–379 of the previous lesson). Students should identify bias and objectivity in these passages (For example; the concluding statement in the passage about Anita Baker reveals the writer's opinion that Baker shouldn't be satisfied with commercial success. The concluding statement in the review of *Ghost* reveals the writer's personal view that movies shouldn't get too "sappy.") To help students practice drawing inferences, ask: What can you assume about Goodman's opinion of ballads and "make-out music"? (Unless they're somehow unique, they're inferior.) What can you assume about Ansen's opinion of movies that take parts from other movies? (They can still be imaginative and funny.)

Lesson Wrap-Up

Exercise Discussion: Before students complete the Lesson 2 Exercise independently, have them discuss the meanings of the following words: *eighth decade, prod, consensus of history, existential anguish, tinsel, slack-jawed authority, amphitheater, collective guilt, preoccupied, panorama, primal cry.* Emphasize that students will be able to figure out what some words mean from context—but not to spend too much time trying to understand every difficult word. It is more important to get a general idea of what the author is saying and how he or she feels about it.

Point out also that it is particularly helpful to try to "picture in your mind" what the writer is saying when he or she is talking about a "visual art" such as painting or photography or sculpture. As they read the descriptions of Francis Bacon's paintings, they should try to imagine what the pictures look like. Give students five minutes to complete the Lesson 2 Exercise on pages 384–385. Before students look at the answer key, discuss each question with the class, eliciting opinions about what the correct answers are, what the wrong choices are, and why. Encourage students to defend different opinions, referring to the passage for supportive evidence, until a consensus is reached.

Answer Key Discussion: Students should compare their reasoning carefully with that outlined in the answer key and discuss what they find. Emphasize how helpful it is to refer to specific sections of the passage when they are mentioned in the question. (For example: Look back at the first paragraph of the passage before trying to predict the answer to question 1.)

Lesson 3: Applying Ideas in Commentary

Lesson Warm-Up

Brainstorming: Review with students what "applying ideas" means by having them brainstorm associations they have with that phrase (using information, building a bridge between old and new situations, figuring out what an author's opinion would be, etc.).

Lesson Activities

Brainstorming: Read and discuss the Prereading Prompt. Tap students' real-life experience with applying ideas in commentary by asking: Do you ever watch movie critics on TV, such as Siskel and Ebert? Is it fairly easy to predict whether Siskel will give a particular movie a "thumbs up" or "thumbs down"? Why or why not?

What are some other situations where you try to predict how a person will react to a new movie, song, book, and so on? (when you are trying to decide what CD, audio tape, book, or video to buy a friend, or what movie to suggest that you see together) How do you make your predictions?

Write these sentences on the board, and have students brainstorm various possibilities for filling in the blanks, then discuss the reasoning behind their choices.

A person who likes _____ (name of a particular movie, book, singing group, etc. e.g., Michael Jackson, a Clint Eastwood movie) would probably like _____ (name of another movie, book, singing group, etc.).

Vocabulary: Write the following words and phrases from the lesson on the board and pronounce them: *inventive use of color and space, spatial designs, representational, spectacular musicals.* Elicit from students what they know about the meanings of each, and explain unfamiliar terms. Have students read the first two sections silently.

Summary Discussion: Break students into small groups and assign them one of the first two sections ("Applying Main Ideas and Details" or "Applying the Author's Attitude"). Group members read the assigned section aloud and discuss it with each other, formulating a one-sentence summary. The entire class reconvenes and a scribe from each group reads the group's summary statement aloud and summarizes particular questions and comments raised by the group. Ask these questions to check for comprehension:

Applying Main Ideas and Details: Why might the reviewer who likes the photographs of gardens also enjoy abstract paintings? (Both emphasize color and use of space.) What kind of novel might the viewer who likes representational paintings enjoy? Why? (realistic novels, since they are lifelike, like representational paintings)

Applying the Author's Attitude: What kind of literature and music might the critic who reviewed *Dick Tracy* like? Why? (fantasy, experimental music; like the movie he praises, they aren't supposed to show life exactly as it is, but go beyond realism)

Reading Strategies Instruction: Before students read the model passage, ask whether any students are familiar with Studs Terkel. What do his books have in common? What is oral history? Have you ever taken down an oral history—for a social studies class, when you were in elementary school perhaps? Discuss the use of italics as used to indicate that the writer is quoting someone else with whom he or she may well not agree. (For example, a feminist might refer to the idea that a *real woman* wears makeup and dresses; a meat-eater might describe a vegetarian's view of the *barbaric* practice of eating hamburger.) Discuss the meanings of the following words from the passage: *solemn-minded historians, oral history, self-serving, suspect, aspiration, speculate.* Ask what two steps they should take before reading the passage itself. (Read the purpose question and the test question.) Have students form pairs and take turns reading the two paragraphs of the passage aloud. (Stop them after they read the purpose question "Why is *Good War* an interesting book?" Ask them to put into their own words what question they should ask themselves as they read the passage (What makes the book *Good War* interesting?) After students have completed the passage, encourage them to put it in their own words, and discuss their thoughts, reactions, and questions about the passage with group members. After students have finished the entire section in groups, reconvene and ask them to say in their own words what the passage is about. (Ask these questions to check for understanding of difficult vocabulary words and comprehension of the main idea: What is oral history? Brainstorm its meaning with students. Why do many historians look down on it? What is Studs Terkel's book like? How is it different from other historical accounts?)

Do the model question together. Remind students that when they are answering questions that require "building a bridge of ideas," it helps to (1) figure out what the writer is saying, then (2) look for similarities between that idea and the idea in each of the choices. Before students read the text explanation on page 388,

ask them to explain in their own words why the right answer is right and why the other choices are wrong. Discuss any differences between their answers.

Debate: Have students examine a TV guide describing the shows of this week. Select five diverse programs and have students debate which one they think the critic (Peter S. Prescott) would most like, and why.

Students still having difficulty with application of nonfiction material might review the Pre-GED *On Your Own: Reading*, Unit 5, and the application sections of the *Threshold* texts in social studies, science, and literature and the arts. For GED work on application with commentary, see *The New Revised Cambridge GED Program: Interpreting Literature and the Arts*, Chapter 5, Lesson 3.

Application: Have students reread pieces of commentary from earlier lessons (such as the passages on pages 383–384 of the preceding lesson). Encourage them to apply these critics' ideas and attitudes to new situations. For example, ask: What do you think Kay Larson would think about having high school students read certain "classics" year after year? (She might be against requiring students to read a particular title just because it has always been considered a classic.) What do you think Denby's opinion of the film, *Batman Returns* would be? (He would probably like it, since—like *Dick Tracy*—it is stylized and uses colorful, experimental special effects.)

Lesson Wrap-Up

Brainstorming: Reiterate how important it is to understand not only what an author says, but how he or she feels about the topic. Homework assignment: Have students look through recent papers and magazines for articles or cartoons that discuss or reveal prejudice based on sex. Students should speculate on what Clive Barnes' attitude toward each might be. (For example: What would Clive Barnes think of the comic strip, *Blondie*? What would he think of the book *Real Men Don't Eat Quiche*?)

Exercise Discussion: Give students five minutes to complete the Lesson 4 Exercise on pages 388–389. Before students look at the answer key, discuss each question with the class, eliciting opinions about what the correct answers are, what the wrong choices are, and why. Have students discuss how they used context clues to figure out what the following words in the passage and questions mean: *social function, colleague, dispel, prejudice, vexed, irrelevant, primitive, inferior, choreographers, break dancing.* Also encourage students to defend different opinions, referring to the passage for supportive evidence, until a consensus is reached. Remind students how crucial it is to focus on the *author's* attitude in answering this type of question. Point out that the reader may have very different ideas about male ballet dancers, but that these are irrelevant to the question.

Answer Key Discussion: Students should compare their reasoning carefully with that outlined in the answer key and discuss what they find.

Lesson 4: Analyzing Commentary

Lesson Warm-Up

Brainstorming: Read aloud the Prereading Prompt. Then write the following on the board:

Chewing gum   Cars   Pizza   Shampoo   Soap

Have students brainstorm advertising jingles they associate with each product and list the phrases underneath each. Then have students identify the complimentary adjectives used by the advertisers.

Vocabulary: Write the Key Word (*diction*) on the board. Point out that in the brainstormed jingles, advertisers are persuading people to buy their product through careful "diction" —word choice.

Lesson Activities

Vocabulary: Break students into small groups and have them discuss the following words and phrases found in the lesson: *generalization, rave reviews, satire, obsessions, formal, informal, wordplay, pretentious.* Students should work together to come up with a group definition for each word or phrase (helping each other find the word in the dictionary, if necessary). Students should also use the words in sentences.

Read the first section (bottom of page 390 and top of page 391) aloud, and ask these questions to check for comprehension: What three parts do you find in most commentary? What are two ways these parts might be arranged? (opinion, support, conclusion; support, opinion, conclusion)

Have student volunteers read the next section, "Diction," aloud. Ask these questions: What are three ways an author might use diction in commentary? (careful choice of comparisons, wordplay, descriptive language) What is being compared in the passage about *Dick Tracy*? (Dick Tracy's attitude toward Breathless is compared with his attitude toward Tess.) How does the author play with words when he says "Forget *Total Recall*"? (He is making fun of the title, which has to do with remembering, by telling us to forget the film.) What are adjectives, and why is it important to pay special attention to the adjectives that a critic uses? (describing words; they are good clues as to whether the critic is praising or criticizing) What is the audience, and how can you tell what audience a critic is writing for? (the group of readers the critic expects to read his or her work; if he or she uses special, technical words, the piece is probably intended for experts)

Summary Discussion: Have each student turn to the student next to him or her. Each summarizes one of the two sections in the lesson (the introduction and "Diction"). Partners then discuss any questions or comments they have about the reading so far.

Reading Strategies Instruction: Before students read the model passage, ask if any are familiar with the name "Satyajit Ray." Point out that there are several difficult vocabulary words in the passage and question: *cinema, aspiring, trajectory, pathetic degeneration, integrity, isolation, climate, sustain, evolution, alternative cinema, promoting, demigod, infallible, oracle, arrogance, egotistical.* Briefly discuss the meanings of these words, but emphasize that on the GED, students should not waste time trying to figure out the meaning of every word. Rather, they should read the passage with the purpose and test questions in mind.

Have students form groups of four and take turns reading the four paragraphs of the passage aloud. (Stop them after they read the purpose question, "What is the lesson of Satyajit Ray's career?" and have students paraphrase it. For example: What can we learn by looking at what this person has done over his lifetime as an artist?)

Encourage them to put the passage in their own words, and discuss their thoughts, reactions, and questions about the review.

After students have finished the entire section in groups, reconvene and ask them to say in their own words what the passage is about. (Ask these questions to check for understanding of difficult vocabulary words and comprehension of the main idea: What sort of artist is Ray? Why is his work a "trajectory"? Why is his Oscar award a "warning"? What are some of the best films he has made? How can you tell that the writer doesn't think that Ray is great today? What are some of the negative, critical words he uses to describe Ray?)

Do the first model question together. Point out that even if students don't know what "egotistical" means, they can figure out the correct answer—that Ray became "removed from life."

Have student pairs do the second model passage (page 393) together. Before they begin reading, discuss these questions: What is a sitcom? What are some sitcoms on TV today? What are some sitcoms from the past? Who are Ward and June and Beaver? What do many sitcoms have in common? After student pairs finish reading the passage aloud, have each partner turn to the other and summarize important points and questions about the passage.

Write these words on the board and encourage partners to discuss how they used context to figure out the meanings: *reinforcing, values of family life, ideological function, domestic chaos, trauma, advent, rampant, domestic violence, rapt, well-appointed, commodity-filled, racism, sexism, social-service agencies.*

Before students read the text explanations on pages 393–394, ask them to explain in their own words why the right answer is right and why the other choices are wrong. Discuss differences among their answers.

Students still having difficulty with the analysis of nonfiction material might review the Pre-GED instruction and practice in *On Your Own: Reading*, Unit 6, and the analysis sections of the *Threshold* texts in social studies, science, and literature and the arts. For more GED work, see *The New Revised Cambridge GED Program: Interpreting Literature and the Arts*, Chapter 5, Lesson 4.

Debate: Encourage students to debate whether or not they agree with Elayne Rapping's viewpoint. Isn't there something to be said for escaping from the world's troubles by watching perfect families on TV? Aren't there some sitcoms that deal well with social issues such as drugs and sexism? Then ask students in each group to note the words (vocabulary) used by the other group in the debate that reveal their point of view.

Application: Have students reread pieces of commentary from earlier lessons (such as the passages on pages 387 and 388 of the preceding lesson). Students should analyze the structure of each (Where is the opinion stated? What support is given? Where is the summary statement?) and analyze the diction (Where does the writer use comparisons? Is there any wordplay? What descriptive language is used?) Also: Students can use reviews from magazines and newspapers; or students can review computer software if they are in a computer class; or students can watch a video together and then write individual reviews.

Lesson Wrap-Up

Brainstorming: Have students close the book and brainstorm the main ideas they will "take from" this lesson. What did they learn that they didn't know before?

Exercise Discussion: Before students complete the Lesson 4 Exercise independently, have them discuss the meanings of the following words: *feminist, self-esteem, monastic, unapologetic, self-actualization, extant, inner child, disillusioned, gossip column, biography.* Then give students five minutes to complete the Lesson 4 Exercise on page 395.

Before students look at the answer key, discuss each question with the class, eliciting opinions about what the correct answers are, what the wrong choices are, and why. Encourage students to defend different opinions, referring to the passage for supportive evidence, until a consensus is reached.

Answer Key Discussion: Students should compare their reasoning carefully with that outlined in the answer key and discuss what they find. Emphasize how important it is to keep in mind not only what the author is saying—but *why*, for what purpose. (Why is the writer telling me this? What does he or she want me to think about? What argument is he or she making?) Point out also how useful it is to try to imagine the writer's voice as you read the passage. Tone of voice is a good clue to the answer to questions about commentary (such as items 1 and 2) and other forms of literature—not just to fiction.

Chapter 1 Whole Numbers

Chapter Warm-Up

Have the students make a list of ten things in the classroom that can be counted. (*Examples*: the number of desks, pencils, pieces of paper, erasers, and so on.) Counting whole things requires the use of whole numbers.

Next have them make a list of ten things that could be measured. (*Examples*: the dimensions of a piece of paper, the height of a student, the weight of a table, the amount of money in your pocket, and so on)

Measuring requires the use of fractions and decimals. The width of a standard piece of paper is 8 ½ inches. You might have $4.32 in your pocket. These quantities cannot be stated with whole numbers alone.

In this chapter, the students will learn about the whole-number system, the four arithmetic operations, and how to solve word problems using whole numbers.

Level 1: Whole-Number Skills

Lesson 1: Our Number System

Lesson Warm-Up

Ask each student to write on a slip of paper a whole number containing from four to seven digits. List the numbers on the board in random order. In small groups, have the students arrange the numbers in order from least to greatest. Put the correct arrangement on the board and have each group check its answers.

Discuss the activity. *Ask*: What made the assignment difficult? How did you approach the task? What was your thought process?

Vocabulary: Write the following terms on the board and discuss their meanings.

- **Digit:** Our math system uses ten digits. A digit is a numeral that takes up only one place. All our numbers are made up of these ten digits.

  Discuss: Our fingers are sometimes called *digits*. What is the connection between fingers and whole numbers? (We can use our fingers for counting.)

- **Place value:** Larger numbers are made up of more than one digit. The position (place) of a digit in a number tells us its value.

Activity

Have the students make their own place-value charts (extending to the billions place). Write the number 4,073,582,691 on the board. Ask the following questions:

1. What is the value of the 5?
2. What is the value of the 1?
3. What is the value of the 3?

   And so on.

   Answers

1. Five hundred thousand
2. One
3. Three million

   Discuss: Although the digit 0 has no value of its own, why is it important in writing numbers? (It serves as a placeholder.)

Error Analysis

Students sometimes have difficulty interpreting the tens and hundreds columns in each group of three. Point out how the pattern repeats in each group of three. From right to left, there are always ones, tens, and then hundreds in each group.

Lesson 2:   Addition of Whole Numbers

Lesson Warm-Up

Count how many students have a last name beginning with a letter from A to M. Now count how many have a last name beginning with a letter from N to Z. Ask the students to find the sum of the two numbers.

Vocabulary: Write the following terms on the board and discuss their meanings.

- **Sum** or **Total:**   These words both refer to the answer of an addition problem. As a memory aid, ask the students to think about one of the many television shows about lawyers. At the end of a trial, the lawyers give a summation. In other words, they "sum" up (or add up) all the facts in the case.

Activity

Invite the students to brainstorm life situations in which people commonly use addition. Have a volunteer tally the number of responses on the board. Have the student use the system of writing the tally marks in groups of five, like these two groups of marks:

   Ask: Why does it help the person counting to group the tally marks? Point out that our place-value system also groups using tens.

Error Analysis

Students often fail to line up place-value columns correctly. Remind them to check alignment from right to left. Graph paper can help students gain the precision they need.

   To emphasize the importance of alignment, have the students solve the following three addition problems. Point out how drastically the answers differ when the problems are lined up incorrectly.

11	11	1
1035	1035	1035
78	78	78
+ 642	+ 642	+ 642
1755	8235	9477

Lesson 3:   Subtraction of Whole Numbers

Lesson Warm-Up

Count how many students have a first name beginning with a letter from A to M. Now count how many have a first name beginning with a letter from N to Z. Ask the students to find the difference between the two numbers.

Vocabulary: Write the following term on the board and discuss its meaning.

- **Difference:**   The word *difference* is much like the word *different*. When you find the difference, you are finding by how much two numbers differ. If Paul earns $7 an hour and Laura earns $9, their hourly wages differ by $2. To find the difference, you should subtract.

Activity

Borrowing is a difficult concept for some students. They may have learned the mechanics but have trouble understanding why it works. Although the following illustration is simple, it works well to help students visualize the concept.

   Tell the students to imagine a neighborhood where everyone gets along very well. If one neighbor is short a few dollars, he can always borrow from the neighbor on the left. Now draw three houses on the board, labeling them *ones*, *tens*, and *hundreds*. Each neighbor always loans the same amount (the amount of the place-value column), and they always give the money in the denomination the borrower needs.

   For example, when the person living in the *ones* house borrows, the neighbor next door always gives $10 in $1 bills. When the person in the *tens* house borrows, the neighbor next door always gives $100 in $10 bills. Work a problem on the board using the houses as place-value columns. A similar example can be used to show how carrying works.

Error Analysis

Students often fail to line up place-value columns correctly. Remind them to check alignment from right to left. Graph paper can help students gain the precision they need.

Lesson 4:   Multiplication of Whole Numbers

Lesson Warm-Up

Multiplication is fast addition. To prove this point, have the students solve the following problem two ways.

   Six employees plan to attend a computer workshop. The registration fee for each worker is $17. What is the total amount the employees will spend to register for the workshop?

4
17
x 6
$102

```
     4
    17
    17
    17
    17
    17
   +17
  $102
```

This example shows that there is no better math shortcut than knowing the multiplication tables. Encourage students who may be rusty on their math facts to study these tables.

Vocabulary: Write the following term on the board and discuss its meaning.

- **Product:**   When you multiply two numbers, the answer is the product. To help the students associate *product* and *multiply*, use this example: In a factory, the workers make products. If you have many workers, the products multiply quickly.

Activity

The most common errors involve the incorrect use of zero as a placeholder.

Direct the students to look at the second example on page 406. *Ask:* How many uses of 0 as a placeholder do you see? (There are three zeros written in the problem and one in the answer.) Actually, three additional zeros are implied in the partial products. Point out that moving each partial product over to the left has the same result as writing the ending zero as a placeholder.

Error Analysis

Because there are addition portions in multiplication problems, alignment continues to be a problem. Graph paper helps students maintain place-value columns.

Carrying in a multiplication problem sometimes presents a problem. Whether they are working with partial products or carrying, remind the students that the rule in math is to multiply before you add.

Lesson 5:   Division of Whole Numbers

Lesson Warm-up

Division is fast subtraction. To prove this point, have the students solve the following problem in two ways.

The 12 players on a softball team need uniform jerseys. A sporting goods store offers to supply the entire team with shirts for $72. How much will each player have to pay for a shirt?

```
    6        72      You had to
12)72       -12      subtract 12
             60      six times, so
            -12      you know that
             48      72 divided by
            -12      12 is 6.
             36
            -12
             24
            -12
             12
            -12
              0
```

This example shows that there is no better math shortcut than knowing the multiplication tables. Encourage students who may be rusty on their multiplication facts to study these tables.

Vocabulary: Write the following term on the board and discuss its meaning.

- **Quotient:**   The answer to a division problem is called a quotient. The Latin word *quotiens* means "how many times." When you are dividing, you are finding how many times one number will go into another. To return to the factory analogy, the number of products needed is divided among the workers, and each worker is given a "quota" to meet.

Activity

The most common errors involve the incorrect use of zero as a placeholder.

Ask: Under what circumstances should you put a zero in the quotient in a division problem? (Whenever the number you are dividing by will not go into a certain digit or number of digits, put a zero in the corresponding place in the quotient.)

Have each student create a division problem that will have a quotient containing a zero used as a placeholder.

Error Analysis

Because there are addition and subtraction portions in division problems, alignment continues to be a problem. Graph paper helps students maintain place-value columns.

Level 2:   Whole-Number Applications

Lesson 1:   Rounding Off

Lesson Warm-Up

Assign the class to find out approximately how much the class members spend on groceries in one week.

Each person should bring in the exact amounts spent during the last week. Since the assignment calls for an approximate total, the amounts can be rounded before they are added. Have the students round to the place-value column of their own choosing and add.

Vocabulary: Write the following terms on the board and discuss their meanings.

- **Rounding, round off, round:**   These terms have the same meaning. They all refer to the practice of expressing an amount in terms of a certain place-value column. Rounding makes calculations easier. It can be used whenever an exact answer is not needed. Rounding can also be used to check quickly whether or not a calculation is reasonable.
- **Estimate:**   The word *estimate* in a problem indicates that an exact answer is not needed. Other words that indicate rounding are *about*, *approximately*, and *approximate*.

Activity

Discuss: How should you decide which place-value column to round to? Think about the grocery bill activity. A bill of $127 is nearly $130; however, it is also closer to $100 than it is to $200. Amounts rounded to the tens column ($130) should lead to a more accurate estimate than amounts rounded to the hundreds column ($100). On the other hand, $100 is an easier figure to work with than $130. As a general rule, the students should round to a lower place-value column when greater accuracy is needed.

Error Analysis

The most common errors are due to carelessness. Occasionally, a student loses track of the digit that he or she is rounding to. Underlining the digit prevents this from happening.

Another error results when the student neglects to change all the digits to the right of the desired place to zeros.

Lesson 2:   Distance and Cost Formulas

Lesson Warm-Up

Formulas are helpful because you can solve problems without figuring out which operations to use. Think of a formula as a set of instructions. Once you find the right formula, you know exactly what to do.

Assign the students to write formulas of their own for these common situations.

1. Figuring out your weekly gross earnings if the hourly wage and number of hours worked are known

2. Figuring out how your share of the cost of a gift when the total cost of the gift and the number of people paying for it are known

Vocabulary: Write the following terms on the board and discuss their meanings:

- **Rate:**   Both formulas use this term. A rate is a number or an amount that remains fixed for a period of time. The rate is shown "per" some unit of measurement. In the following expressions, the rate comes before the word *per*: 16 miles per gallon, $8 per hour, 50 words per minute, and so on.
- **Per:**   In a word problem, the word *per* indicates either multiplication or division. It is used to express a rate. It means *for each*. For example:

  Jane earns $12 per hour.
  Jane earns $12 for each hour she works.

Activity

Assign the students to write word problems that require the use of the distance and cost formulas (one for each). Have them trade papers with a partner and solve.

Error Analysis

If the students have difficulty identifying the rate, point out that the word *per* usually follows the rate. Another word that signals the rate is the word *at* which comes before the rate.

Lesson 3:   Powers and Roots

Lesson Warm-Up

Which of these expressions has the greater value: 10^2 or 10^3?

10^2 is read "Ten to the second power." Its value is 100 (10 x 10).

10^3 is read "Ten to the third power." The value of 10^3 is 1000. The value of 10^3 is greater than 10^2.

Discuss: What is the opposite of addition? (subtraction) What is the opposite of multiplication? (division) Point out that in the same way, finding a root is the opposite of finding a power.

Ask the students to imagine an avalanche. Now, as if the image in your mind were a movie, run the film backward. The snow rushes back up the mountain decreasing in intensity until you see the starting moment of the avalanche. This process is the same as tracing a problem back to its root. When you find a root, you begin with a value and work back to find a certain root.

Vocabulary: An understanding of the following terms is necessary to do the work in Lesson 3.

- **Base:** In normal usage, a base is a foundation. It holds something up. A basement is the foundation for a house. In the expression 5^2, the base is 5.
- **Exponent:** The exponent is a small number written slightly above and to the right of the base. It tells you how many times to write the base to find the value of a power. In the expression 5^2, the exponent is 2. The value of 5^2 is 5 x 5, or 25.
- **Square:** Finding a number to the second power is finding a square. For example, the square of 6 or 6^2 is 36.
- **Square root:** When you find a square root, you are figuring out what number squared is equal to a certain value. In other words, finding a square root is finding a base. For example: $?^2 = 36$ The missing base is 6. The sign for square root is $\sqrt{\ }$ $\sqrt{36} = 6$.

Activity

This explanation can be used to help students remember the meaning of powers and roots. Ask the students to imagine an avalanche. An avalanche may start small, but as it picks up momentum, it becomes more powerful. The same principle is true of a tidal wave, an earthquake, and many other forces in nature. Things that multiply increase in power.

When there is an earthquake, the experts on television show us maps of the epicenter—the place where the earthquake started. When there is a crisis of some kind, the experts look for the root of the problem. The root is the base before it begins to multiply.

To practice finding square roots, assign each student to take a number between 21 and 99 and square it (multiply it by itself). Have the student write the result on a small slip of paper. Then collect the slips and draw them out one at a time. Ask for volunteers to estimate an answer. Encourage the students to use the table to make the best estimate possible.

Error Analysis

Mistakes involving powers occur when students multiply the base the number of times stated by the exponent. 2^4 means that the base 2 appears four times in the multiplication problem. It does not mean that the student should multiply by 2 four times.

To pass the GED, students need to know the common square roots. Create a table by squaring the numbers from 1 to 15. Memorizing this table will allow students to solve most problems easily.

Lesson 4: Perimeter and Area of Polygons

Lesson Warm-Up

Each side of shape A (a square) measures 6 inches in length. Each side of shape B (a triangle) also measures 6 inches. Ask for volunteers to draw the shapes on the board. Have these students find the perimeter of the square and the triangle. (The square has a 24-inch perimeter. The perimeter of the triangle is 18 inches.)

Discuss: Did the volunteers use a formula or some other method to solve the parts of the problem?

Activity

Cut a rectangle 5 inches by 4 inches out of heavy paper. Now cut a square with 1-inch sides. To find the perimeter of the rectangle, the students measured the outside edge. To find the area, the students need to measure the surface space inside. They can do this by finding how many "square inches" will fit inside the rectangle. Choose two volunteers to demonstrate for the class how the area can be measured using the paper "square inch." Afterward, demonstrate that the same result can be found by multiplying 5 x 4.

Vocabulary: An understanding of the following terms is necessary to do the work in Lesson 4.

- **Perimeter:** The distance around the outside of any flat figure. Notice that the word *meter* is part of *perimeter*. A meter is a measure of length.
- **Length** and **Width:** Rectangles have both length (the measure of the longer side) and width (the measure of the shorter side). Squares do not have both length and width because all four sides are of the same length. Triangles have only three sides and all three may be of different lengths.
- **Area:** The measure of the surface area of a flat figure.
- **Square unit:** We measure lines using other marked lines (rulers). To measure surface area, we need to use units of surface area. Any unit of measure can be squared. A square inch is a square that measures 1 inch on each side. A square meter is a square that measures 1 meter on each side.

Activity

Have the students determine the perimeter and the area of the classroom.

Ask: Assuming that the room is either a perfect square or a perfect rectangle, is it necessary to measure all four walls to solve the problem?

Discuss: The lesson presents three formulas for finding perimeter. Is it necessary to use the formulas to calculate perimeter? Ask for two volunteers to calculate the perimeter of a room that is 9 feet by 12 feet, writing either on paper or on the board. Assign one student to use addition only and the other to use the formula for finding the perimeter of a rectangle.

$$
\begin{array}{ll}
\begin{array}{r}
12 \\
12 \\
9 \\
\underline{+\ 9} \\
42 \text{ feet}
\end{array}
&
\begin{aligned}
p &= 2l + 2w \\
&= 2(12) + 2(9) \\
&= 24 + 18 \\
&= 42 \text{ feet}
\end{aligned}
\end{array}
$$

Take a vote as to which method seems easier. Many students will probably opt for adding only, but once they understand the ideas behind the formula, doubling the two numbers and adding is actually a very fast method for solving the problem.

Brainstorming: Ask the class to brainstorm work situations in which finding area would be necessary. Possible answers include laying carpeting, flooring, and tiles, and finding the amount of material needed for a bedspread.

Error Analysis

Using the rectangle formula involves an understanding of the order of operations. The students must multiply before they add.

Common errors in finding area include:

1. Forgetting to label the answer in square units of measure

2. Finding perimeter when area is needed

Encourage students to visualize the problem before doing any calculations. They must make sure that they know exactly what they are solving for before they do the work.

Lesson 5: Volume

Lesson Warm-Up

Define volume as the amount of space inside a three-dimensional figure. Remind the students that you measure lines with a marked line. You measure the surface area of a flat figure with a square unit (another flat figure). Following the pattern, what would be the best way to measure volume? (With a three-dimensional unit)

Vocabulary: An understanding of the following terms is necessary to do the work in Lesson 5.

- **Three-dimensional figure:** A figure that has length, width, and height. In other words, to describe the figure, you need to talk about three dimensions.
- **Volume:** The measure of the space inside a three-dimensional figure.
- **Cube:** A three-dimensional figure that has equal length, width, and height measures.

Activity

The floor of a storage unit measures 3 feet by 5 feet. The unit has a height of 8 feet. How many boxes measuring $1 \times 1 \times 1$ feet (in other words, a cube) could fit into the storage unit?

Have the students describe how they could solve the problem physically. Then teach them the two volume formulas used on the GED.

Brainstorming: Have the students brainstorm examples of work situations that might require solving for volume.

Error Analysis

Students often fail to label their answers correctly. You may want to post a chart that states:

Perimeter	Linear units
Area	Square units
Volume	Cubic units

To help the students further understand volume, you may want to have them build three-dimensional figures with cubes. Divide the class into small groups and assign each group to build a figure, keeping track of the number of blocks used. Then ask the groups to find the volume of the figures using the formulas they know.

Lesson 6: Mean and Median

Lesson Warm-Up

On the board, list the numbers from 50 to 78. Tell the students that these numbers represent inches. Ask them to calculate their heights in inches. As the students report their height, put tally marks next to the appropriate numbers on the board. *Ask:* what do you notice about the pattern forming on the board? (Unless you have a very unusual class, there will be more tally marks near the center of the column of numbers than at either end.)

People who work with numbers often collect sets of numbers or measurements. As individual values, the numbers are difficult to use. Instead, a number from the center or middle is calculated to represent the entire group. Mean and median are two ways to find the measurement that best represents the group.

Vocabulary: An understanding of the following terms is necessary to do the work in Lesson 6.

- **Average** or **mean:** This measurement is found by adding together all the individual measures and dividing by the total number of measurements collected.

   Discuss: How could you find the average height of the members of the class? (Add the measurements together and divide by the number of students.)

- **Median:** The median is the middle number in a set of numbers. The word *median* sounds like *medium*, a measurement halfway between large and small, tall and short, and so on. Help the students find the median value in the set of heights.

Activity

The following table represents grocery bills for the months of June and July. Find the mean and median for each month.

Week	June	July
1	$ 99	$104
2	113	120
3	87	109
4	101	90
5		112

   Answers: June: mean $100; median $100. July: mean $107; median $109

   Discuss: Why aren't the mean and median always the same? (They are two different ways of finding a central value. When very large samples are taken, the mean and median are often the same.)
   When you are finding the median, how can you know whether there will be two numbers in the middle even before you put the numbers in order? (Count the values. If there is an odd number, there will be one middle value; if there is an even number, there will be two middle values.)

Error Analysis

Most errors in calculating the mean are careless. Because two operations are involved, there is room for computational errors. Teach the students to ask: Is my answer reasonable? Remember, the mean is

one way to find a central measure. They should question whether their answer could reasonably fall in the middle.

Level 3: Whole-Number Problem Solving

Lesson 1: Setup Answers

Lesson Warm-Up

Write the following problem on the board. Margo and Andrew are on a vacation in southern California. They have a $100 bill to cover their expenses for the day. Margo decides to go on an all-day whale watch. She buys a ticket for $12.50. After paying for the ticket, she splits her change with Andrew. Which expression below shows the amount of money she gave Andrew?

(a) $100 - \dfrac{\$12.50}{2}$

(b) $\dfrac{\$100 - \$12.50}{2}$

(c) $\dfrac{\$100}{2} - \$12.50$

The correct answer is (b).

Vocabulary: An understanding of the following terms is necessary to do the work in Lesson 1.

- **Setup problem:** A word problem on the GED test that asks you to choose the way to solve the problem. You don't have to solve the problem.
- **Expression:** A number sentence. Using numbers and symbols, an expression shows the reader how to do the work of solving a problem.

Activity

Use the word problems on pages 412, 417, and 421 to practice writing expressions.

   Discuss: How important are parentheses in writing expressions? Remind the students that they should always do the work in this order:

1. Exponents
2. Operations in parentheses
3. Multiplication and division operations from left to right

4. Addition and subtraction operations from left to right

The best strategy for solving a setup problem is to write your own expression and compare it to the answer choices.

Error Analysis

Students who have difficulty interpreting expressions may be unaccustomed to the order of operations. It may be helpful for them to write a few setup problems of their own. Emphasize the importance of deciding which operations are needed before evaluating the expressions.

Lesson 2:   Multistep Problems

Lesson Warm-Up

Leona is a teacher's aide at a public elementary school. She works 25 hours per week with a kindergarten class and 15 hours with a fourth grade class. If she earns $7 per hour, how much does she earn during the week?

Ask the students to describe what facts they need to know to find out how much she earns. (They need to know her total hours and her hourly rate.) Point out that they have been given the rate ($7 per hour). Ask them what they need to do to find the other fact (total hours). (They need to add 25 and 15.)

Discuss: How can you figure out which operation to do first?

Vocabulary: No new terms are presented in this lesson.

Activity

Divide the students into small groups. Have each group write at least two multistep problems. Solve the problems on the board having the students answer the following questions.

1. What does the problem ask me to find?
2. What operations would I use to find the solution?
3. What facts would I need to find the solution?
4. What facts do I have?
5. What could I do first to have all the facts I need?

Then they are ready to solve the problem.

Error Analysis

If students are making errors, they are probably doing the operations in the wrong order. Take these students through the list of questions above. Point out that they won't save time by guessing. Also point out that on the GED test they will sometimes be given extra information. They do not need to do something with every number.

Lesson 3:   Estimating

Lesson Warm-Up

Five friends want to chip in together to buy a birthday present for a mutual friend. If the present they plan to buy will cost $44, about how much will they each have to contribute?

1. Ask for a volunteer to solve the problem using estimation. The student should round $44 to $45 and divide by 5.
2. Now ask a volunteer to solve for the exact answer. Which process took longer?
3. Have the students compare the difference in answers: $8.80 (exact) compared to $9. The difference, $0.20, is small.

Point out that if this problem appeared on the GED test with the following answer choices, estimation would be most practical. In fact, the GED testing service suggests that over 50% of the items on the test can be solved using estimation.

Choices:

(a) about $6
(b) about $7
(c) about $8
(d) about $9
(e) about $10

Vocabulary: Some words that indicate the need to estimate are *approximate* and *about*. Point out that some GED problems do not require an exact answer. Since estimating an answer usually takes less time than solving for an exact answer, knowing when to estimate can save valuable test time.

Activity

Divide the students into small groups and have each create a word problem that can be solved using estimation. Solve the problems on the board.

Discuss: Why is it important to see whether your answer makes sense (or is reasonable)? How do you decide which place-value column to round to?

Error Analysis

Students who have problems with the exercise may be choosing the wrong operation. Have them underline clue words and develop a plan for solving before they estimate.

Lesson 4: Item Sets

Lesson Warm-Up

Write the following paragraph on the board: Jan ordered 24 pizzas for an office party from a pizza parlor six blocks away. Each pizza cost $9.25. Each pizza contained 12 slices. She also ordered 8 six-packs of soda pop and 12 side orders of garlic bread. When the food was delivered, she paid the delivery person a $10 delivery charge.

Now present the following word problem: If each person at the party eats two-thirds of a pizza, how many people can be fed? Ask the students what fact from the paragraph is needed to solve the problem. (the number of pizzas: 24) The rest of the information is unnecessary.

Vocabulary: No new terms are presented in this lesson.

Activity

Divide the class into small groups. Have them construct problems using the passage above. Count up how many different problems the class can create. Clearly, a small number of facts can yield a large number of problems.

When students encounter GED passages like the one above, they should:

1. Read the passage once for an overview of the facts contained within it.
2. Read the first word problem.
3. Determine what facts are needed to solve the problem.
4. Find the necessary facts in the passage.
5. Do the work.

They should not do any calculations based on the passage alone. Don't waste time solving the wrong problem.

Error Analysis

If students are having difficulty interpreting passages, encourage them to underline the key facts in the passage. It may be helpful to draw pictures or diagrams of the information in some passages. For example: Using the passage from the warm-up activity described above, the student could draw several pizzas, dividing them into thirds. By shading appropriate amounts, the student can quickly see that two pizzas will feed three people.

For additional help on the topics covered in Chapter 1, refer to *On Your Own: Basic Math,* a volume in a Cambridge Pre-GED series. The following table shows the correlation between the lessons in this GED Comprehensive Book text and the chapters in this Pre-GED series, in the *Threshold* Pre-GED math text, and in the GED satellite text, *The New Revised Cambridge GED Program: Mathematics.*

Cambridge GED Math (Comprehensive Book)		On Your Own: Basic Math
Level 1	Lesson 1	Chapter 1
	Lesson 2	Chapter 2
	Lesson 3	Chapter 3
	Lesson 4	Chapter 4
	Lesson 5	Chapter 5
Level 2	Lesson 1	Chapter 1, Lesson 7
	Lesson 4	Chapter 6
	Lesson 6	Chapter 5, Lesson 10
Level 3	Lessons 1–4	Chapter 6

Cambridge GED Math (Comprehensive Book)		Threshold Math Book 1
Level 1	Lesson 1	Unit 1, Ch. 1, Lessons 1–3
	Lesson 2	Unit 1, Chapter 2
	Lesson 3	Unit 1, Chapter 3
	Lesson 4	Unit 1, Chapter 4
	Lesson 5	Unit 1, Chapter 5
Level 2	Lesson 1	Unit 1, Ch. 1, Lesson 4
	Lesson 2	Unit 1, Ch. 4, Lesson 33
	Lesson 4	Unit 1, Ch. 6, Lessons 15 & 16
	Lesson 6	Unit 1, Ch. 6, Lesson 17
Level 3	Lesson 1	Unit 1, Ch. 6, Lesson 18
	Lesson 2	Unit 1, Ch. 6, Lesson 19
	Lesson 3	Unit 1, Chs. 5 & 6, Lesson 18

Cambridge GED Math (Comprehensive Book)		Cambridge GED Math (Satellite Book)
Level 1	Lesson 1	Chapter 1, Lesson 1
	Lesson 2	Chapter 1, Lesson 2
	Lesson 3	Chapter 1, Lesson 2
	Lesson 4	Chapter 1, Lesson 3
	Lesson 5	Chapter 1, Lesson 3
Level 2	Lesson 1	Chapter 1, Lesson 4
	Lesson 2	Chapter 1, Lesson 5
	Lesson 3	Ch 1, Lessons 7 & 8
	Lesson 4	Ch. 1, Lessons 9 & 10
	Lesson 5	Chapter 1, Lesson 11
	Lesson 6	Chapter 1, Lesson 6
Level 3	Lesson 1	Chapter 1, Lesson 18
	Lesson 2	Chapter 1, Lesson 15
	Lesson 3	Chapter 1, Lesson 14
	Lesson 4	Chapter 1, Lesson 17

Chapter

2 Fractions

Chapter Warm-Up

Point out that common fractions are used to express part of something. Another common fraction system all of us use is the decimal system. Which fraction system is best for expressing the following? Why?

1. Part of a dollar (decimals)
2. Part of a pizza (fractions)
3. A fraction of an inch (fractions)
4. A fraction of a kilometer (decimals)
5. Part of a yard of fabric (fractions)
6. Part of a mile (either)
7. Part of an hour (either)
8. Part of a cup in a recipe (fractions)
9. The part of a baseball player's times at bat in which he gets a hit (decimals)
10. Part of a year (fractions)

Level 1: Fraction Skills

Lesson 1: Reducing Fractions

Lesson Warm-Up

Scott orders a large pizza. He tells the waiter that he wants $\frac{5}{10}$ of the pizza to be pepperoni and pineapple and $\frac{4}{8}$ to be sausage and mushroom. What is he really saying?

Point out that $\frac{5}{10}$ and $\frac{4}{8}$ are both equal to $\frac{1}{2}$. Fractions are best understood when they are in lowest terms. On the board, use cross multiplication to prove that $\frac{5}{10}$ and $\frac{4}{8}$ are equal to $\frac{1}{2}$.

$$\frac{5}{10} \times = \frac{1}{2} \qquad \frac{4}{8} \times = \frac{1}{2} \qquad \frac{5}{10} \times = \frac{4}{8}$$

When cross products are equal, we know that the fractions are equivalent.

Vocabulary: An understanding of the following terms is necessary to do the work in Lesson 1.

- **Fraction:** Like a decimal, a common fraction shows part of a whole. A common fraction is written with two numbers. The top number (numerator) shows how many parts you have. The bottom number (denominator) shows how many equal parts there are in the whole.
- **Numerator:** The top number in a common fraction.
- **Denominator:** The bottom number in a common fraction.
- **Reducing fractions:** Dividing both the numerator and the denominator of a fraction by the same number. The result is an equivalent fraction.
- **Lowest terms:** A fraction is said to be in lowest terms when it cannot be reduced further.

Activity

Discuss: How can you tell that a fraction needs to be reduced? When taking the GED test, students can look at the answer choices for clues. If an answer does not match one of the choices, perhaps it needs to be reduced.

Error Analysis

Students who are having difficulty may need work on the multiplication tables.

Lesson 2: Raising Fractions to Higher Terms

Lesson Warm-Up

How can you prove that $\frac{5}{20}$ is equal to $\frac{1}{4}$? (In the activity for Lesson 1, you used cross-multiplication to prove that two fractions were equal. That method can be used here. The students can also explain that dividing both the numerator and the denominator by the same number does not change the value because dividing by 1 does not change the value of a number.)

Point out that multiplying by 1 also does not change the value of a number; therefore, multiplying both the numerator and the denominator by the same number raises a fraction to an equivalent fraction in higher terms.

Vocabulary: An understanding of the following terms is necessary to do the work in Lesson 2.

- **Raising fractions:** Multiplying both the numerator and the denominator of a fraction by the same number. Raising a fraction does not change its value.
- **Equivalent fractions:** Two or more fractions that have the same value.

Activity

Divide the class into small groups. Have them raise the fractions ⅔, ¾, and ⅜, using multiples of their own choosing. Then put the raised fractions on the board and ask for volunteers to reduce the fractions.

Error Analysis

Students who are having difficulty may need work on the multiplication tables.

Lesson 3 Mixed Numbers and Improper Fractions

Lesson Warm-Up

In Lesson 2 you had the students practice raising fractions to higher terms. Now test their understanding of mixed numbers.

Maggie is ordering pizzas this time. She is planning a party for 10 people. She estimates that they will each eat 3 slices of pizza. She will need 30 slices. If the policy of the pizza parlor is to cut large pizzas into 8 slices, how many pizzas would she need?

Have them draw the pizzas on the board to support their answer. They need $^{30}\!/_{8}$ or 3 $^{6}\!/_{8}$ pizzas. Point out that 3 $^{6}\!/_{8}$ reduces to 3 ¾. Of course, Maggie will have to order 4 whole pizzas to get enough slices.

Vocabulary: An understanding of the following terms is necessary to do the work in Lesson 3.

- **Raising fractions:** Multiplying both the numerator and the denominator of a fraction by the same number. Raising a fraction does not change its value.
- **Change:** In this lesson, the word *change* is used instead of *rewrite*, *rename*, or *convert*. Point out that

this process does not change the value of the fraction. Use cross-multiplication to prove this point.

- **Higher terms:** Raising a fraction changes the numerator and denominator to greater numbers. However, the value of the fraction does not change.

Activity

Put the fraction $^{15}\!/_{6}$ on the board and the mixed number 2 ½. Ask for a volunteer to change $^{15}\!/_{6}$ to a mixed number and another volunteer to change 2 ½ to an improper fraction. Have a third volunteer use cross-multiplication to prove that $^{15}\!/_{6}$ and 2 ½ have the same value.

Error Analysis

Students who are having difficulty may need further review of the multiplication tables.

Lesson 4: Adding Fractions and Mixed Numbers That Have Like Denominators

Lesson Warm-Up

Denise works as a waitress in a coffee shop. After the dinner rush ends, Denise notices that there are parts of three pies left over. There are 3 slices of a peach pie left, 5 of a cherry pie, and 7 of a rhubarb pie. Each of the pies was originally cut into 8 pieces. Write a fraction for the leftover part of each pie and add to find the total pie left over.

$$\tfrac{3}{8} + \tfrac{5}{8} + \tfrac{7}{8} = {}^{15}\!/_{8} = 1\,\tfrac{7}{8}\text{ pies}$$

Point out that they would probably not have written fractions unless they had been asked to. As long as the pies were cut into the same number of pieces, the problem could be solved by adding the slices. This problem shows clearly why it works to add fractions that have like denominators.

Vocabulary: An understanding of the following term is necessary to do the work in Lesson 4.

- **Like denominators:** Fractions that have the same denominator. 1/4 and 3/4 have like denominators. 3/5 and 3/4 do not.

Activity

Point out that the denominator on a fraction is a kind of label. Just as it wouldn't make sense to add 5 inches to 3 pounds, it doesn't make sense to add fractions with different denominators.

Divide the class into groups of three or four students. Assign each group a denominator from 5 to 12. Have each member of the group write a numerator on a slip of paper. Then have the group come to the board and demonstrate how to add the fractions and reduce the answer.

Error Analysis

Common errors include adding the denominators as well or making errors when converting improper fractions to mixed numbers.

Lesson 5: Common Denominators

Lesson Warm-Up

Mario works out every three days. Sandra works out every four days. How many days will pass before they meet at the gym on the same day?

Make a chart on the board to solve the problem.

Day 1	*Day 2*	*Day 3* Mario	*Day 4* Sandra
Day 5	*Day 6* Mario	*Day 7*	*Day 8* Sandra
Day 9 Mario	*Day 10*	*Day 11*	*Day 12* Mario Sandra

The answer is day 12. We can say that Mario works out every *third* day and Sandra works out every *fourth* day. The lowest common denominator for thirds and fourths is 12. In other words, 12 is the lowest number that both 3 and 4 will divide into evenly.

Vocabulary: An understanding of the following terms is necessary to do the work in Lesson 5.

- **Common denominator:** A number into which each denominator in a problem divides evenly
- **Lowest common denominator** The lowest number into which each denominator in a problem divides evenly

Activity

Phil and Nita want to buy bicycles. They both have chosen the same bike which sells for $120. Nita has saved $\frac{2}{3}$ of the cost of the bike. Phil has saved $\frac{5}{6}$ of the cost. Who has saved the most money toward the purchase of the bike?

There are two ways to solve this problem. The student could find $\frac{2}{3}$ of $120 and $\frac{5}{6}$ of $120 and compare the amounts, or the student could compare the fractions. Raise $\frac{2}{3}$ to $\frac{4}{6}$ and compare. Since $\frac{5}{6} > \frac{4}{6}$ Phil has saved the most money. Using the second approach, the problem can be worked mentally.

Point out that many of the items on the GED test can be solved without performing any calculations.

Error Analysis

The most common error is confusing the numerator and the denominator. Remind the students that the numerator shows the number of parts. It does not need to be the same since the number of parts may be different. The denominator is like a label. The denominators must be the same to add and subtract.

Lesson 6: Adding Fractions and Mixed Numbers That Have Unlike Denominators

Lesson Warm-up

Put the following problem on the board:

$\frac{3}{4} + \frac{5}{6} + \frac{2}{3} =$

Have the students work the problem at their desks. The answer is 2 $\frac{1}{4}$. Invite a member of the class to come to the board and demonstrate how to work the problem.

Vocabulary: No new terms are presented in this lesson.

Activity

Sam spent $\frac{1}{2}$ of his day at work and $\frac{1}{3}$ at school. How much of his time did he spend in these two activities? ($\frac{5}{6}$)

Discuss: Will the answer be the same if you do not use the lowest common denominator to solve it? (Yes) Ask for three volunteers to solve the problem on the board. Have the first student use 12 for a denominator; the second, 18; and the third, 24.

Ask: If using the lowest common denominator is not necessary, why is it desirable? (Because you are able to do less reducing at the end of the problem, which saves time. Also, using greater numbers may make the math more difficult for some.)

Error Analysis

Students who are having difficulty may need further practice with the multiplication tables. Remind the students that they need to use multiplication and division to raise and reduce fractions, but once the denominators are the same, they are ready to add.

Lesson 7: Subtracting Fractions and Mixed Numbers

Lesson Warm-Up

Kim and Lee are making cupcakes for a charity bake sale. Kim will need 12 ¾ cups of flour for his cupcakes. They buy a bag of flour that contains 20 cups. How many cups of flour will be left over for Lee?

Have the students work the problem at their desks. They can solve the problem by drawing a picture instead of doing the math if they choose. The correct answer is 7 ¼ cups. Invite class members who solved the problem correctly to share different ways of solving the problem with the class.

Vocabulary: An understanding of the following term is necessary to do the work in Lesson 7.

- **Borrowing:** Remind the students that they do know what this word means. Ask for volunteers to explain in their own words what borrowing means.

  When you borrow when working with fractions, you borrow 1 from the whole-number column and express it as a fraction with the denominator that you need.

  Discuss: How is borrowing in a fraction problem different from borrowing with whole numbers? How is it the same?

Activity

Divide the class into pairs. Have each student number a sheet of paper from 1 to 4 and write down four mixed numbers. Have the pairs create subtraction problems from their lists. Have them compare the mixed numbers they have written next to number 1. Have them work together to subtract the lesser number from the greater one. They should repeat the procedure for each of the mixed-number pairs on their lists.

Error Analysis

Remind students that the steps for adding and subtracting fractions must be completed in order. A common denominator and equivalent fractions must be found before any operation can take place.

A common mistake when borrowing is forgetting to take 1 from the whole-number column. Another common mistake occurs when the student forgets to add the borrowed amount to the fraction in the number being subtracted from.

Lesson 8: Multiplying Fractions and Mixed Numbers

Lesson Warm-Up

To better visualize the multiplication of fractions, have the students complete this activity:

1. Take a piece of paper and fold it into thirds as shown. Color ⅓ of the paper pink.

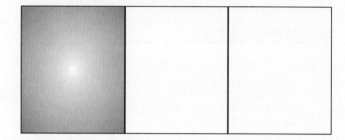

2. Now fold the same piece of paper into fourths as shown, and color ¾ of the pink part blue.

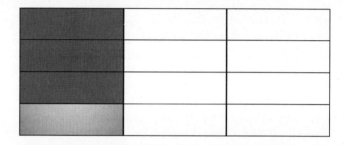

3. You have colored 3 out of 12 parts blue. That fraction can be expressed as ³⁄₁₂ or ¼.
4. You have found that ¾ of ⅓ is ¼, or ¾ x ⅓ = ¼.

Emphasize that when you multiply fractions, you are finding a part of a part.

Vocabulary: An understanding of the following term is necessary to do the work in Lesson 8.

- **Canceling:** A shortcut that makes the multiplication of fractions easier. When you cancel, you are reducing the answer to lowest terms before you work the problem. Instead of waiting to reduce the answer, you reduce the fractions within the problem.

Activity

Is canceling necessary? Have two students work the following problem on the board. Allow one to cancel. The second should multiply only and reduce the fraction answer.

$\frac{5}{8} \times \frac{4}{15}$

Discuss: Is canceling necessary? Does it actually save time?

Error Analysis

Remind students that mixed numbers must be changed to improper fractions before multiplying. Also, remind students to check their answers to make sure that they have been reduced to lowest terms. If they missed something during the canceling step, they may still need to reduce.

Lesson 9: Dividing Fractions and Whole Numbers

Lesson Warm-Up

One serving of Sugar Sparkle Breakfast Cereal is ½ cup. If a box of cereal contains 15 cups, how many servings are in the box?

Before the students do the work, *ask*: Will the answer be less than or greater than 15? (Greater than) Have the students solve the problem. They can use a drawing or diagram to do the work if they choose. The answer is 30 cups.

Vocabulary: An understanding of the following terms is necessary to do the work in Lesson 9.

- **Invert:** The word *invert* commonly means to turn something upside down. When you invert a fraction, you write the numerator on the bottom and the denominator on the top.
- **Reciprocal:** When you invert a fraction, the result is the reciprocal of the fraction you started with. $\frac{3}{2}$ is the reciprocal of $\frac{2}{3}$.

Activity

In the warm-up activity, the students were asked to divide by ½. Point out that the answer 30 is two times the number of cups in the cereal box (15). This observation proves that dividing by ½ is the same as multiplying by its reciprocal $\frac{2}{1}$.

Have the students do the following problem:

$1 \frac{1}{5} \div \frac{3}{10} =$

The answer is 4.

Before they do the work, *ask*: Will the answer be less than or greater than $1 \frac{1}{5}$? (The answer will be greater.) Why? (When you divide by a fraction, you are finding out how many times the fraction will go into the other number. If the fraction is less than the

number it is divided into, the answer will be greater than that number.)

Error Analysis

Common mistakes include:

1. Inverting the wrong fraction
2. Forgetting to invert the second fraction before multiplying
3. Not changing mixed numbers to improper fractions

Level 2: Fraction Applications

Lesson 1: Ratio

Lesson Warm-Up

Have the class find what part the number of women in the class is of the number of students in the class.

To find the answer, the two numbers are written as a fraction and reduced. This fraction is actually the ratio of women students to total students.

Present the following problem: During the first month of the season, the Mudhens won 9 home games and lost 6. What is the ratio of games won to games lost? ($\frac{9}{6}$ or $\frac{3}{2}$)

Vocabulary: An understanding of the following term is necessary to do the work in Lesson 1.

- **Ratio:** A comparison of two numbers, written as a fraction. A ratio can be used to make three kinds of comparisons:
  1. Part/part (in the example above, the ratio of games won to games lost)
  2. Part/whole (the ratio of games won to home games played)
  3. Whole/part (the ratio of home games played to games won)

Activity

Choose 20 students to participate in a consumer survey. If you do not have 20 students in your class, the student could ask these questions of their families and friends. Have the participants answer the following: What brand of (1) soda pop, (2) laundry soap, (3) potato chips do you buy?

For each brand, assign your class to calculate the ratio of the number of consumers who chose the brand compared to the total consumers in the survey.

Activity

Bring several copies of a daily newspaper to class. Divide the class into small groups. You will need one paper for each group. Assign the groups to find the following ratios.

1. The number of pages devoted to sports compared to the number devoted to editorials
2. The number of comic strips about families compared to the total number of comic strips
3. The total number of movie ads compared to the number of movie ads with an "R" rating

Error Analysis

The most common error is writing the numbers in the ratio in the wrong order. Stress the importance of order in a ratio. On the GED test, some of the wrong choices will show ratios written in the wrong order. The students should be aware of this mistake and avoid making it.

Lesson 2:   Proportion

Lesson Warm-Up

Michelle drove 40 miles on 2 gallons of gas. Her gas tank holds 12 gallons. How many miles could she drive on a full tank of gas? (240 miles).

Have the students explain how they solved the problem. Many probably used a mix of common sense and arithmetic. Set the problem up on the board as a proportion and show how it can be solved.

Vocabulary: An understanding of the following terms is necessary to do the work in Lesson 2.

- **Proportion:**   A mathematical statement that two ratios are equal: for example: $\frac{3}{6} = \frac{1}{2}$.
- **Cross products:**   Multiplying diagonally across the equals sign produces cross products. When the cross products are equal, the ratios are equal. For example:

$$\overset{6}{\underset{}{\frac{3}{6}}} \overset{}{\underset{}{=}} \overset{6}{\underset{}{\frac{1}{2}}}$$

This same method can be used to find equivalent fractions.

Activity

The following table shows the number of times each baseball player walked during a certain number of "at bats." Calculate how many walks the players will have at the end of the season if they each have 600 at bats.

Player	Walks	At Bats
Boggs	8	50
Duncan	1	40
Canseco	14	100
Deer	3	25

Answers:

Boggs	96 walks
Duncan	15 walks
Canseco	84 walks
Deer	72 walks

Error Analysis

The most common error is setting up the terms of the proportion in the wrong order. Encourage students who are having difficulty to label each term.

Lesson 3:   Probability

Lesson Warm-Up

Divide the class into small groups and give each group a six-sided die. Have the group predict how many times they can roll a 6 if they roll the die 30 times. Have the groups roll their dice and keep a tally. How close were the results to their predictions? Discuss the results. Point out that probability allows us to make more accurate predictions, but there is no way to know in advance exactly what will happen.

Vocabulary: An understanding of the following term is necessary to do the work in Lesson 3.

- **Probability:**   The chance that something will happen. An impossible event would have a probability of 0. A certain event would have a probability of 1. All other probabilities are represented by fractions greater than 0 but less than 1.

Activity

Describe this situation to the class: There are 3 red, 5 green, and 4 blue marbles in a bag. You draw one marble randomly from the bag.

1. What is the probability that the marble is red? (¼)
2. What is the probability that the marble is green? (⁵⁄₁₂)
3. What is the probability that the marble is either red or green? (⅔)
4. What is the probability that the marble is green or blue? (¾)
5. What is the probability that the marble is yellow? (0)
6. How many green marbles would you have to add

to the bag so that the probability of choosing a green marble is ½? (2)

Error Analysis

Students who are having difficulty should be encouraged to draw diagrams and pictures to visualize more accurately the information in the problems.

Level 3:   Problem Solving

Lesson 1:   Setup Problems

Lesson Warm-Up:

This activity gives students a chance to see how GED test items are constructed. Read your students the following problem: The scale on a map shows that 2 inches equals 500 miles. If the distance between two cities on the map measures 1 ½ inches, what is the actual distance between the cities?

Write the number choices 1 through 5 on the board. Next to (5) write "Not enough information is given." Have the students work the problem correctly and put their answer next to a numbered choice. Now have them work it wrong three times and put those choices on the board.

Discuss: Although you are not penalized for guessing on the GED, why is guessing a poor strategy for taking the GED? (The people who wrote the test have anticipated what you might do wrong. Any of the answer choices might seem right if you don't do the work.)

Vocabulary: No new terms are presented in this lesson.

Activity

Many of the items on the GED test are setup problems. Read again the problem from the lesson warm-up. Instead of writing solutions, have the students write an expression to solve the problem. Compare answers. Point out that there may be more than one expression that will solve the problem.

Have the students add four incorrect choices. Point out that the incorrect distractors on the test are written based on the common mistakes that people make.

Error Analysis

Students sometimes feel overwhelmed at this point in their studies. They may be tempted to throw their math skills out the window and resort to guessing or performing the first operation that comes to mind. Walk them through a problem-solving approach that includes:

- Reading the entire problem
- Identifying necessary information
- Writing an expression
- Solving the problem
- Making sure the answer makes sense

Lesson 2:   Extraneous Information

Lesson Warm-Up

Mark and Risa have started a small business. They agree to divide the profits in a 3:2 ratio (Mark:Risa) because Mark is investing more startup money. The setup costs for their business total $1000. If they make a profit of $1200 the first year, how much do they each receive?

Discuss: What facts do you need to know to solve the problem? (the ratio and the total profit) What fact in the problem is unnecessary? (the setup costs—$1000)

The correct answer to the problem is $720 for Mark and $480 for Risa.

Why is it important to disregard unnecessary information? Give examples of wrong approaches that a student might take to the problem if he or she takes into account the unneeded $1000.

Vocabulary: No new terms are presented in this lesson.

Activity

Divide the students into pairs. Each person in the pair should write two ratio/proportion problems and then give the problems to his or her partner. The partner should add unnecessary information to the problems. Have the pairs present their problems orally to the class. The class should identify the unnecessary information. Select some problems for solution on the board.

Error Analysis

Unnecessary information is a trap for students who decide to guess. Many problems on the GED test have "too much information." Students who are having difficulty need to approach each word problem by asking, "What do I need to solve this problem?" Then they should use only those facts.

For additional help on the topics covered in Chapter 2, refer to *On Your Own: Basic Math*, a volume in a

Cambridge Pre-GED series. The following table shows the correlation between the lessons in this book and the chapters in this Pre-GED series, in the *Threshold Pre-GED* text, and in the satellite GED text, *The New Revised Cambridge GED Program: Mathematics.*

Comprehensive GED Math

Cambridge GED Math (Comprehensive Book)		On Your Own: Basic Math
Level 1	Lessons 1–3	Chapter 7
	Lessons 4–6	Chapter 8
	Lesson 7	Chapter 9
	Lesson 8	Chapter 10
	Lesson 9	Chapter 11
Level 3	Lessons 1, 2	Chapter 12

Cambridge GED Math (Comprehensive Book)		Threshold Math Book 2
Level 1	Lesson 1	Unit 1, Ch. 1, Lessons 1 & 2
	Lesson 2	Unit 1, Ch. 1, Lesson 3
	Lesson 3	Unit 1, Ch. 1, Lesson 6
	Lesson 4	Unit 1, Ch. 2, Lessons 7 & 8
	Lesson 5	Unit 1, Ch. 1, Lesson 4
	Lesson 6	Unit 1, Ch. 2, Lesson 9
	Lesson 7	Unit 1, Chapter 3
	Lesson 8	Unit 1, Chapter 4
	Lesson 9	Unit 1, Chapter 5

Cambridge GED Math (Comprehensive Book)		Cambridge GED Math (Satellite Book)
Level 1	Lesson 1	Chapter 3, Lesson 1
	Lesson 2	Chapter 3, Lesson 2
	Lesson 3	Chapter 3, Lesson 2
	Lesson 4	Chapter 3, Lesson 3
	Lesson 5	Chapter 3, Lesson 3
	Lesson 6	Chapter 3, Lesson 3
	Lesson 7	Chapter 3, Lesson 4
	Lesson 8	Chapter 3, Lesson 5
	Lesson 9	Chapter 3, Lesson 6
Level 2	Lesson 1	Chapter 3, Lesson 14
	Lesson 2	Ch. 3, Lessons 15, 17, 18
	Lesson 3	Chapter 3, Lesson 16
Level 3	Lesson 1	Chapter 3, Lesson 20
	Lesson 2	Chapter 3, Lesson 19

Chapter 3

Decimals

Chapter Warm-Up

Would you rather pay $1.13 or $1.31 for a tank of gas?

Discuss: Obviously, $1.13 is less than $1.31, but how do you know that? Point out that the students are comparing the tenths and hundredths decimal places to find the answer. This problem is easy because we have a great deal of experience handling money.

Actually, your students probably have more experience with decimals than with any other fraction system. Unfortunately, their experience comes almost solely through the handling of money. You may want to point out to your students that in other countries, decimals are a regular part of every person's life through the use of the metric system. Americans are still resistant to learning about metrics, but the metric system is ultimately easier than our own.

Level 1:   Decimal Skills

Lesson 1:   Reading and Writing Decimals

Lesson Warm-Up

Put the amount $35.86 on the board. Ask for a volunteer to read it. The student should have no trouble reading *thirty-five dollars and eighty-six cents.*

Now put the mixed decimal 35.86 on the board. Ask for a volunteer to read it. The correct reading is *thirty-five and eighty-six hundredths.*

Vocabulary: An understanding of the following terms is necessary to do the work in Lesson 1.

- **Decimal point:**   the dot (.) that separates the whole number from the decimal fraction (*Note:* In some countries, a comma is used for this function.)

- **Mixed decimal:**   a number that contains both a whole number and a decimal: for example, 8.2, which is read *eight and two tenths*

Activity

After reading the text, have each student write a decimal or a mixed decimal on a piece of paper. Go around the room and have the students read their numbers aloud. The other students should try to write down the number the student has read. You should also write down the numbers to create a master list to check the students' work.

Discuss: What kinds of numbers are most difficult to read? Point out that zeros make a number more difficult to read and write. Zeros are placeholders; without them, it would be difficult to tell what place a digit occupies. However, since zero is not read aloud, it can be difficult to "hear" when one is needed.

Error Analysis

The most common mistake is not using the word *and* to represent the decimal point. Remind the students that the word *and* should not be used when reading whole numbers.

Lesson 2:   Adding Decimals

Lesson Warm-Up

Ask the students to add the following: 15.49, 6.005, and 0.8. Invite a volunteer to come to the board to show his or her work. As the student writes the problem, emphasize the importance of lining up the decimal points. The student's work should look something like this.

$$
\begin{array}{r}
\overset{1\ \ \ 1}{15.490} \\
6.005 \\
+\ 0.080 \\
\hline
21.575
\end{array}
$$

The student may add zeros as placeholders to the right to make the columns have an equal number of digits.

Vocabulary: No new terms are presented in this lesson.

Activity

Have the students examine closely the sample problems in the text.

Discuss: What can you learn about the placement of the decimal point in addition problems from this example? The students should notice that the decimal point in the answer is exactly in line with the decimal point in the numbers in the problems. The decimal point anchors the numbers in the problem so that the place-value columns in each number also line up.

Error Analysis

If students are having trouble, they may be making the problems more difficult than they are. Once the decimal points are lined up, adding decimals is no more difficult than doing the same operations with whole numbers.

Lesson 3:   Subtracting Decimals

Lesson Warm-Up

Ask the students to subtract 0.16 from 1.5. Ask a volunteer to work the problem on the board. Emphasize the importance of alignment. Remind the students that adding zeros to the right of the last digit in a decimal number does not change the value of the decimal. The student's work should look like this.

$$\begin{array}{r} \overset{4}{\cancel{1}}{}^{1} \\ 1.50 \\ -\ 0.16 \\ \hline 1.34 \end{array}$$

Vocabulary: No new terms are presented in this lesson.

Activity

Divide into small groups. Have each group write five word problems involving the use of decimals. Invite groups to read problems to the class and let volunteers work the problems on the board.

Error Analysis

If students are having trouble, they may be making the problems more difficult than they are. Once the decimal points are lined up, adding decimals is no more difficult than doing the same operations with whole numbers.

Lesson 4:   Multiplying Decimals

Lesson Warm-Up

Ask the students to solve the following problem:

Multiply 5.4 by 0.81.

Then invite a volunteer to do the work on the board. Point out as the problem is written that it is not necessary to line up decimal points when multiplying decimals. Instead, you have to make sure that the decimal point is placed correctly in the answer.

The students' work should look as follows:

$$\begin{array}{r} 5.4 \\ \times\ 0.81 \\ \hline 54 \\ 432 \\ \hline 4.374 \end{array}$$

Vocabulary: No new terms are presented in this lesson.

Activity

If students have access to calculators for class use, have them perform the following multiplication problems.

1. $25 \times 0.1 =$
2. $25 \times 0.01 =$
3. $25 \times 0.001 =$

The answers are:

1. 2.5
2. 0.25
3. 0.025

Discuss: What do you notice about the number of decimal points in the answer? (The number of decimal points in the answer matches the number in the problem.) What do you notice about the size of the numbers in the answer? (As you multiply by increasingly smaller numbers, the answers decrease in size.)

Error Analysis

Students who are having difficulty may need further study of the multiplication tables or the multiplication process. Placing the decimal point rarely poses a problem when multiplying decimals.

Lesson 5:   Dividing Decimals

Lesson Warm-Up

Ask the students to solve the following problem:

> Divide 0.63 by 3.5.

Then invite a volunteer to do the work on the board. As the problem is written, point out that it is not necessary to line up decimal points when dividing with decimals. Instead, you have to make sure that the decimal point is placed correctly in the answer.

The students' work should look as follows:

```
              0.18
    3.5 ) 0.6 30
         - 3 5
           2 80
         - 2 80
              0
```

Vocabulary: An understanding of the following terms is necessary to do the work in Lesson 5.

- **Divisor:**   In a division problem, the number by which you are dividing. Point out that we often use the ending *-or* on words that name someone doing something: actor, instructor, and so on. The divisor is doing something. It is going into the dividend.
- **Dividend:**   In a division problem, the number you are dividing.

Activity

If the students have access to calculators, have them work the following problems on their calculators.

- **1.** $25 \div 0.1$
- **2.** $25 \div 0.01$
- **3.** $25 \div 0.001$

The answers are:

- **1.** 250
- **2.** 2500
- **3.** 25,000

Discuss: What do you notice about the size of the numbers in the answers? (The answers increase in size as you divide by increasingly smaller decimals.)

Error Analysis

The placement of the decimal point in a division problem can be difficult. Have the students follow these steps:
- **1.** Count the number of decimal places in the divisor.
- **2.** Move the decimal point in the dividend that number (from step 1) of places.
- **3.** Put the decimal point in the answer directly above the new placement of the decimal point in the dividend.
- **4.** Divide.

Lesson 6:   Interchanging Fractions and Decimals

Lesson Warm-Up

Assign the class to solve the following problems:

- **1.** $160 \times 3/4 =$
- **2.** $160 \times 0.75 =$

Discuss: Which problem was easier to solve? There is no right answer. Some students prefer to work with decimals, and some prefer fractions. Make the point that knowing how to convert fractions and decimals can make your work easier. Some problems can be solved more easily with fractions and others with decimals.

Vocabulary: No new terms are introduced in this lesson, but you may want to introduce the concept of the repeating decimal. Have the students convert 2/3 to a decimal to see what happens. It will not be necessary to carry out a division problem past three decimal places on the GED test.

Activity

Have the students create a table of common conversions.

Error Analysis

Remind students who are having difficulty that decimals and fractions are both ways to show part of a whole. In a fraction, the denominator shows how many parts are in the whole. In a decimal, the decimal place farthest to the right shows how many parts are in the whole. The decimal 0.75 (which means 75 parts out of 100) has the same value as 3/4 (which means 3 parts of of 4). All students should memorize the most common conversions. Most of the fractions encountered on the GED test will be from this group.

Level 2:   Decimal Applications

Lesson 1:   Rounding Decimals

Lesson Warm-Up

Imagine that you are going to the store to buy disposable diapers and baby formula. You know that the diapers are usually $9.95 and the formula is $3.89. Excluding sales tax, how much, to the nearest whole dollar, will you need to make your purchase?

You know you need about $10 for the diapers and about $4 for the formula. The total $14 is an estimate that you arrived at by rounding.

Point out that the students already know how to round decimals when working with money. Now they need to apply that knowledge to all decimal numbers.

Vocabulary: No new terms are presented in this lesson.

Activity

Discuss: Why is rounding decimals an important skill to have? When would rounding be particularly helpful?

Bring out the following points:

1. Problems often have more than one step. If you continue to use all the decimal points at each step, the problems will take longer to work and you will only increase the number of decimal places.
2. Most of the problems on the GED can be solved by carrying out work to one or two decimal places. Being able to round an answer partway through a division problem saves time.
3. Some division problems result in repeating decimals that would never end. Being able to recognize them and round at the appropriate time is critical.

Error Analysis

The most common errors result when students are still not sure of the decimal-place-value system. Having students make their own place-value charts can be a good learning tool.

Lesson 2:   Decimal Word Problems

Lesson Warm-Up

The cost for mailing a first class letter is based on the weight of the document. It costs $0.029 for the first ounce and $0.23 for each additional ounce. How much will it cost to send a 10-ounce letter first class?

Answer:

$$9(\$0.23) + \$0.29 =$$
$$\$2.07 + \$0.29 = \$2.36$$

Vocabulary: No new terms are presented in this lesson.

Activity

Divide the class into small groups. Have each group write four word problems that involve the use of decimals. At least one of the problems should involve more than one step. No more than two of the problems should involve money. After the problems are written, the students should create five GED-style answer choices for each. Then have the groups trade problem lists and solve. Put some of the more difficult problems on the board and discuss solving strategies.

Error Analysis

Remind students who are having difficulty that solving word problems with decimals is no different than working with whole numbers. Use key words to identify the operations, then solve.

Lesson 3:   Metric Measurement

Lesson Warm-Up

The prefix *kilo-* means *one thousand.* How many meters are there in a kilometer? (1000) How many grams are there in a kilogram? (1000) How many liters are there in a kiloliter? (1000) Point out that the metric system begins with a basic unit of measure and then adds prefixes to tell how many.

If *centi-* means *one hundredth,* how many meters are there in a centimeter? (1/100 or 0.01) Now reverse the question. How many centimeters are there in a meter? (The answer must be 100.) The trick in understanding metrics is to learn which units are lesser and which are greater than the basic unit (meter, gram, and liter).

Vocabulary: An understanding of the following terms is necessary to do the work in Lesson 3.

- **Metric system:**   A system of measurement used throughout the world. In fact, only the United States holds to the standard or Imperial system of measurement.
- **Meter:**   A measure of length. It is a little longer than a yard. Meter sticks are common in other countries, just as yard sticks are common in the United States.
- **Gram:**   A measure of weight (mass). One gram is substantially less than an ounce.

- **Liter:** A measure of liquid (volume). A liter is a little more than a quart.

Activity

Using the information presented in the lesson, have the students estimate the following equivalents.

1. The weight in grams of an 8-pound newborn baby (about 3600)
2. The height of a doorway in meters (about 2)
3. The number of liters in a gallon (about 4)

Using the equivalencies listed in the chapter, have the students state what would be the best unit of measure for measuring each of the following:

1. The width of a paper clip (millimeters)
2. The length of a piece of paper (centimeters)
3. The distance between San Francisco and Los Angeles (kilometers)
4. The weight of a car (kilograms)
5. The amount of aspirin in a capsule (milligrams)
6. The amount of punch needed for a party (liters)

Brainstorming: Have the class identify uses they have noticed of metrics in the United States. Point out that since U.S. markets have become more competitive with overseas markets, we have had to change our view of the metric system.

Discuss: What are the advantages of using the metric system? What are the disadvantages?

Error Analysis

U.S. students have internalized the measurement units they have experienced most often. To learn metrics, they need a picture in their minds of these new units. For each unit and subunit within the metric system, have the students think of an object that is equal in length, weight, or volume. To aid visualization, you may want to make a chart with these objects.

Lesson 4: Circumference and Area of Circles

Lesson Warm-Up

Remind the class that they have learned to find the perimeter and area of square and rectangular objects. Using chalk and a string, draw a circle with a 20 inch diameter on the board. Then ask the students: How could you find the distance around the

outside of the circle (circumference)? How could you find the area of the circle?

To find circumference, the students could measure the distance around the circle with a string and then measure the string. To find the area, they could mark off 1-inch squares and then estimate the remaining area. If the students come up with these or other alternative methods, let them use them. Point out that at best these measurements are estimates.

Vocabulary: An understanding of the following terms is necessary to do the work in Lesson 4.

- **Diameter:** The distance across the widest part of the circle. Point out that the diameter passes through the center of the circle. Draw and label the diameter on the circle on the board.
- **Radius:** The distance from the center of the circle to the outside. The radius is always exactly one half of the diameter.
- **Circumference:** A special name for the perimeter of a circle.
- **Pi:** A special number found by dividing the circumference of a circle by its diameter. Every circle yields the same result for pi. To work problems on the GED test, the students should use the value 3.14 for pi. When less accuracy is needed, the students can estimate an answer using the value 3 for pi.

Activity

Present the formulas for finding the circumference and area of a circle.

$C = \pi d$ where $\pi = 3.14$ and d = diameter
$A = \pi r^2$ where $\pi = 3.14$ and r = radius

Help the students use the formulas to find the circumference and area of the circles on the board. Have them evaluate the accuracy of their estimates.

If you used a circle with a 20-inch diameter for the exercise, you can solve the problems as follows:

$$\begin{aligned} C &= \pi d \\ &= 3.14(20) \\ &= 62.8 \text{ inches} \end{aligned}$$

$$\begin{aligned} A &= \pi r^2 \\ &= 3.14(10 \times 10) \\ &= 3.14(100) \\ &= 314 \text{ square inches} \end{aligned}$$

Error Analysis

Remind the students that formulas make their work easier. A formula can be trusted to work every time.

Lesson 5:   Volume of a Cylinder

Lesson Warm-Up

Put a circle on the board and label its diameter as measuring 20 inches. This is the same circle that the students worked with in Lesson 4.

Ask the students to imagine that the circle on the board is representative of the ends of a cylinder that is 20 inches in height. Have them think of some way to measure the number of cubic inches in the cylinder. (They might suggest filling up the cylinder with 1-inch cubes and estimating the remaining space.)

Point out that the most accurate measure can be found using the formula $V = \pi r^2 h$; where $\pi = 3.14$, $r =$ radius, and $h =$ height. *Ask:* What is the relationship between the formula for volume and the formula for area? (You can find volume by multiplying the area by the height of the cylinder.) The volume of the cylinder described above is

$$
\begin{aligned}
V &= \pi r^2 h \\
&= 3.14(10 \times 10)(20) \\
&= 3.14(100)(20) \\
&= 314(20) \\
&= 6280 \text{ cubic inches}
\end{aligned}
$$

Vocabulary: An understanding of the following terms is necessary to do the work in Lesson 5.

- **Pi:**   A special number found by dividing the circumference of a circle by its diameter. Every circle yields the same result for pi. To work problems on the GED test, the students should use the value 3.14 for pi. When less accuracy is needed, the students can estimate an answer using the value 3 for pi.
- **Cylinder:**   A three-dimensional figure shaped like a can. Ask the students to visualize a can of frozen orange juice. If they wanted to measure the amount of orange juice concentrate that could fit in the can, they would need to find the volume of the can.

Activity

Bring several cylinders to class and have the class members, working in small groups, calculate the volumes of the cylinders. Some possibilities might be a coffee can, a trash can, a flowerpot, and so on.

Error Analysis

Help students who are having trouble see the relationship between finding circumference, area, and volume of a circle/cylinder and finding perimeter, area, and volume of a rectangle/prism.

Lesson 6:   Comparing Decimals

Lesson Warm-Up

Which is greater: 75 or 80? Point out that they have no trouble with this because of their understanding of place value. *Now ask:* Which is greater: 0.75 or 0.8? The same digits have been placed in the same relationship on the other side of the decimal point. Do the numbers still have the same size relationship? (Yes.)

Point out that 0.8 (eight tenths) is equal to 0.80 (eighty hundredths). In fact, the students can add as many zeros as they want to the right of the last digit of a decimal number without changing its value. The decimal 0.8 is also equal to 0.8000 (eight thousand ten-thousandths).

Now ask the students to compare 0.80 and 0.75. Clearly, 0.80 is greater. Isn't $0.80 greater than $0.75?

Vocabulary: No new terms are presented in this lesson.

Activity

Have the members of the class write down decimals (no mixed decimals) expressed as tenths, hundredths, or thousandths. Then ask the students to read their decimal aloud as you make a list on the board. Break the class into small groups and, working together, have them arrange the decimals from greatest to least.

Discuss: What was difficult about this assignment? Did you find any shortcuts to make it easier? What were they?

Error Analysis

Students who are having difficulty have not mastered place value as it applies to decimal numbers. Review the relationship between the decimal place value and whole-number place value.

Level 3:   Insufficient Data

Lesson Warm-Up

Present the following scenario to your students: Imagine that you work at a grocery store. The owner wants to collect some demographics about her customers. She asks you to find out how many shoppers go through the checkout lines between noon and 5 P.M. You dutifully count every shopper for one week (seven days) and find out that the store had 560 shoppers during that period. Then your boss asks you to figure out how many more women shoppers there were than men on weekdays. Could you figure it out from the information you have? Why not? What information would you need to solve the problem? (the total number of shoppers on weekdays and either the number of male or female shoppers for the same days) What would an employee in this situation have to do? (Start over the next week and gather the right information.)

Vocabulary: No new terms are presented in this lesson.

Activity

Make the following points: In real life, we often lack vital pieces of information. Luckily, we can usually go back and get it once we see that something is missing. On the GED, you will be expected to recognize when necessary facts are missing. The best way to do this is to read the question posed in the word problem and figure out what facts you would need to find that answer. Do not simply perform operations with the numbers you have. Many of the wrong choices are selected because they can be calculated by using the numbers in the problem in the wrong way.

Divide the class into small groups. Each person in the group should create two word problems. Have each student read the question from a word problem and ask the group what information they would need to solve the problem. When a member of the group asks for one of the necessary facts, the student posing the problem should give it. When the group has enough information, they can solve the problem.

Example: A student reads: How many more dresses did Bill make than Amy? The first student asks: How many dresses did Amy make? (The presenter answers "12.") Another student asks: How many dresses did they make in all? ("The problem doesn't say," the presenter answers.) A third students asks: How many dresses did Bill make? (The presenter answers "14.") The third student says: We have enough information to solve the problem. The answer is 2.

Error Analysis

Students who are having trouble may be guessing an answer. Problems that present only a few numbers seem "obvious" to these students. They use clue words to perform an operation using the numbers and choose an answer from the choices below. Unfortunately, this doesn't always work. Have these students first write the information they will need before they begin solving.

For additional help on the topics covered in Chapter 3, refer to *On Your Own: Basic Math*, a volume in a Cambridge Pre-GED series. The following table shows the correlation between the lessons in this GED Comprehensive Book text and the chapters in this Pre-GED series, in the *Threshold* Pre-GED math text, and in the GED Satellite text, *The New Revised Cambridge GED Program: Mathematics.*

Cambridge GED Math (Comprehensive Book)		On Your Own: Basic Math
Level 1	Lesson 1	Chapter 13
	Lessons 2, 3	Chapter 14
	Lesson 4	Chapter 15
	Lesson 5	Chapter 16
	Lesson 6	Chapter 17
Level 2	Lesson 2	Chapter 18

Cambridge GED Math (Comprehensive Book)		Threshold Math Book 1
Level 1	Lesson 1	Unit 2, Ch. 1, Lessons 20 & 21
	Lesson 2	Unit 2, Chapter 2, Lesson 24
	Lesson 3	Unit 2, Ch. 2, Lesson 25
	Lesson 4	Unit 2, Ch. 3, Lesson 26
	Lesson 5	Unit 2, Ch. 3, Lesson 27
	Lesson 6	Unit 2, Ch. 1, Lesson 22
Level 2	Lesson 1	Unit 2, Ch. 1, Lesson 23
	Lesson 2	Unit 2, Ch. 4, Lessons 28 & 34
	Lesson 3	Unit 2, Ch. 4, Lesson 29
	Lesson 4	Unit 2, Ch. 4, Lesson 32
	Lesson 6	Unit 2, Ch. 1, Lesson 22

Cambridge GED Math (Comprehensive Book)		Cambridge GED Math (Satellite Book)
Level1	Lesson 1	Chapter 2, Lessons 1 & 2
	Lesson 2	Chapter 3, Lesson 3
	Lesson 3	Chapter 2, Lesson 3
	Lesson 4	Chapter 2, Lesson 4
	Lesson 5	Chapter 2, Lesson 4
	Lesson 6	Chapter 2, Lesson 5
Level 2	Lesson 1	Chapter 2, Lesson 6
	Lesson 2	Chapter 2, Lesson 12–14
	Lesson 3	Chapter 2, Lesson 7 & 8
	Lesson 4	Chapter 2, Lesson 10
	Lesson 5	Chapter 2, Lesson 10
	Lesson 6	Chapter 2, Lesson 5
Level 3		Chapter 2, Lesson 14

Chapter

4

Percents

Chapter Warm-Up

Have the students brainstorm a list of situations in which they have heard information expressed as a percent. (*Examples:* tax rates, voter turnout, interest, polls and surveys, budgets, test scores, sports, sales and discounts).

    Point out that percent is another way to show part of a whole.

Discuss: Why is the use of percent to describe a part more common than the use of fractions? Why are percents easier for people to understand? (Percents make comparisons easier to understand because the whole is always 100%.)

Level 1:   *Percent Skills*

Lesson 1:   Interchanging Percents and Decimals

Lesson Warm-Up

1. Change 35% to a decimal.
2. Change 0.5 to a percent.

Discuss: Why is it necessary to change decimals and percents? (Percents are useful expressions, but they must be converted to decimals before you can perform math operations with them.)

Vocabulary: An understanding of the following term is necessary to do the work in Lesson 1.

- **Percent:**   This word literally means "out of one hundred" so that when we say 50%, we mean 50 out of 100, $^{50}/_{100}$, or 0.50.

Activity

Divide the class into small groups. Provide a national daily newspaper for each group. Have the groups search

the newspaper for examples of percents. Have them write down the sentence in which they found the percent. Then have them convert the percents to decimals.

Error Analysis

Common errors are:

1. Failing to drop the percent sign when a percent is changed to a decimal: 30% = 0.3%
2. Failing to add a zero when a decimal is changed to a percent: 0.3 = 3%

Lesson 2:   Interchanging Percents and Fractions

Lesson Warm-Up

Leona and Philip earn the same salary. Leona pays ⅕ of her earnings in taxes. Philip pays 20% of his earnings in taxes. Which one pays a greater amount in taxes?

    The problem asks the students to compare ⅕ and 20%. Since ⅕ = 20%, both Leona and Philip pay the same amount in taxes.

Vocabulary: No new terms are presented in this lesson.

Activity

Divide the class into small groups. Have the students use the chart on page 487 to write 12 sentences. Four of the sentences should use percents; four, decimals; and four, fractions.

Examples:

1. This credit card company charges 12 ½% annual interest.
2. Four-fifths of the students voted for a longer spring break.
3. Bob donated 0.2 (two-tenths) of the proceeds from the sale of his book to the World Wildlife Fund.

Have the groups exchange sentences. For each sentence, the groups should write the other possible ways of expressing the fractional part.

Examples:

1. 12 ½% = 0.12 ½ or ⅛
2. ⅘ = 0.8 or 80%
3. 0.2 = 20% or ⅕

Error Analysis

The purpose of this lesson is to familiarize the students with the common equivalencies. Students who are having difficulty may need drill work with the chart. You may want to have them construct their own chart from scratch.

Lesson 3: Common Equivalent Fractions, Decimals, and Percents

Lesson Warm-Up

The Martin family spent 33 1/3% of their net income on housing last month. If the family's net income was $2400 last month, how much did they spend on housing?
    Which of the following would be the easiest way to solve the problem?

(a) $2400 x 0.33 ⅓ =
(b) $2400/3 =

Obviously, the second method is easier. Since the GED test uses mostly common percents, fractions, and decimals, knowing the common conversions can make a student's work go more quickly.

Vocabulary: No new terms are presented in this lesson.

Activity

Hold a "spelling bee" to drill students on the table on page 487.

Error Analysis

Students who are having difficulty need help seeing the patterns in the table. Have them create their own table, grouping fractions with similar patterns.

Lesson 4: Recognizing Components of Percent Problems

Lesson Warm-Up

Francine took a $400 cash advance on a credit card.

The credit card company charged her an $8 fee, or 2% of the amount she borrowed. Ask the students to identify the base, part, and the rate in the situation above.

Vocabulary: An understanding of the following terms is necessary to do the work in Lesson 4.

- **Whole:** Sometimes called the *base*, the whole is the foundation for the problem. The whole is the entire amount.
- **Rate:** The rate is the percent. The rate is always followed by the % sign.
- **Part:** The number that represents part of the whole. The part is never followed by the % sign.

Activity

Divide the class into small groups. Have the groups choose one of the following places of business:

1. Bank
2. Grocery store
3. Clothing store
4. Stadium
5. Car dealership
6. Computer store
7. Restaurant
8. School

    Assign the groups to create five problems that relate to the setting they choose. Help the students identify the elements in the problems they have written. You may want to create extra practice using the problems the students have written.

Error Analysis

Students who are having difficulty may benefit from drawing a diagram to represent the parts of the problem. Have them draw a whole circle, then ask them what element of the problem the circle could represent. The part can be represented by shading part of the circle. The rate is one way to describe the fraction represented by the shaded portion of the circle.

Lesson 5: Finding a Part of a Number

Lesson Warm-Up

Write the following statement on the board: 10% of $500 is $50.
Have the students identify the whole, rate, and part.

    Answers: whole, $500; rate, 10%; part, $50

Vocabulary: No new terms are presented in this lesson.

Activity

Ask a student to solve the following problem on the board: Find 25% of 60. (The answer is 15.)

Now demonstrate that the problem can also be solved using proportion:

$$\frac{25}{100} = \frac{x}{60}$$
$$100x = 1500$$
$$x = 15$$

Error Analysis

One common error is forgetting to change the percent to a decimal or fraction before multiplying. For students who are having difficulty, using proportion to solve percent problems may be a good strategy.

Lesson 6: Finding What Percent One Number Is of Another

Lesson Warm-Up

Write the following problem on the board:

20 is what percent of 40?

Discuss: How can you recognize a rate problem? The rate is always followed by the percent (%) sign. Since none of the numbers have that sign, you know that the rate is the missing element.

Help the students to identify the part and the whole. Point out that the base usually follows the word *of.* Invite a volunteer to solve the problem on the board.

Vocabulary: No new terms are presented in this lesson.

Activity

Ask the students to solve the following problem: What percent of 12 is 3? (The answer is 25%.)

Now demonstrate that the problem can also be solved using proportion:

$$\frac{3}{12} = \frac{x}{100}$$
$$12x = 300$$
$$x = 25$$

Be sure to add the percent sign to your answer. (The answer is 25%.)

Error Analysis

The most common error is forgetting to include the percent sign in the answer. Another common error is

mixing up the part and the whole. Remind the students that the part is not always less than the whole.

Lesson 7: Finding a Number When a Percent Is Given

Lesson Warm-Up

Write the following problem on the board:

45 is 30% of what number?

Ask a volunteer to identify the elements of the problem. Point out that the word *of* usually comes before the whole. Since the word *of* comes before *what number,* you know that you need to solve for the whole. Invite a student to solve the problem. (The answer is 150.)

Vocabulary: No new terms are presented in this lesson.

Activity

Ask the students to solve the following problem: 60 is 75% of what number? (The answer is 80.)

Now demonstrate that the problem can also be solved using proportion:

$$\frac{60}{x} = \frac{75}{100}$$
$$600 = 75x$$
$$80 = x$$

Error Analysis

When students see a number and a percent, they tend to multiply automatically. Remind students to identify all the elements in the percent problem before they begin solving the problem.

Level 2: Percent Applications

Lesson 1: Word Problems involving Percents

Lesson Warm-Up

Present the following problems to the class. Have the students identify the elements and solve.

1. The South City Hornets, a softball team, won 75% of the games they played this season. If they played 20 games, how many games did they win? *Ask:* How do you know the number 20 is the whole? Point out that the word *of* precedes *the games they played this season.* That number of

games (20) is given in the next sentence. Therefore, you know that 20 is the whole. (The Hornets won 15 games.)

2. Max works in a clothing store. A shirt that originally sold for $36 has been marked down to $18. What percent of the original price is the new sale price? (The new price $18 is the part. The original price $36 is the whole. The answer is 50%.)

3. Pat is trying to remember how much she and her husband paid for their TV. She knows they put down $35 which was 10% of the total price. Does she have enough information to figure out the price of the television? (Yes, she does. She has the rate 10% and the part $35. She needs to solve for the whole. Problems that ask you to solve for the whole often sound incomplete. Watch for the word *of* to help you identify the whole. In this problem, the word *of* preceded *the total price.* Therefore, you know that the missing total price is the whole. The price of the television set was $350.)

Vocabulary: No new terms are presented in this lesson.

Activity

Discuss the three computation methods for solving percent problems: using proportion, changing the percent to a decimal, and changing the percent to a fraction.

Ask: How do you decide which method to use? Some suggestions are to use proportion if you are having trouble setting up the problem or identifying the relationship between the elements. Change the percent to a fraction if the fraction is a simple one to use. Change the percent to a decimal in all other situations.

Error Analysis

Common errors include:

1. Forgetting to change the percent to a decimal or fraction before multiplying
2. Not identifying the problem elements correctly

Lesson 2:   Simple Interest

Lesson Warm-Up

Stuart borrows $2400 from his uncle to buy a computer. He agrees to pay his uncle 10% interest. If he pays his uncle back in 2 years, how much interest does Stuart owe?
    Have the students identify the principal, rate, and time elements in the problem before solving.

Vocabulary: An understanding of the following terms is necessary to do the work in Lesson 2.

- **Interest:**   An amount of money paid in order to use someone's else money. If you borrow money from a bank, you are using the bank's money, so you pay interest. If you put your money in a savings account, the bank is using your money, so the bank pays you interest.
- **Principal:**   The amount of money borrowed or invested.
- **Rate:**   The interest rate is always expressed as a percent.
- **Time:**   The amount of time (expressed in years) that the money is used by someone else.

Activity

Divide the class into small groups. Have the students work together to evaluate the following situation: Monica has a chance to buy a car. Her car loan will be a simple-interest loan. Which of the following financing companies would charge her the least amount of interest?

(A) Price of car: $4000
      Length of loan: 3 years
      Interest rate: 12.5%
(B) Price of car: $4000
      Length of loan: 2 years
      Interest rate: 14%
(C) Price of car: $4000
      Length of loan: 30 months
      Interest rate: 11%

Answer: Financing company A would charge $1500 in interest. Company B would charge $1120. Company C would charge $1100.

Error Analysis

The most common error is to forget to write the time period as a fractional part of a year. Point out that the rate of interest is an annual (or yearly) rate. The period of time has to be expressed in the same terms (annual or yearly).

Level 3:   *Problem Solving That Involves Percents*

Lesson 1:   Multistep Percent Problems

Lesson Warm-Up

Pat decides to finance her car through American Auto Financing Corp. She borrows $4000 at 9% annual interest for 4 years. What is the total amount she will have to pay the finance company?

This problem has two steps. First, you have to find the amount of interest that Pat will owe. Second, you have to find the amount that she will pay to the finance company.

Work backward to analyze multistep problems. *Think:* What do I need to know to find the total amount that she will pay the financing company? (I need the amount she borrowed plus the amount of interest she owes.) *Ask:* Which one of these facts do I already have? [the amount she borrowed ($4000)]. *Do:* Find the amount of interest that she will owe.

$$i = prt$$
$$= (4000)(0.09)(4)$$
$$= \$1440$$

Then add it to $4000.

$$\$1440 + \$4000 = \$5440$$

Pat will pay a total of $5440 to the financing company.

Vocabulary: No new terms are presented in this lesson.

Activity

Last year, the Conservation Society planted 220 trees on Arbor Day. This year they were able to plant 50% more. How many did they plant this year?

Write these sentences on the board:

1. What facts do you need to solve the problem?
2. Which of these facts do you have?
3. Solve for the remaining fact.
4. Solve the problem.
5. Does your answer make sense?

Have the students work the problem by using the steps on the board.

Error Analysis

Students who are having difficulty often skip steps. Asking if the answer makes sense is an important step in solving a problem. Especially when working with percents, working the problem incorrectly usually results in an unreasonable answer.

Lesson 2: Percent Increase and Percent Decrease

Lesson Warm-Up

When she started her new job, Jane was paid $8 per hour. Now she earns $10 per hour. By what percent have her wages increased? (25%)

Vocabulary: An understanding of the following terms is necessary to do the work in Lesson 2.

- **Original amount:** When a problem shows a change in an amount, the original amount was first.
- **Percent of increase/decrease:** The percent of change in a number or amount over time.
- **Discount:** A percent of decrease. Stores often discount items to put them on sale.
- **Markup:** A percent of increase. Stores mark up items to make a profit.

Activity

The following proportion can be used to solve problems dealing with percent of increase/decrease:

$$\frac{change}{original} = \frac{x}{100}$$

For students who are having difficulty, proportion may be the best approach to rate-of-change problems. Be sure to point out that the students have to solve for the amount of change in order to use the proportion.

Error Analysis

The most common error is forgetting to write the percent (%) sign after solving for the rate.

Lesson 3: Using Ratio and Proportion

Lesson Warm-Up

Chances are that you have already presented the use of ratio and proportion to solve word problems. When students are having difficulty, this method seems best because there is no need to manipulate the percent formula.

Discuss: Invite the class members to share their feelings about the two methods. Point out to those who prefer using ratio and proportion that they still need to understand the percent formula because many of the GED test items are setup problems.

Vocabulary: No new terms are presented in this lesson.

Activity

Randomly choose problems from Lessons 5 through 7 (pages 489–492). For each problem, ask two students to come to the board. Assign one student to solve the problem using the percent formula. The other should use ratio and proportion.

Discuss: What are the similarities between the two methods? How are they different?

Error Analysis

Common mistakes when using ratio and proportion to solve percent problems:

1. Converting the rate to a decimal or a fraction. It is not necessary to convert the rate when using proportion. Writing the rate over 100 is writing it as a fraction.
2. Forgetting to write a % sign after the rate when solving for rate. It is not necessary to convert the number to a percent. Simply write the percent sign after the answer.

For additional help on the topics covered in Chapter 4, refer to *On Your Own: Basic Math*, a volume in a Cambridge Pre-GED series. The following table shows the correlation between the lessons in this GED Comprehensive Book text and the chapters in this Pre-GED series, in the *Threshold* Pre-GED math text, and the GED satellite text, *The New Revised Cambridge GED Program: Mathematics*.

Cambridge GED Math		On Your Own: Basic Math
Level 1	Lessons 1–4	Chapter 19
	Lesson 5	Chapter 20
	Lesson 6	Chapter 21
	Lesson 7	Chapter 22
Level 2	Lesson 2	Chapter 24
Level 3	Lesson 2	Chapter 23

Cambridge GED Math (Comprehensive Book)		Threshold Math Book 2
Level 1	Lesson 1	Unit 2, Ch. 1, Lessons 27–29
	Lesson 2	Unit 2, Ch. 1, Lessons 30–32
	Lesson 3	Unit 2, Ch. 1, Lesson 32
	Lesson 4	Unit 2, Ch. 2, Lesson 33
	Lesson 5	Unit 2, Ch. 2, Lesson 34
	Lesson 6	Unit 2, Ch. 2, Lesson 35
	Lesson 7	Unit 2, Ch. 2, Lesson 36
Level 2	Lesson 1	Unit 2, Chapter 3

Cambridge GED Math (Comprehensive Book)		Cambridge GED Math (Satellite Book)
Level 1	Lesson 1	Chapter 4, Lesson 1
	Lesson 2	Chapter 4, Lesson 2
	Lesson 5	Chapter 4, Lesson 3
	Lesson 6	Chapter 4, Lesson 4
	Lesson 7	Chapter 4, Lesson 5
Level 2	Lesson 1	Chapter 4, Lessons 6–8
	Lesson 2	Chapter 4, Lesson 9
Level 3	Lesson 1	Chapter 4, Lessons 10–12
	Lesson 3	Chapter 4, Lesson 13

Chapter 5 Graphs

Chapter Warm-Up

Bring a newspaper to class that contains many graphs and charts. *USA Today* is always a good choice. Show the class examples of the various kinds of graphs in the paper. Point out that a graph is only as good as its labels.

Discuss: Why are graphs better than text for presenting some kinds of information? (Graphs make it easier to compare numerical information. For example, large numbers may be represented by long bars and small numbers may be represented by short bars on a bar graph. The reader can quickly compare the numbers by comparing the lengths of the bars. For exact calculations, tables and charts may be more helpful.

Lesson 1:   Tables

Lesson Warm-Up

Bring in a newspaper or magazine that contains tables. Have the students find several examples of tables. From the examples, have the students define *table* in their own words.

Vocabulary: An understanding of the following terms is necessary to do the work in Lesson 1.

- **Column:**   A vertical (up and down) list of information.
- **Row:**   A horizontal (left to right) list of information.

Activity

Point out that a table usually presents more information than the student will need to solve the problem. Interpreting the table is the first step in solving the problem.

Divide the class into small groups. Ask the groups to use the table in the lesson text to make as many problems as they can. The activity will help the students see that a table of information can yield a large number of problems.

To make the best use of a table, the student should always:

1. Read all titles and column headings.
2. Read the word problem and determine what information will be needed to solve it.
3. Find the information on the table.
4. Solve the problem.

Error Analysis

The main source of errors in using a table is misreading the table. Following the procedure shown above will guard against errors. Tables generally contain more information than students will need. On the other hand, a table may not contain the necessary information. When taking the GED test, students need to be on their guard to spot problems in which "not enough information is given."

Lesson 2:   Circle Graphs

Lesson Warm-Up

Conduct a survey of class members. Have each student write on a slip of paper the number of days in a week that he or she formally exercises. The students should not write their names on the slips. Collect the papers and tally the results. Assign students to figure (to the nearest whole percent) the percent of the class that exercises 0 days, 1 day, 2 days, and so on, through 7 days.

Ask for a volunteer to create a circle graph on the board. Make sure that the graph is labeled appropriately.

Discuss: What are some possible word problems that could be based on this graph?

Vocabulary: An understanding of the following term is necessary to do the work in Lesson 2.

- **circle graph:** A circle graph shows how a whole is divided into parts. Circle graphs are especially effective at illustrating percents.

Activity

Have the students use the following table of information to create a circle graph titled "The Martinez Family Monthly Expenses."

Expense	Percent	Dollar Amount
Rent	32	960
Taxes	17	510
Groceries	10	300
Clothing	6	180
Recreation	4	120
Other	31	930

Discuss: Besides adding the dollar amount column, what other way could you use to find the family's total monthly income? Is it better to label the graph with percents or with dollar figures?

Have the students suggest word problems based on the circle graph. [*Example:* What expense is equal to the amount spent on both clothing and recreation? (groceries)]

Error Analysis

Students who are having trouble may be unsure of how to interpret the percent figures. When you see a circle graph labeled with percents, you do not have to worry about converting percents. You can compare the percents directly: A slice labeled 20% is twice as great as a slice labeled 10%.

Lesson 3:   Bar Graphs

Lesson Warm-Up

Write the months of the year on the board and ask the class members to state the months in which they were born. Tally their answers on the board. Then ask for volunteers to draw a bar graph of the information on the board. Make sure that the graph is labeled appropriately. Discuss the best way to mark the scale line. Now have the students divide the bars to show the number of male and female students born in each month.

Discuss: What kind of applications could be respresented well in a divided-bar graph?

Vocabulary: An understanding of the following terms is necessary to do the work in Lesson 3.

- **Bar graph:** A graph that uses bars or thick lines to compare sizes of numbers. The bars are com-

pared to a scale (either along the left side or across the bottom of the graph.)
- **Horizontal:** A line running left and right
- **Vertical:** A line running up and down
- **Divided-bar graph:** A divided-bar graph breaks the amounts represented by one bar into parts.

Activity

The following table shows the percent distribution of the U.S. population for selected age groups for the year 1990.

Age (years)	Percent of U.S. Population, 1990
5–13	12.5
18–24	10
35–44	15
65 and over	12.5

Source: U.S. Bureau of the Census.

Assign the students to create a bar graph of the information.

Discuss: Why don't the percents on the table total 100%? (Only certain age groups are represented on the table.) What range would be best for the scale for this graph? (Showing percents up to 20% would be adequate. The scale could be labeled "Percent" and include the numbers 0, 5, 10, 15, and 20.)

Have the students suggest word problems based on the bar graph. (*Example:* From the age groups on the chart, which is the greatest percent of the U.S. population?)

Activity

Have the students use the following table of information to create a divided-bar graph. The graph should be titled "Trailers and Rental Vans: Third Quarter Sales."

Salesperson	Number of Sales in: July	Aug.	Sept.
Al Fillmore	6	8	13
Brad Allen	7	11	9
Carrie Butler	10	12	13
Barbara Prow	5	7	14

Discuss: What are some possible word problems that could be based on this graph?

Error Analysis

Remind students to read the scale before attempting to solve the problems. Scales can be deceptive. Although you can see which bar is longest, you cannot make number comparisons until you read the scale.

Students who are having difficulty may make errors when comparing sections of a bar. Divided-bar graphs present a large amount of information in a small space. The students must read the labels carefully in order to interpret the sections of the bars correctly.

Lesson 4:   Line Graphs

Lesson Warm-Up

Marta has taken four different GED math practice tests. Each test had 28 items. Have the students use the following table to make a line graph of her test scores.

Test 1	Test 2	Test 3	Test 4
15	18	20	24

Discuss: Would the graph look any different if you use percents instead of actual scores? Try it. Which might be easier for someone else to read and understand? (Although the graphs would show the same trend, the percent graph would be more meaningful.)

Vocabulary: An understanding of the following terms is necessary to do the work in Lesson 4.

- **Line graph:**   A graph that uses a line to show changing amounts over a period of time. A line that rises (goes up) from left to right shows an increase. A line that falls (goes down) from left to right shows a decrease.
- **Trend:**   A tendency to rise or fall. A line that continues to rise shows an upward trend.

Activity

The following table shows the changing cost of 1 quart of milk over a select period of years.

Year	Cost (cents)
1890	7
1910	8
1930	14
1950	21
1970	33

Assign the students to create a line graph of the information.

Have the students suggest word problems based on the bar graph. [*Example:* Find the percent of increase from 1910 to 1930. (75%)]

Error Analysis

Students who are having difficulty should read the scale carefully before using the line to make comparisons. Some students find it helpful to use a ruler to help them read the point on the line against the scales at the side or bottom of the graph.

For additional help on the topics covered in Chapter 5, refer to *On Your Own: Basic Math*, a volume in a Cambridge Pre-GED series. The following table shows the correlation between the lessons in this GED Comprehensive Book text and the chapters in this Pre-GED series, the *Threshold* math text, Book 2, and *The New Revised Cambridge GED Program: Mathematics*.

Cambridge GED Math	On Your Own: Basic Math
Lesson 1	Chapter 30
Lesson 2	Chapter 26
Lesson 3	Chapter 28
Lesson 4	Chapter 29

Cambridge GED Math (Comprehensive Book)	Threshold Math Book 2
Lesson 1	Unit 3, Ch. 1, Lesson 40
Lesson 2	Unit 3, Ch. 1, Lesson 42
Lesson 3	Unit 3, Ch. 1, Les. 40, 42, 43
Lesson 4	Unit 3, Ch. 1, Lesson 41

Cambridge GED Math (Comprehensive Book)	Cambridge GED Math (Satellite Book)
Lesson 2	Chapter 5, Lesson 2
Lesson 3	Chapter 5, Lessons 3 and 4
Lesson 4	Chapter 5, Lesson 5

Chapter 6 Algebra

Chapter Warm-Up

Ask: What do you think of when you think of algebra? (Some answers might be "solving for *x*" or "equations" or "getting frustrated.") Now is a good time for students to vent their frustrations with algebra.

Many students have had bad experiences with algebra. You can do much to promote a positive atmosphere by pointing out that they have already had prior experience with algebraic principles in these lessons. They have used variables in formulas to solve problems. They have also solved proportion equations. By building on their prior knowledge they can learn the algebra they need for the GED test.

Level 1: Algebra Skills

Lesson 1: The Number Line

Lesson Warm-Up

Draw a thermometer on the board. Invite a student to estimate and mark the current temperature on the thermometer.

Ask: What will the temperature be if it increases 5 degrees? What if it decreases 15 degrees? 50 degrees? Discuss how we talk about temperatures that are below zero. Point out that 0 is not the least number on the scale. The temperature can drop below 0 degrees.

Vocabulary: An understanding of the following terms is necessary to do the work in Lesson 1.

- **Positive number:** A number with a value greater than zero
- **Negative number:** A number with a value less than zero
- **Number line:** A visual representation of the order of numbers

Activity

Have the students create a number line showing the whole-number values from -10 to +10. Have them plot the following values on the number line.

1. -5.5
2. +7½
3. -2/3
4. +1¼
5. -3.8

Error Analysis

Tie the concept of signed numbers to students' prior experience. Brainstorm activities that use signed numbers. [*Examples:* Football losses and gains, having your checking account be overdrawn, playing a game in which your score drops below zero (often called "going in the hole"), and so on.]

Lesson 2: Adding and Subtracting Signed Numbers

Lesson Warm-Up

Mike deposits a $200 check into his checking account. How much money does he have now if his prior balance was:

(a) $0? (+$200)
(b) $100? (+$300)
(c) -$100? (+$100)

The highest recorded temperature for February 7 in Rockford is 42 degrees Fahrenheit. The lowest temperature for that day is -32°F (Fahrenheit). By how many degrees do these temperatures differ?

42 - (-32) = +74°F (Fahrenheit)

Vocabulary: An understanding of the following terms is necessary to do the work in Lesson 2.

- **Absolute value:** The distance from 0. The signed numbers +8 and -8 have the same absolute value.
- **Positive direction:** Moving to the right on the number line
- **Negative direction:** Moving to the left on the number line

Activity

A football team takes control of the ball on the 50-yard line. On their first play, they gain 6 yards. On the second play, they take a 2-yard loss. On the third play, they gain 22 yards. Then the quarterback is sacked for a 10-yard loss. How many total yards closer to the opponents' goal line did the team move during the four plays?

Map out the results of the plays on the board using a number line. Point out that the 50-yard line on a football field is like the number 0 on a number line.

Now write an expression using the numbers from the problem.

(+6) + (-2) + (+22) + (-10) = +16

For extra practice, have the students solve the following problems.

1. Give a value for x that will make $x + 5$ negative. (any number less than -5)
2. Give a value for x that will make $5 - x$ positive. (Any number less than +5)
3. Give a value for x that will make $x - 5$ positive. (Any number greater than +5)
4. Give a value for x that will make $5 + x$ positive. (any number greater than -5)

Error Analysis

Writing down the wrong sign is the most common error. Point out to the students that when they are adding two signed numbers, they can determine the sign of the answer and write it down before they add or subtract.

Another common error occurs when a student forgets to change both signs when subtracting a negative number.

Problem: 8 - (-3) =
Error: 8 + (-3) = 5
Correct: 8 + (+3) = 11

Lesson 3: Multiplying and Dividing Signed Numbers

Lesson Warm-Up

Solve the following problems:

1. (+6)(-6) =
2. (-6)(-6) =
3. (+3)(-3)(+3) =
4. (+2)(-2)(+2)(-2) =

Answers: **1.** -36; **2.** +36; **3.** -27; **4.** +16

5. $\dfrac{-8}{-4} =$
6. $\dfrac{+9}{-3} =$
7. $\dfrac{+10}{+2} =$
8. $\dfrac{-15}{+5} =$

Answers: **5.** +2; **6.** -3; **7.** +5; **8.** -3

Vocabulary: No new terms are presented in this lesson.

Activity

Discuss: What will be the sign of the answer if you multiply as follows?

1. Three negative numbers (negative)
2. Three positive numbers (positive)
3. Four negative numbers (positive)
4. Four positive numbers (positive)

Have the students explain their answers.

To reinforce the rules for dividing numbers, have the students solve the following problems.

1. What number would you divide +12 by to get +3? (+4)
2. What number would you divide +12 by to get -3? (-4)
3. What number would you divide -12 by to get +3? (-4)
4. What number would you divide -12 by to get -3? (+4)

Error Analysis

The most common error is putting the wrong sign in the answer. Remind the students that they can figure out the correct sign before they multiply or divide.

Lesson 4: Adding and Subtracting Monomials

Lesson Warm-Up

Have the students solve each of the following problems.

1. $9x + 3x =$
2. $15y - 9y =$
3. $(2r) + (-5r) + (-9r) =$
4. $(5p) - (p) =$
5. $(+4x) - (+5x) =$
6. $(6n) - (-2n) =$
7. $(-7m) - (3m) =$

Answers: **1.** $12x$; **2.** $6y$; **3.** $-12r$; **4.** $4p$; **5.** $-x$; **6.** $8n$; **7.** $-10m$

Vocabulary: An understanding of the following terms is necessary to do the work in Lesson 4.

- **Expression:** A combination of letters and numbers that expresses a mathematical relationship.
- **Terms:** The building blocks of an algebraic expression. It may contain a number or a letter or both.
- **Monomial:** An expression with only one term.
- **Coefficient:** The number part of a term.
- **Variable:** The letter part of a term.

Activity

Call for two and three signed numbers at a time. List them horizontally on the board leaving space between. Put a variable after each number and put parentheses around the monomial. Then separate the monomials with addition and subtraction signs. Invite volunteers to come to the board and solve the problems.

Point out that monomials cannot be added unless the variables are exactly the same. Review the rules for adding signed numbers.

Error Analysis

Common errors include:

1. Performing operations with unlike monomials
2. Adding signed numbers incorrectly

Students sometimes have difficulty subtracting a negative number from a positive one: $(-7m) - (3m) = ?$. Should they add or subtract? Remind them that plus and minus signs also show direction. They start at -7 on the number line and move an additional 3 in a negative direction. The answer is $-10m$.

Lesson 5: Multiplying and Dividing Monomials

Lesson Warm-Up

Have the students solve each of the following problems.

1. $x^2 \cdot x^4 =$
2. $c \cdot c^2 =$
3. $m^2 \cdot x^2 =$

Answers: **1.** x^6; **2.** c^3; **3.** m^2x^2

4. $\dfrac{b^4}{b^2} =$
5. $\dfrac{-15cd^5}{3cd^2} =$
6. $\dfrac{4x^4y^3}{-12x^3y^5} =$

Answers: **4.** b^2; **5.** $-3d^3$; **6.** $\dfrac{x}{-3y^5}$

Vocabulary: An understanding of the following terms is necessary to do the work in Lesson 5.

- **Raised dot ($\cdot$):** In algebra, means to multiply.
- **Exponent:** A small number written to the right and slightly above a variable or number that shows how many times the base should appear in a multiplication problem. For example; x^3 means $x \cdot x \cdot x$.

Activity

Write the following problem on the board:

$(x^3y^2)(xy^3z) =$

Then expand the monomials as follows:
$(x \cdot x \cdot x \cdot y \cdot y)(x \cdot y \cdot y \cdot y \cdot z) =$

Remind the students that an exponent tells how many times the base appears in the problem. Demonstrate how to solve the problem. The answer is x^4y^5z. The exponents show how many times the x and y variables appeared in the problem.

Activity

Write the following problem on the board:

$$\dfrac{-4x^6 yz^5}{-2x^4y^3z}$$

Now expand the problem as follows:

$$\dfrac{-4 \cdot x \cdot x \cdot x \cdot x \cdot x \cdot x \cdot y \cdot z \cdot z \cdot z \cdot z}{-2 \cdot x \cdot x \cdot x \cdot x \cdot y \cdot y \cdot y \cdot z}$$

Demonstrate how to cancel the variables.

$$\frac{-4 \cdot \cancel{x} \cdot \cancel{x} \cdot x \cdot x \cdot \cancel{y} \cdot \cancel{z} \cdot z \cdot z \cdot z}{-2 \cdot \cancel{x} \cdot \cancel{x} \cdot \cancel{x} \cdot \cancel{y} \cdot y \cdot y \cdot \cancel{z}}$$

The answer is:

$$\frac{2x^2 z^4}{y^2}$$

Error Analysis

For multiplication, the most common errors are to multiply instead of adding exponents and to apply incorrectly the rules for multiplying signed numbers.

For division, the most common errors are to divide instead of subtracting exponents and to incorrectly apply the rules for dividing signed numbers.

Level 2: Algebra Applications

Lesson 1: Solving One-Step Equations

Lesson Warm-Up

Have the students solve each equation.

1. $x + 6 = 11$
2. $x - 4 = 8$
3. $5x = 35$
4. $\frac{x}{6} = 5$

Answers: **1.** $x = 5$; **2.** $x = 12$; **3.** $x = 7$; **4.** $x = 30$

Vocabulary: An understanding of the following terms is necessary to do the work in Lesson 1

- **Equation:** A mathematical statement which says that two amounts are equal
- **Unknown:** A variable for which you do not know the value
- **Inverse operation:** The opposite operation. Addition and subtraction are opposites, and multiplication and division are opposites.
- **Solving an equation:** Finding the value for the variable that will make the equation true

Activity

Divide the class into small groups. Assign each group to write ten equations using all four arithmetic operations. Have the groups exchange problems and practice solving. If any problems prove to be particularly difficult, invite volunteers to put those equations on the board.

Discuss: Why does performing the inverse operation work to solve the equation? (It isolates the variable. Once the variable is by itself on one side, the solution is apparent.)

Error Analysis

Students who are having difficulty sometimes forget to perform the same operation on *both* sides of the equation. Point out that this changes the relationship between the two sides so that the equation no longer states the same fact.

Lesson 2: Solving Multistep Equations

Lesson Warm-Up

Have the students solve the following equations.

1. $3x + 6 = 18$
2. $\frac{x}{4} - 8 = 2$

Answers: **1.** $x = 4$; **2.** $x = 40$

Discuss: How can you tell by looking at an equation that it will take more than one step to solve it? (When the side of the equation that contains the variable shows more than one operation taking place, there will be more than one step involved in solving the equation.)

Vocabulary: No new terms are presented in this lesson.

Activity

Give the class members an assignment to write the following problems.

1. An equation that will require addition and division to solve
2. An equation that will require subtraction and division to solve
3. An equation that will require addition and multiplication to solve
4. An equation that will require subtraction and multiplication to solve

Invite volunteers to put equations on the board and demonstrate how to solve them.

Error Analysis

The most common error is to forget to perform an operation on *both* sides of the equation. Remind the students that this error changes the relationship between the sides of the equation forming a new equation.

Lesson 3:   Solving Inequalities

Lesson Warm-Up

Have the students solve the following inequalities.

1. $2(x + 4) < 12$
2. $5c + 3 \geq 9c - 5$

Answers: **1.** $x < 2$; **2.** $c \leq 2$

Vocabulary: An understanding of the following term is necessary to do the work in Lesson 3.

- **Inequality:**   A statement which says that two sides are not equal. The symbol used to connect the two sides tells the relationship that exists between the sides.

Activity

In this activity, the students will learn to graph the answer to an inequality. Write this inequality on the board:

$$x + 4 \geq -2$$

Have the students solve it:

$$\begin{array}{r} x + 4 \geq -2 \\ \underline{-4 \quad -4} \\ x \quad\;\; \geq -6 \end{array}$$

To graph it, draw a number line and make a heavy line over the values that are greater than or equal to -6. The closed circle on -6 shows that -6 is a possible solution.

Solve and graph: $x + 3 > -4$

$$\begin{array}{r} x + 3 > -4 \\ \underline{-3 \quad -3} \\ x \quad\;\; > -7 \end{array}$$

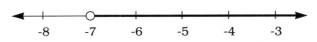

The open circle shows that -7 is not one of the possible solutions.

Error Analysis

Have students who are having difficulty graph solutions on a number line.

Lesson 4:   Multiplying Binomials

Lesson Warm-Up

Have the students multiply the following binomials.

1. $(x + 3)(x + 2) =$
2. $(x - 2)(x - 5) =$
3. $(x + 4)(x - 6) =$

Answers: **1.** $x^2 + 5x + 6$; **2.** $x^2 - 7x + 10$; **3.** $x^2 - 2x - 24$

Vocabulary: An understanding of the following terms is necessary to do the work in Lesson 4.

- **Binomial:**   An algebraic expression that has two terms. For example: $x + 8$
- **Monomial:**   An expression that consists of a single number, a single variable, or a product of one or more variables. Examples: x, 3, $3x$, or $3xy$

Activity

Have each student write down a binomial. All students should use the variable x. Then pair students randomly and have them multiply the factors they have written. Choose several pairs to put their problem on the board.

Discuss: What situations make problem solving more difficult? (Dealing with negative numbers usually presents the most problems.)

Error Analysis

Students who are having difficulty often confuse the rules for adding and multiplying signed numbers. Remind them that they always multiply first, then add when multiplying binomials.

Lesson 5:   Factoring Trinomials

Lesson Warm-Up

Have the students factor the following expressions.

1. $4x + 16 =$
2. $5y - 10 =$
3. $s^2 - 4s =$

Answers: **1.** $4(x + 4)$; **2.** $5(y - 2)$; **3.** $s(s - 4)$

Vocabulary: An understanding of the following term is necessary to do the work in Lesson 5.

- **Factors:**   Numbers that are multiplied together to find a product. For example, 2 and 5 are factors of

10 because 2 x 5 = 10. The expressions 4 and $x + 4$ are factors of $4x + 16$ because $4(x + 4) = 4x + 16$.

Activity

Have each student write a binomial. (*Example:* $3x + 4$.) Write the numbers 4, 5, and 6 on the board. Have the students multiply their binomial by each of the numbers on the board. For the example:

4   $4(3x + 4) = 12x + 16$
5   $5(3x + 4) = 15x + 20$
6   $6(3x + 4) = 18x + 24$

Now choose volunteers to put one of their binomials on the board. Ask other students to come up and factor the binomials.

Error Analysis

One common error is to neglect the second term in the binomial when factoring. Remind the students that they can check their answers by multiplying.

Level 3:   Algebra Problem Solving

Lesson 1:   Writing Algebraic Expressions and Equations

Lesson Warm-Up

Have the students write algebraic expressions for the following word expressions.

1. The product of seven and a number
2. Twelve decreased by a number
3. The sum of three and a number
4. A number divided by two

   Answers: **1.** $7x$; **2.** $12 - x$; **3.** $3 + x$; **4.** $x/2$

Now have them write equations for the following and solve:

5. Fifteen more than twice a number is equal to 23. What is the number?
6. Three times the difference of a number and one equals 12. Find the number.

Answers:

5. $2x + 15 = 23$
     $\quad\, -15 \quad\; -15$
     $\dfrac{2x}{2} = \dfrac{8}{2}$
     $x = 4$

6. $3(x - 1) = 12$
     $3x - 3 = 12$
     $\quad\; +3 \quad\; +3$
     $\dfrac{3x}{3} = \dfrac{15}{3}$

V*ocabulary:*   An understanding of the following terms is necessary to do the work in Lesson 1.

- **Algebraic expression:**   A mathematical statement that shows the relationship between unknown and known quantities.
- **Equation:**   A mathematical statement that two expressions are equal. Words such as *is* and *equals* tell you to write the = sign.

Activity

The following equations are the answers. Have the students make up possible situations for these equations. For example,

   Answer: $\$115 + x = \$165$

   Question: Pat is saving up to buy a bike that costs $165. She has saved $115 so far, how much more does she have to save?

   Use these "answers."

1. $21 - x = 14$
2. $\frac{1}{2}(x + 5) = 6$
3. $2(x + 1) = 12$
4. $3x + 2 = 11$
5. $13 + x - 5 = 16$

   Discuss: In an algebra problem, what does the variable represent? (The unknown; it is often signaled by the words "a number" or "what number.")

Error Analysis

Students who are having difficulty need to identify the key words in the word problem. Have them write the numbers and symbols under the words. After translating each part of the statement into mathematical symbols, they are ready to write an equation.

Another common error is solving for x and stopping. The value for x may not be the solution for the word problem. Remind the students that they may need to do something with that value to find the answer. Point out that the one of the wrong choices among the distractors in a GED test item may be the value for x. The best advice you can give students taking the test is to read each algebra problem one last time to be sure the solution makes sense.

Lesson 2: Algebra Setup Problems

Lesson Warm-Up

On Friday, the Colorado Rockies scored twice as many runs as they did on Thursday. On Saturday, they scored 2 more runs than they did on Thursday. The total number of runs scored during the three days was 10. Which expression represents the number of runs the Rockies scored on Thursday (represented by x)?

(a) $x + 2x + (x + 2) = 10$

(b) $2x + (x + 2) = 10$

(c) $2x - x = 10$

(d) $x + 2(x + 2) = 10$

(e) Not enough information is given.

Answer:

Thursday	Friday	Saturday
x	$2x$	$x + 2$

Equation: $x + 2x + (x + 2) = 10$

Present the following solution to prove the equation can be used to solve the problem; however, remind the students that they do not have to solve setup problems on the GED test.

Solve:

$$x + 2x + x + 2 = 10$$
$$4x + 2 = 10$$
$$\underline{\quad -2 \quad -2 \quad}$$
$$\frac{4x}{4} = \frac{8}{4}$$
$$x = 2$$

They scored 2 runs on Thursday. (They scored 4 on Friday and 4 more on Saturday.)

Vocabulary: An understanding of the following term is necessary to do the work in Lesson 2.

- **Setup problem:** A GED item that does not require a solution. Instead, the student chooses the option that shows the correct way to solve the problem.

Activity

Many setup problems can be solved using formulas. Have the students read the following problem and create five choices based on distance formula: $d = rt$. The wrong choices should use the formula incorrectly or use incorrect operations.

Cathy walks 4 miles every morning. If she walks at a rate of 8 miles per hour, how long will it take her to complete her walk?

Discuss how the students arrived at the incorrect answer choices. Point out that this is the same process used by GED item writers. They work the problem wrong to come up with wrong choices.

Error Analysis

Many setup problems can be solved using formulas. Review the use of the formulas page for the students. Remind them that they do not have to memorize these formulas, but they should be able to find the formula they need and use it correctly.

Further GED instruction and practice can be found in *The New Revised Cambridge GED Program: Mathematics.* See the following correlation chart for lessons in it corresponding to those in this chapter.

Cambridge GED Math (Comprehensive Book)		Cambridge GED Math (Satellite Book)
Level 1	Lesson 1	Chapter 6, Lesson 1
	Lesson 2	Chapter 6, Lessons 2 and 3
	Lesson 3	Chapter 6, Lessons 4 and 5
	Lesson 4	Chapter 6, Lessons 7 and 8
	Lesson 5	Chapter 6, Lessons 9 and 10
Level 2	Lesson 1	Chapter 6, Lesson 12
	Lesson 2	Chapter 6, Lessons 13–15
	Lesson 3	Chapter 6, Lesson 16
	Lesson 4	Chapter 6, Lesson 17
	Lesson 5	Chapter 6, Lessons 18–21
Level 3	Lesson 1	Chapter 6, Lesson 22
	Lesson 2	Chapter 6, Lessons 26–27

Chapter 7 Geometry

For the purposes of the GED test, geometry involves the measure of lines, angles, surfaces, and three-dimensional figures. Your students have already learned to figure perimeter, area, and volume. Now they need to learn the more abstract concepts of geometry relationships.

In your teaching of this section, one of the bigger challenges is involving the student's prior knowledge. To be successful, you need to convince the students that the information in the chapter will be useful to them. It can be helpful to point out that the majority of the geometry items on the GED test take very little time to solve. Most test knowledge of concepts with very little computation involved. By learning the basic geometry concepts presented in these lessons, the students can be assured of moving quickly through these items on the test and doing well on them.

Level 1: Geometry Skills

Lesson 1: Points, Lines, and Planes

Lesson Warm-Up

Ask the following questions:

1. Which mathematics symbol is formed by two parallel lines? (an equal sign)
2. Which two operations signs are formed using perpendicular lines? [the plus (+) sign and the times (x) sign]

Vocabulary: An understanding of the following terms is necessary to do the work in Lesson 1.

- **Point:** A dot
- **Line:** The shortest distance between two points
- **Perpendicular lines:** Two lines that intersect at an angle of 90 degrees
- **Parallel lines:** Two lines that will never intersect

Activity

Have the students take a sheet of notebook paper. Point out that plane geometry governs the points, lines, and figures that can be drawn on that piece of paper.
   Have the students draw:

1. A point
2. A second point and a line connecting the two points
3. Two parallel lines
4. Two perpendicular lines

   Ask: When would two lines that intersect not be perpendicular? (when the angle the lines form is greater than or less than 90 degrees)

Error Analysis

Students who are having difficulty need to apply the terms to familiar items. A road map can be useful for more practice with points and lines.

Lesson 2: Relationships of Angles

Lesson Warm-Up

Draw an angle on the board (approximately 45°).

   Ask: What can you tell me about this figure? As the students describe features of the angle, introduce the vocabulary terms defined below. Invite students to draw examples of acute, obtuse, straight, and reflex angles based on the definitions below.

Vocabulary: An understanding of the following terms is necessary to do the work in Lesson 2.

- **Angle:** A figure formed when two lines (called *rays*) share a common endpoint
- **Ray:** Part of a line that has one endpoint and extends in one direction without ending
- **Vertex:** The point from which the lines of an angle extend

There are many types of angles.

- **Right angle:** An angle containing 90°. A right angle always has a box at the vertex.
- **Acute angle:** An angle containing less than 90°.
- **Obtuse angle:** An angle containing more than 90°.
- **Straight angle:** An angle containing exactly 180°. A straight angle looks like a straight line.
- **Reflex angle:** An angle containing more than 180°. A reflex angle looks like it has been bent backward.

Activity: Draw a horizontal line on the board. Now draw a diagonal line that intersects the horizontal line as shown. Number the angles as follows:

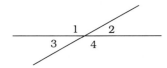

Ask: What can you tell me about angles 1 and 2? about angles 2 and 3? about angles 1 and 3? As the students describe the relationship between the angles, introduce the following vocabulary terms.

- **Complementary angles:** Two angles that add up to 90°
- **Supplementary angles:** Two angles that add up to 180°
- **Vertical angles:** Vertical angles are formed when two straight lines intersect. Vertical angles are opposite each other and they have the same measure.
- **Adjacent angles:** Angles that share a common ray. These angles lie next to each other.

Activity: Invite three students to come to the board and draw three different kinds of angles. Have each label their angles in different ways.

Discuss: What are the three ways to refer to an angle? Emphasize that the students may see all three ways used on the GED test.

Activity: Invite volunteers to the board and ask them to draw and label:

1. A right angle
2. An acute angle and its complement
3. An obtuse angle and its supplement

Then draw two intersecting straight lines. Ask volunteers to identify:

1. All opposite angles
2. All adjacent angles
3. All vertical angles

- **Parallel lines:** Two lines that run in the same direction and will never cross
- **Transversal:** The name of a third line that crosses two parallel lines
- **Corresponding angles:** Equal angles. A transversal creates corresponding angles.
- **Interior angles:** Angles (created by the transversal) that fall between the parallel lines
- **Exterior angles:** Angles (created by the transversal) that fall outside the parallel lines

Activity: Have a student come to the board and draw two parallel lines intersected by a diagonal transversal. Point out the "Z" shape formed by the transversal (see below).

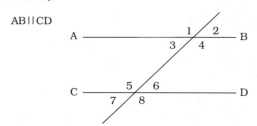

Ask for volunteers to identify:

1. All pairs of corresponding angles
2. All alternate interior angles
3. All alternate exterior angles

Discuss: How could knowing about corresponding and alternate interior and exterior angles save you time on the GED test? (Knowing which angles have equal measures could be helpful in making quick calculations.)

Activity: Assign students to use a street map to find two streets that appear to be parallel, with a third street forming a transversal. Have the students make a copy of the map (enlarging it if possible). Then have them use a protractor to determine if the streets are actually parallel.

Error Analysis

Students who are having difficulty should be taught to use protractors and receive plenty of practice in drawing all kinds of angles. Emphasize that they may be asked to identify angles on the GED. They may also need to know the kinds of angles in order to interpret the information in a problem.

Lesson 3: Triangles

Lesson Warm-Up

Have the students use their prior knowledge to answer the following questions.

1. Could a right triangle ever have more than one right angle? Why or why not? (No. Since the sum of the measure of the angles of a triangle is 180° and a right triangle measures 90°, it would not be possible for a second angle to measure 90°.)

2. Could an equilateral triangle ever be a right triangle? Why or why not? (No. A right triangle has to have one 90° angle. An equilateral triangle has to have three equal angles. It would not be possible to have three angles measuring 90°.)

Vocabulary: An understanding of the following terms is necessary to do the work in Lesson 3.

- **Triangle:** A flat figure that has three sides and three angles. The sum of the measure of the angles of a triangle is 180°.
- **Equilateral triangle:** This triangle has three equal sides and three equal angles (each measuring 60°).
- **Isosceles triangle:** This triangle has two equal sides (called base angles). The third side is called the vertex angle.
- **Scalene triangle:** This triangle has no equal sides and no equal angles.
- **Right triangle:** This triangle has one right angle.
- **Hypotenuse:** The side opposite the right angle in a right triangle.

Activity: Provide protractors if possible. Have students come to the board to draw and label the following kinds of triangles.

1. Right triangle
2. Equilateral triangle
3. Isosceles triangle
4 Scalene triangle

Using the protractors, have the students find the measures of two of the three angles for each triangle. Have the class solve for the measure of the remaining angle. Have volunteers check the answers with the protractors.

Error Analysis

Students who are having difficulty might benefit from a picture dictionary of the terms and figures presented in Lessons 1 through 3. The class could work on this project in small groups and copies could be made as study guides.

Level 2: Geometry Applications

Lesson 1: Congruent and Similar Triangles Congruence

Lesson Warm-Up

Which of these figures are always similar?

1. Two circles
2. Two rectangles
3. Two right triangles
4. Two squares
5. Two equilateral triangles

The answers are (1), (4), and (5) because the degrees of the angles in each of these figures never varies.
Have the students consider the following questions.

1. Two rectangles have exactly the same area. How could you find out whether they are congruent? (Compare the measures of the sides of both rectangles.)
2. The perimeters of two triangles are equal. How could you find out whether they are congruent? (Compare the measures of the sides and the measures of the angles for both triangles.)

Vocabulary: An understanding of the following terms is necessary to do the work in Lesson 1.

- **Similar:** In geometry, this term tells you something about the relationship between two figures. Geometric figures are similar when they have the same shape, although they may not have the same size. You can tell if figures are similar by comparing their angles.
- **Congruent:** When similar figures are the same size, they are also congruent. Congruent figures have the same shape *and* the same size.

Activity

Review the concept of proportion with the students using this problem: You can buy 10 pencils for $3. How much would it cost to buy 25 pencils? ($7.50)
To solve this problem, you need to apply the relationship between the number of pencils and the cost that exists in the first ratio to the second ratio. The same principle applies to geometric figures.
Draw a right triangle on the board. Ask a student to come to the board and draw a larger right triangle in the same proportion as the first.

Discuss: What would be the best way to approach the task? (Some answers might include doubling the length of every side or measuring each angle to make sure that the larger triangle has the same angle measures.)

Activity

The students will need protractors and rulers to complete the activity. Have each student draw a triangle.

The students should not label the lengths of the sides or measure the angles. Now have them trade papers. Tell the students to construct a congruent triangle without tracing.

Error Analysis

Students who are having difficulty need more hands-on practice. If you have access to a photocopier that can reduce and enlarge, have the students draw several figures (rectangles and triangles) and reduce and/or enlarge them. Have the students use protractors to prove the figures are similar although they are not the same size.

Lesson 2: The Pythagorean Relationship

Lesson Warm-Up

A ladder is leaning up against a house. If the base of the ladder rests at a point 3 feet from the house and the top of the ladder rests at a point 4 feet up the wall, how long is the ladder? (5 feet)

Vocabulary: An understanding of the following terms is necessary to do the work in Lesson 2.

- **Pythagorean relationship:** The sides of a right triangle have a unique relationship. This relationship is true for every right triangle. We express this relationship with a formula (which will be found on the formulas page of the GED test). The formula can be used to find the length of the hypotenuse when the other legs of a right triangle are known.
- **Hypotenuse:** The side opposite the right angle in a right triangle

Activity

Have the students draw and label triangles to illustrate the following problems. Invite students to solve the problems on the board.

1. The legs of a right triangle measure 5 inches and 12 inches. What is the measure of the hypotenuse? (13 inches)
2. The hypotenuse of a right triangle measures 15 inches. If one leg measures 12 inches, what is the measure of the other leg? (9 inches)

Error Analysis

Students who are having difficulty may benefit greatly from using calculators at this stage. There are two main sources of error: (1) using the formula and (2) dealing with square roots. Point out that the square roots the students will encounter on the GED test will be common ones.

Level 3: Coordinate Geometry

Lesson 1: Rectangular Coordinates and Plotting Points

Lesson Warm-Up

Provide each student with a grid. Have them label the *x*-axis and *y*-axis and plot the following coordinates.

$A = (+1, +2)$
$B = (0, -3)$
$C = (+2, -4)$
$D = (-3, -2)$

Vocabulary: An understanding of the following terms is necessary to do the work in Lesson 1.

- **Rectangular coordinate system:** A tool for drawing pictures of algebraic and geometric relationships. This system is made on a flat plane which two perpendicular axis lines.
- **X-axis:** The horizontal axis line
- **Y-axis:** The vertical axis line
- **Origin:** The point at which the two axis lines intersect. It is labeled (0, 0).
- **Coordinates:** A system of describing any point within the plane by describing the relationship of the point to the *x* and *y* axis lines

Activity

Bring an atlas to class and show how a grid system is used to locate places on a map. Point out that entire cities have been set up using a grid system. Many cities in Utah are built around two perpendicular streets which are similar to the *x* and *y* axes in the rectangular coordinate system. These streets usually have names such as Main Street and State Street. The remaining streets are numbered as in the grid below.

Discuss: Do you think a grid system would be easier or more difficult for visitors to a city to understand?

Error Analysis

Students who are having difficulty need more hands-on experience. You may want to have them use the atlas to get a better feeling for how places can be given an "address" based on their relationship to a grid.

Lesson 2:   Slope and Intercepts

Lesson Warm-Up

Draw the following diagram on the board.

Ask: What can you tell me about the slope of these items in the picture?

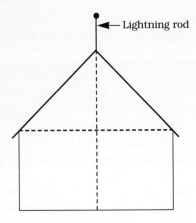

← Lightning rod

1. The left side of the roof
2. The right side of the roof
3. The vertical lightning rod
4. The horizontal beam at the base of the roof

Vocabulary: An understanding of the following terms is necessary to do the work in Lesson 2.

• **Slope:**   How much a line slants or leans
• **Intercept:**   The point where two lines cross

Activity

Have the class brainstorm occupations and activities in which finding the slope of a line would be necessary. Some possible answers include measuring distance down a hill, determining the angle at which a baseball pitcher throws to the batter, finding the pitch of a roof, and figuring out how much force will be needed to push an object up an inclined plane.

Error Analysis

Students who are having difficulty need more hands-on experience using the formula slope of a line formula. Remind the students that the formula will appear on the GED test formulas page. They do not have to memorize it.

Lesson 3:   Finding the Distance Between Points

Instructor's Note: The ideas in this lesson come under the *difficult* classification on the GED test. Remind the students that the formulas they will need will be given on the formulas page in the test booklet. They do not need to memorize the formula presented in this lesson.

Lesson Warm-Up

Write the formula for finding the distance between two points on the board:

$$d = \sqrt{(x_2 - x_1)^2 + (y_2 - y_1)^2}$$

Instruct the students to use the formula to find the distance between point A (1, 5) and point B (4, 0). Choose from the following:

(a)   Between 3 and 4
(b)   Between 4 and 5
(c)   Between 5 and 6
(d)   Between 6 and 7

The correct answer choice is (c). The distance is approximately 5.83.

Vocabulary: An understanding of the following term is necessary to do the work in Lesson 3.

• **Subscripts:**   These numbers are used to keep track of which numbers belong in which coordinate. Think of them as meaning *first* and *second*.

Activity

Point out that the students are actually finding the hypotenuse of a right triangle. Divide the class into small groups. Have the students draw right triangles on graph paper and identify the coordinates that mark the endpoints of the hypotenuse. Have them first estimate the length of the hypotenuse and then use the formula to solve for it. The use of calculators at this point may be desirable. Remind the students that the square roots they will encounter on the GED test will be common ones.

Error Analysis

Common mistakes include entering the coordinates in the formula backward and forgetting to find the square root in the final step when working the formula.

For further GED instruction and practice, see the following correlation chart connecting the lessons in this chapter with corresponding lessons in *The New Revised Cambridge GED Program: Mathematics.*

Cambridge GED Math (Comprehensive Book)		Cambridge GED Math (Satellite Book)
Level 1	Lesson 2	Chapter 7, Lessons 1–3
	Lesson 3	Chapter 7, Lesson 4
Level 2	Lesson 1	Chapter 7, Lessons 5 and 6
	Lesson 2	Chapter 7, Lesson 7
Level 3	Lesson 1	Chapter 7, Lesson 8
	Lesson 2	Chapter 7, Lesson 12
	Lesson 3	Chapter 7, Lessons 9 and 10

Using the Tests

Using the Predictor Test

The Predictor Test should be taken in class under timed conditions to help students identify strengths and weaknesses. A student's performance on the Predictor Test will be very useful in planning how to work with the rest of this book. On the GED exam, a student must get more than 50% of the items correct to pass. Therefore, a Predictor Test score under 50% means that the student probably would not pass the GED if he or she were to take it. Even a score of 60% or so is a signal to the student that he or she has major work to do in preparing for the actual exam. A student having trouble with any of the GED test areas might be referred to Cambridge's Pre-GED *Threshold* series, which parallels this GED series, or the Pre-GED *On Your Own* texts in writing process, grammar, basic math, and reading. On the other hand, a score of about 75% probably means that the student has a good grasp of much of the material, with certain areas of deficiency. While taking the Predictor Test, the teacher might call out when the time allotted is half over so that the students can circle the item they are on before they proceed to finish the exam. In that way, students will have an idea of how much they need to work on speed versus how much they have to work on content (i.e., a poor score may result from the need to work faster rather than a poor grasp of the material.) Like the other two tests, the Predictor Test should be gone over in class. Students who get the correct answers should volunteer to explain the reasoning they used to select the right choice and to eliminate the incorrect ones.

Using the Performance Analysis Charts

At this point, the teacher should meet individually with students and go over their Performance Analysis Charts (pp. 57–59), pointing out what the charts show about the areas each student needs to focus on in using this text. *These charts are a unique feature of the New Revised Cambridge GED Program.* They are particularly useful because they categorize every item on every test according to item type as well as according to content area and branch of con-

tent area. They therefore target thinking skills and test-taking in combination with content instruction, an approach that is central to this entire series and is the most effective preparation for passing the GED exam. Students should fill out their own charts according to the directions: they circle the number of each item they got right and enter the total number correct at the bottom of each content area column, next to the total number of items. Point out that the uncircled numbers indicating wrong answers are useful clues to the areas they especially need to study and review.

Using the Practice Items

The Practice Items (pp. 564–650) are grouped together according to the major content areas on the GED exam: Writing Skills, Social Studies, Science, Interpreting Literature and the Arts, Mathematics. Items are also grouped according to the branches of each area (for example, the Mathematics Practice Items are grouped according to Arithmetic, Algebra, and Geometry), with the exception of the grammar section of Writing Skills, where the items are mixed as on the GED exam. Because of this format, the Practice Items (again, except for Writing Skills) might be used as chapter tests or assigned as homework after the corresponding lessons in the book have been completed, as described below.

Guide for Using Practice Items as Homework

Social Studies: After Lesson 2, you might assign any of the items on graphs in any of the content areas: items 30 and 31 on p. 590, items 45 and 46 on p. 595, items 55–58 on p. 598, item 64 on p. 600. After Lessons 3 through 5, assign History items 1–17 on pp. 578–584.

After Lesson 6, assign Political Science items 38–51 on pp. 593–596. After Lesson 7, assign Economics items 26–37 on pp. 588–592. After Lesson 8, assign Geography items 18–25 on pp. 585–588. After Lessons 9 and 10, assign Behavioral Science items 52–64 on pp. 597–600.

Science: After Lessons 1 through 5, assign Biology items 1–33 on pp. 602–612. After Lessons 6 and 7, assign Earth Science items 34–44 on pp. 612–615. After Lessons 8 and 9, assign Chemistry items 45–55 on pp. 615–618. After Lesson 10, assign Physics items 56–66 on pp. 618–621.

Interpreting Literature and the Arts: After Chapter 1, assign Nonfiction items 1–12 on pp. 623–626. After Chapter 2, assign Fiction items 13–24 on pp. 627–630. After Chapter 3, assign Drama items 25–36 on pp. 631–633. After Chapter 4, assign Poetry items 31–36 on pp. 632–633. After Chapter 5, assign Commentary items 37–45 on pp. 634–636.

Mathematics: After Chapters 1 through 5, assign Arithmetic items 1–29 on pp. 638–643. After Chapter 6, assign Algebra items 30–46 on pp. 643–645. After Chapter 7, assign Geometry items 47–56 on pp. 643–645. After Chapter 7, assign Geometry items 47–56 on pp. 646–649. [*Note:* You may want to use the Mathematics Practice Items as a unified test, since each math chapter has a Chapter Quiz of 15 to 20 items (Algebra and Geometry quizzes have 25 each); these appear on the following pages: Chapter 1 Quiz, pp. 432–433; Chapter 2 Quiz, pp. 459–460; Chapter 3 Quiz, pp. 481–482; Chapter 4 Quiz. pp. 503–505; Chapter 5 Quiz, pp. 513–514; Chapter 6 Quiz, pp. 538–540; Chapter 7 Quiz, pp. 561–563.]

Going over the answers in class is useful whether the Practice Items are used as homework, chapter tests, or a unified practice test. Discuss each of the questions, encouraging students to explain why the incorrect choices are wrong. As a conclusion to discussion you can refer to the detailed, explanatory answer keys for the Practice Items on pp. A-53 to A-77, which demonstrate the steps of reasoning used to eliminate wrong answers and select correct ones. Students should be strongly encouraged to study these explanations to acquire the thinking skills they teach.

Using the Simulated Test

This test (pp. 651–738) should be taken under test conditions: each of the five tests should be taken separately, in one supervised sitting, within the time limits of the actual GED examination, as follows:

Content Area	Number of Items on Test	Time Limit for Test (minutes)
Writing Skills (Part I, Grammar)	55	75
Writing Skills (Essay)		45
Social Studies	64	85
Science	66	95
Literature and Arts	45	65
Mathematics	56	90

Note: On the actual GED examination, students sometimes take two of these tests—any two of their choice—in a single sitting; it is recommended, however, that they take only one at a sitting for best performance.)

Like the actual GED test, the Simulated Test contains items randomly mixed from all five areas of the text is completed and after the Practice Items have been taken and discussed. However, the high-level student or the student who needs to meet a GED deadline for entry into a training program or a college might take the Simulated Test before finishing the text. Other, lower-level students might want to take sections of each test in different stages—an approach that is less useful for familiarizing them with the actual test situation but which still teaches valuable test-taking skills. As with all the exercises, quizzes, and tests in this book, items should be corrected and discussed with students as soon as possible. Tell students to carefully fill out the Performance Analysis Chart for each test as described above and go over it with them; this is a useful way of assessing the student's capabilities and deficits as he or she considers taking the GED examination and a handy guide for further study.